Occupational Crime

Deterrence, Investigation, and Reporting in Compliance with Federal Guidelines

Praise for *Occupational Crime: Deterrence, Investigation, and Reporting in Compliance with Federal Guidelines*

"…captured my attention …aided me with understanding the impact occupational crime has on my staff, myself and the organization I am employed to support and protect. [The book] does a succinct job of outlining the problems, the costs, and the solutions. …provides well-researched and practical support materials to assist the proactive security conscious individual with development of a security awareness/loss contingency program."

— **Paul P. Donahue, CMA, CBM, ACFE**

"A well-written eye opener, the subject of which is very timely and definitely needed in the current economic turmoil we are in. A 'must read' for all business management and auditors."

— **Richard J. Kamentz, CIA**

"The compelling insight [the author has] provided regarding the development of a culture for ethical corporate behavior transcends various diverse industries. I found this book to be an excellent resource for anyone who cares about the conduct and survival of their business. [It] not only provided great insight as to 'why' anyone in today's business environment would need to develop a meaningful corporate compliance program, but also a demystified and commonsense 'how to' approach."

— **Steven Mellion, MBA, MHA, CNHA**

Occupational Crime

Deterrence, Investigation, and Reporting in Compliance with Federal Guidelines

Ernest C. Blount

CRC PRESS

Boca Raton   London   New York   Washington, D.C.

Library of Congress Cataloging-in-Publication Data

Blount, Ernest C.
   Occupational crime : deterrence, investigation, and reporting in compliance with federal guidelines / Ernest C. Blount
         p.   cm.
   Includes index.
   ISBN 0-8493-1377-5 (alk. paper)
   1. Employee crimes--United States--Prevention. 2. Industries--United States--Security measures. 3. Criminal investigations--United States. 4. White collar crime investigation--United States. 5. Criminal law--United States. I. Title.

HF5549.5.E43 B583 2002
658.3′8--dc21   2002025926

This book contains information obtained from authentic and highly regarded sources. Reprinted material is quoted with permission, and sources are indicated. A wide variety of references are listed. Reasonable efforts have been made to publish reliable data and information, but the author and the publisher cannot assume responsibility for the validity of all materials or for the consequences of their use.

Visit the CRC Press Web site at www.crcpress.com

© 2003 by CRC Press LLC

No claim to original U.S. Government works
International Standard Book Number 0-8493-1377-5
Library of Congress Card Number 2002025926
Printed in the United States of America 1 2 3 4 5 6 7 8 9 0
Printed on acid-free paper

Dedication

For Shirley Ann Brickell of Halifax, North Carolina
— My wife and best friend

Introduction

The central focus of this book is occupational crime: its prevention, detection, reporting, and incident management. Its motivation originates not only with management concerns about internal loss prevention, but also the consequences in the event an employee is convicted of a federal crime and the organization is subsequently charged. More on how these interests correlate as you proceed.

Occupational crime is defined as those crimes committed by employees on behalf of or against an organization — public or private — with or without the express or implied consent, approval, or knowledge of management. The purpose herein is to provide organizational management, their internal staffs, and contract professionals who provide ancillary support services an informational resource that will aid in the prevention, detection, and reporting of illegal behaviors occurring within an organization.

When occupational crime is prevented, deterred, or detected post commission, with reported and effective remedial action initiated, many obvious benefits accrue to the organization. Those benefits are explored herein. And there is more. An additional incentive may not be so obvious and, under certain circumstances, hold critical significance to a particular organization. If you have not heard of the United States Sentencing Commission and, more specifically, *Chapter Eight, Sentencing of Organizations*, of the *United States Sentencing Guidelines*, perhaps it's now time to learn.

The United States Sentencing Commission is an independent agency of the federal judicial branch of government. The Commission was created by Congress through provisions of the Sentencing Reform Act of the Comprehensive Crime Control Act of 1984. Congress was not pleased with the perceived lack of certainty and disparity at the federal level in sentencing for criminal behavior. Crime control issues had also gained its attention. Congress wanted to rein in federal judicial sentencing discretion and add formal structure where none had previously existed. It also wanted heavier penalties imposed on white-collar criminals and on violent and repeat offenders in all categories.

The Commission was to create, among other tasks, a national set of sentencing guidelines to be used by federal criminal court trial judges in making their sentencing decisions. The inaugural set of the *United States Sentencing Guidelines* took effect November 1, 1987. They have, of course, been amended over the years. The controversy generated by the Guidelines continues to this day. Many question their constitutionality, which has been tested for constitutionality in the U.S. Supreme Court. Challenges were initiated almost immediately and centered on the Sentencing Reform Act and allegations of improper legislative delegation and violation of the separation-of-powers doctrine. On January 18, 1989 the Court rejected the challenges, upholding the Commission as a judicial-branch agency (see *Mistretta v. United States*).

While the constitutional debate was ongoing, not much sympathy existed for convicted individuals. In the years since the U.S. Supreme Court's decision upholding the Commission, there has been a continuing debate as to whether the Guidelines unreasonably restrict judicial discretion and are, therefore, unfairly harsh to some defendants. This debate continues and, in all probability, will never be resolved to everyone's satisfaction.

In the period between November 1987 and the Court's ruling on the constitutionality of the Commission in January 1989, congressional interest in controlling organizational crime did not abate. Thus, on November 1, 1991, *Chapter Eight* of the Commission's Guidelines became effective, expanding the *Guidelines*. *Chapter Eight,* entitled *Sentencing of Organizations,* drew the attention of an entirely new set of the organization's interests. The provisions of *Chapter Eight* covered "corporations, partnerships, labor unions, pension funds, trusts, nonprofit entities, and governmental units." Things had changed.

Federal sentencing guidelines were no longer limited to individual miscreants — they now covered organizations. Like individuals, organizations can be indicted, criminally charged, prosecuted, and found guilty of criminal conduct. *Chapter Eight* sets forth punishments for organizations convicted of federal crimes, including felonies and Class A misdemeanors. It also offers incentives that can mitigate sanctions. The enactment of *Chapter Eight* and its provisions got the attention of organizational managers, at least those who knew about it. The term, *Compliance Program,* took on a new meaning and level of importance.

Judicial discretion in the sentencing of convicted organizations is now statutorily defined and limited. Organizational entities cannot be sent to prison — but they can be and are heavily fined, ordered to make restitution, placed on probation, forced to forfeit property, suffer public and stakeholder recriminations, and can be forced out of business. The rules of the game changed with the post-November 1, 1991 implementation of *Chapter Eight* — and fundamentally so. It is prudent for organizational management to be familiar with and understand the implications of the new rules or suffer the consequences if ever convicted of a federal crime. Statistically, organizations are most frequently convicted of violating criminal laws related to fraud, environmental waste discharge, taxes, antitrust, and food and drug offenses. There are many reasons why management should pay closer attention to organizational crime prevention, detection, and reporting — those that pre-date November 1, 1991 and those post November 1st.

Criminal liability can attach to an organization whenever an employee of the organization commits an act within the apparent scope of his or her employment, even if the employee acted directly contrary to company policy and instructions. An entire organization, despite its best efforts to prevent wrongdoing in its ranks, can still be held criminally liable for any of its employees' illegal actions.

Read that last paragraph again; you'll have to read it at least twice for the gravity of it to sink in.

Organizational sentencing guidelines offer convicted organizations an opportunity to mitigate potentially harsh sentencing impacts through incorporation of incentives that take the form of credits. These potential credits are set forth in *Chapter Eight*, § 8C2.5 — Culpability Score. Credits earned can substantially mitigate the size of a potential fine and other types of sanctions. The essential qualifier or credit trigger, if you will, is whether the miscreant organization had an effective compliance program in place. The operative term being *effective*. Eye wash compliance programs will not meet federal effectiveness criteria and should be avoided. Within the provisions of *Chapter Eight* is the architectural framework that sets forth the seven criteria for establishing an effective compliance program. Those seven criteria are:*

Compliance standards and procedures reasonably capable of reducing the prospect of criminal activity

Oversight by high-level management

Due care in delegating substantial discretionary authority

Effective communications to all levels of employees

Reasonable steps to achieve compliance, which include systems for monitoring, auditing, and reporting suspected wrongdoing without fear of reprisal

---

* From: *An Overview of the Organizational Guidelines*, by Paula Desio, Deputy General Counsel, United States Sentencing Commission. (January 1999).

Consistent enforcement of compliance standards including disciplinary mechanisms

Reasonable steps to respond to and prevent further similar offenses upon detection of a violation

These seven criteria establish the necessary basis for the evaluation of and suitability for issuance of mitigation credits in federal criminal courts. They define the core components of an effective compliance program but do not provide precise details for their design and implementation. Each organization is, therefore, left with the flexibility and independence to design a program that is responsive to its specific requirements and circumstances.

What is a "compliance program?" In the absence of industry-specific regulatory requirements and definitions a compliance program may be viewed as the totality of those actions taken by an organization to set the legal and ethical tone of the organization and to prevent, detect, report, and legally manage internal criminal behavior. Such a program will encompass a broad spectrum of policies and procedures that includes ethics, integrity components, employee education, incident investigation, disciplinary issues, reporting requirements, and managerial and audit oversight. Program design should incorporate Guidelines criteria as an integral part of its architecture if mitigation credits are to be sought should the organization ever be convicted of a federal crime. In some industries like banking and securities, there are specific statutorily defined compliance programs and oversight mandates that must be met.

Congress has now emphasized the importance it places on organizational efforts for internal crime-control measures and the effectiveness thereof. Allocation of any mitigating credit, however, is contingent upon the miscreant meeting two basic requirements: (1) prompt reporting of a violation to proper authorities and (2) no involvement of high-level personnel in the commission of the violation. That's right, management must not only report a crime, known or suspected, but also fully cooperate with authorities in the investigation of itself — and the results of the investigation better not show high-level involvement.

If these two requirements are not met, mitigation of sanctions becomes highly problematic. A management dilemma is thus created. Here are some options: do nothing and take the risks, or put an eyewash program in place and hope its transparency is not discovered, and then hope your attorney effectively pleads ignorance or comes up with some creative defense upon conviction. With both options there is no possibility of mitigating federal sanctions, and the results could be disastrous. Conversely, management can design and implement an effective compliance program and if ever prosecuted and convicted sanctions can be mitigated. What about self-incrimination; are you required to waive that protection? No, not if you do not intend to seek sanction-mitigation credits and are willing to take your chances in federal criminal court. But, if you intend to collect credits for sanction mitigation, then the answer is yes. In the latter instance, if you report internal criminal behavior, you may have voluntarily incriminated your organization.

Are the key criteria outlined in *Chapter Eight* mandated by law? The answer is no. Given, however, the pervasive all-encompassing number and complexity of federal criminal laws and the number of federal investigative agencies, the potential exposure to and risk of an employee committing violative behavior are substantially increased. Even in the absence of the aforementioned significant motivators exist for creation and implementation of internal crime and loss-prevention programs. When benefits are considered, it seems that good and sufficient cause exists to produce and implement such a worthwhile program. Even if an organization never has to deal with a federal crime conviction, the upside in internal loss prevention may just be sufficient justification for such a program.

Illegal, unethical, and irresponsible employee behavior is a multifaceted organizational problem. When this behavior is manifested, it is often described as fraud, theft, embezzlement, corruption, or white-collar crime. That is the legal context. Concurrently, unethical behavior can have moral and legal ramifications. Irresponsible behavior encompasses careless inattention to blatant illicit actions; it has become a national quagmire.

Preventing, deterring, and detecting such behavior and responding appropriately upon discovery have become significant concerns for the managers of America's commercial interests and for those individuals who run our societal and governmental institutions. In each venue abusive employee behavior and occupational crime are costly and intricate issues demanding vigilant management attention and diverse remedies.

A review of the elements necessary for the prevention, deterrence, detection, reporting, and management of wrongful employee behavior is included here. The means recommended to enhance existing management practices and controls is the employee security-awareness program. The employee security-awareness program is an expansive educational, motivational, and procedural approach custom-designed to accommodate the needs of a specific organization. Providing management with the essential "How tos" of such a program is the purpose of the present book.

If your intent is to design and implement a compliance program that incorporates the seven criteria of the Guidelines, then this material will assist you. You and your legal and other professional contributors, however, will have to ensure that the burdens of effectiveness are met and that each of the seven criteria is sufficiently incorporated into the compliance program to meet the requirements of law. Given the uniqueness of each organization, no attempt is made herein to provide a model compliance program, and no attempt is made to produce a "one size fits all" approach. Each compliance program, therefore, must be custom designed to fit the individual requirements of the organization it is intended to serve.

The author has tried to create a resource in an easy-to-use and readable form: a book that connects the practical and the philosophical aspects of planning for producing and operating a successful employee security-awareness program — a resource that will assist the user from start to finish, from recognition of a problem to determination of need and program design and from program implementation through maintenance; a guide for those starting a program from scratch or for those who wish to enhance an existing one; and a source of information that will provide a framework for success if properly used and applied. Depending on the organization, the design, scope, audit, and other essential functions and components of a successful program will vary from the relatively simple to the highly complex. Each must be custom designed. The contents set forth herein cover the "big picture," and each organization must provide the details that fit and fulfill their specific requirements.

Organizational crime and other abusive acts committed by employees are management problems. This book is intended for management use; any discussion of the referenced problems will require some analysis by management, which will include an examination of management's ethics, business practices, and attitudes. We examine how those three areas influence the existence of abusive employee behavior or, conversely, how they work to eliminate it.

The book is organized as follows:

- Chapter 1: The Problem — Reviews and places organizational crime and the abusive-employee behavior problem into perspective; discusses management's contribution to the problem and suggests remedial action.
- Chapter 2: The Cost — Examines the price business, institutions, individuals, and the nation pay for organizational crime and abusive employee behavior, and how to calculate those costs.
- Chapter 3: The Solution — Provides specifics for the development, implementation, and maintenance of an employee security-awareness program. The intent is to prevent, deter, and detect organizational crime and other abusive employee conduct. Input is interfaced with criteria proscribed by the federal sentencing guidelines for organizational crimes.
- Chapter 4: Support Materials — Provides supplemental materials used for program planning, records, and communications media.

Two points must be made prior to review and use of this book. First, any discussion of abusive employee behavior has negative overtones and implications that are inherent and unavoidable. Second, when management is taken to task about an issue, the author is not indicting every current or former business or institutional manager. The emphasis is on those issues, attitudes, and practices that apply to or come under the auspices of management. Keeping these two points in mind will assist you in keeping the purpose of the book balanced and in proper perspective.

Furthermore, I would be negligent in my treatment of management if I did not acknowledge the leaders — those ethical, highly competent, entrepreneurial, imaginative, empathic, and concerned business and institutional managers — who set the standard for managerial excellence in America and throughout the world. It is those individuals who by their actions contribute immeasurably to the richness of our daily lives and the American experience. It is their commitment to excellence, entrepreneurial spirit, and determination that moves America. It is their character, integrity, and vision of the future that will take us into many tomorrows.

The use of the pronouns "he" and him" throughout this text are used generically and not intended to singularly imply the male gender. Thus, "he and "him" are simply used in place of "he or she" and "him or her." This convention has been adopted to convey the point with an economy of words.

In closing, a word of caution about the use of the book. The author provides some basic discussion and input on a few legal, accounting, and personnel matters and references federal sentencing guidelines for organizations. However, such information is not a substitute for professional advice in those areas. The author is neither a lawyer nor a certified public accountant; therefore, you are encouraged to seek and use the services of professional advisors in all matters where such input is dictated.

Ernest C. Blount, CFE

About the Author

Ernest C. Blount is a seasoned business executive with extensive management, corporate security, and law enforcement experience that encompasses a broad range of investigative and executive posts. In business he has served as a vice president with a major multinational security firm, heading up their public services division. Mr. Blount has been the director of internal affairs and director of corporate security for two large Florida corporations over a period of 25 years. In government he has served as a chief of police, the organizer and first administrator of the Office of Safety and Security for the Palm Beach County Public School System, and as a part-time instructor in the Criminal Justice Degree Program at Palm Beach Community College. He is a graduate of Florida Atlantic University.

Mr. Blount's experience in the investigation and prevention of fraud and white-collar crime began as criminal investigator for the Palm Beach County Sheriff's Department. He is a Certified Fraud Examiner and has served as a business consultant and expert witness in federal court. This is Mr. Blount's second book. His first book is entitled *Model Guidelines for Effective Police-Public School Relationships.*

Mr. Blount is a member of the Association of Certified Fraud Examiners. He has been a member of the International Association of Chiefs of Police and The Florida Association of Chiefs of Police.

Acknowledgments

Anyone who has ever undertaken a research and writing project of the nature contained herein soon finds many of his or her weaknesses exposed. During the time it took to complete the project the support, encouragement, suggestions, criticism, factual analysis, and other inputs from those persons who took an interest in the project were very important to its completion. For that help, I shall always be appreciative.

In saying thank you I acknowledge the many industrial security professionals who pioneered and contributed so much to the body of knowledge now identified with professional security management, loss-prevention, and employee security-awareness programs. Through the years I have drawn on and grown with that knowledge. So much of what this manual contains reflects what I have learned from others. I give credit, then, to those professionals who through their written or personal input have influenced my professional life.

There are a few friends and professional colleagues who I wish to acknowledge and thank as well: Jim Manor, Paul Duffy, Margaret Devine, Mario Martinez, Paul Johnson, Jim Kirkland, and Ken McNabb. There were others who added their two cents' worth. Several senior executives took a look at the manuscript and, while they squirmed at the criticism of management, acknowledged the truth it contained. All recognized the problems illustrated and the need for solutions.

Ernest C. Blount

"Where the law ends, tyranny begins......."

William Pitt, 1770

Contents

The Problem

1

Objective: Provide a critique of occupational crimes and abusive employee behavior with a focus on management's contribution to the problem and its existence and growth in business, government, and institutions.

1.1 Overview

What is the problem? The problem is occupational crime and other abusive employee behavior characterized by illegal, unethical, and irresponsible acts. Such behavior exists at all levels — from the highest-ranking levels of executive management to rock-bottom subordinate positions. And while private sector interests are often perceived as the most egregious violators, the problem is not unique to business. The reality is that our government and our most trusted institutions are not immune to the problem and suffer from the same behaviors.

What to do about the "problem" is a controversy currently languishing in the boardrooms, executive suites, and governmental and institutional centers of this nation. This is a problem of monumental scope, with a price tag in the billions of dollars. It is a problem that threatens the free enterprise system and our way of life, one that raises issues and concerns about societal trends indicative of the erosion of the ethics, morals, and values of the American people.

At the nucleus of this problem are questions that strike at the very root of the controversy, questions and answers that raise doubts about the fundamental honesty, ethics, and integrity of America's business and institutional leadership and of their subordinates. In all instances — that's us. The nature of the problem calls into question many of management's current attitudes and practices. Certainly, leadership attitudes and practices bear on and influence cause-and-effect considerations of peers and subordinates.

Many contributors impact the current situation. The workplace is but a microcosm of American society, its ethics and integrity. Organizational management cannot be held responsible for every individual act of misconduct perpetrated by a co-worker in or out of the workplace, and no one, to the author's knowledge, advocates such a position. Management, however, has a powerful influence on whether — and to what degree — abusive behavior exists in an organization.

The information provided herein might enlighten you and provide a fresh perspective on the subject, or it might validate what you already know. In either instance the evidence is clear and compelling: wrongful workplace conduct is pervasive, and current trends in internal corruption must be reversed. Failure to do so will result in the nation's commercial and social institutions being altered in the most harmful way.

As you proceed, occupational crimes and abusive employee behavior will be defined. Also provided is a discussion of many of the objective and philosophical considerations that bear directly on and contribute to the defined conduct. In this review many elements that influence the existence and growth of occupational crime and abusive employee behavior are clarified. The adverse impact on business, our institutions, and nation will become apparent. You will also be alerted to crucial points and issues you might not have thought of or may not have considered in the detail provided herein.

Dealing with issues associated with occupational crime and abusive employee behavior can be very distasteful to management, and oftentimes it is avoided by them. The fact that managing specific instances of wrongful behavior can be unpleasant is not the only distraction for management. Many other underlying contributors add significantly to management avoidance and lack of interest in the subject generally. Many of these contributing factors are identified and examined in this text.

Volumes of material have been written on the subject of internal crime and loss prevention; many professions specialize in the field. Corporate lawyers, public accountants, security practitioners, and internal and outside auditors are but a few examples of those specialists. Most organizations focus their internal crime-prevention and other loss-prevention efforts on internal controls, audits, disciplinary practices, security policies and procedures, investigations, locks, lights, fences, CCTV, access controls, intrusion detection, security personnel, and management oversight; thus, the need for specialists.

This approach, while established in the literature of security and business management, results in a sometimes fragmented approach that tends to isolate responsibility for maintaining organizational integrity with the specialists. The material contained in this book offers a prescription that links together all internal crime- and loss-prevention programs, various loss-prevention disciplines, and all employees in a cooperative effort of shared responsibility. This is accomplished with improved employee security awareness, a change in management attitudes and practices, motivated employees, and specific security policies and procedures.

Preventing, deterring, and detecting corruptive behavior are not just the exclusive domain of crime- and loss-prevention experts. Protecting the assets and integrity of an organization is the job and responsibility of everyone who derives benefit from that association. In a business context the net result of a sound employee security-awareness program is a substantial positive impact on the bottom line and on operational effectiveness. Governmental and institutional impacts have a positive influence on cost of service and the level of clientele trust in the organization.

If properly designed, implemented, and maintained, an employee security-awareness program can improve an individual employee's self-esteem, loyalty, ownership mentality, work ethic, quality and quantity of production, employer–employee relations, and pride of membership in the organization. It can reduce incidents of internal crime and other abusive conduct. This is no minor payback for a program that, on a relative basis, can be so economical to implement.

No matter the organization or its purpose, the character, drive, determination, competence, creativeness, leadership, and entrepreneurial spirit of management ultimately determine the level of that organization's success or failure. All of the aforementioned are epitomized in one word — leadership. That simple fact is the immutable law of organizational success.

The foregoing statement is a meaningful framework to keep in mind as you begin to use this book. From the very beginning of your journey through the book to its end, keep an open mind and commit yourself to make an honest introspective personal and organizational analysis; that is the only way to fully benefit from the information you'll find throughout the book.

It is through the aforementioned analysis that you determine individual and organizational strengths and soft spots, key information you will need to know — if not already acquired. The knowledge and wisdom encompassed in this work will assist in and stimulate the prerequisite evaluation, that is, if it is used properly. The fact that you are now reading this overview is not only an indication of interest, but of your probable concern. Whatever your motivation in acquiring the book, be it personal or organizational, this material will aid in satisfying that motivation or in resolving many of your concerns relating to the topic.

Loss-prevention programs are designed and intended to prevent, deter, and detect corruptive and abusive behavior. Employee security-awareness programs may be used to enhance loss-prevention efforts and are designed to meet compliance program criteria as set forth in *Chapter Eight, Sentencing of Organizations,* of the *U.S. Sentencing Guidelines.* Through review of the material contained in this book, you will gain an understanding of the scope of the problems addressed and receive sufficient input to write your own prescription for preventing the occurrence or correcting such exposures in your own organization. Through the use and application of the tactics, techniques, and programs set forth herein, motivated managers can effectively dispense with an existing problem or set in place the mechanisms to prevent or deter its occurrence.

By focusing on the problem of internal corruption and employee misconduct, the quality of management, the individual employee, and the entire organization can be fundamentally improved. If that is the objective, then this book will show you how to achieve it. The material is tough, biting, and sometimes "preachy," but in all aspects it is an accurate analysis of the management practices, attitudes, ethics, and honesty and integrity levels of many of our nation's business managers and those individuals who manage our governmental and other societal organizations. The costs, while often unbelievable, are as accurate as could be obtained. The picture you will view is often unattractive.

1.2   What are Occupational Crimes and Abusive Employee Behavior?

For our purposes occupational crimes and abusive employee behavior are defined as any illegal, unethical, or irresponsible act committed by an employee acting alone or in concert with a co-worker or nonemployee that results in a loss to an organization, co-worker, customer, or vendor. Corruption and fraud are addressed in this definition. When you change from good to bad morals, manners, actions, or illegal activity, you meet the *Webster's New Collegiate Dictionary* definition of corruption. So, when the abusive employee is addressed, you are also addressing and working to reverse any fraud or corruptive influences that may exist in your organization.

To the author's knowledge, the first definition of "abusive employee behavior" to incorporate illegal, unethical, and irresponsible actions into one concept was created by an Atlanta, Georgia-based company known as The Network. The above definition incorporates The Network's central thesis, but is somewhat expanded to serve the purpose of this book. Both definitions incorporate crime, moral, work ethic, and character issues.

There are other definitions of abusive employee behavior, but most focus on crime losses and omit direct references to employee honesty, ethics, integrity, and irresponsibility. In this book occupational crimes and abusive employee behavior are viewed as multidimensional and, therefore, require a broader definition. To omit references to unethical and irresponsible behavior is to miss the nature of the problem and perhaps the most damaging aspect of the abusive employee issue.

The definition of abusive employee behavior used herein is straightforward enough. That, however, is not where discussion will end; actually, it's where discussion begins. What appears to be simple can become very complex in its application and interpretation. Any definition of its nature raises legitimate security, personnel, and legal issues and questions. Each of the questions and issues raised have the potential to create more difficulties than those the definition was originally intended to resolve. You can develop your own definition if you find the one noted unsatisfactory. Attorney review should be undertaken prior to use of any definition to ensure legal application.

The following questions typify those you will want to address in the design of your loss-prevention or compliance program(s)

- What is a crime?
- What is unethical and irresponsible behavior?
- Because there are degrees of abuse, how will they be defined?
- How will violators be disciplined?
- What crimes will be prosecuted?
- What violations require termination, suspension, or verbal or written warnings?
- How will due process impact disciplinary actions?
- Do policies have to be written or rewritten?
- Are administrative or other legal remedies available or proscribed by law, policy, or contract?
- Is the intent to produce a program that meets *Chapter Eight* criteria for compliance?

The foregoing questions initiate the evaluation process. Additional questions, along with answers relevant to the needs of a particular organization, will have to be developed by you. Brainstorming with management associates can be very productive when it comes to compiling a worthwhile series of pertinent questions and answers. Management involvement in the developmental process will enhance their understanding of the problem and will assist in effecting buy-in. If your employee security awareness program is intended to meet *Chapter Eight* criteria as a compliance program, then careful attention to those criteria must be applied.

Addressing issues, asking questions, finding answers, and discovering strengths and soft-spots of any proposed or existing employee security-awareness or loss-prevention program, etc., are not impossible tasks. They are tasks that require thoughtful preparation prior to making changes in an existing program. The same logic applies when planning the adoption and incorporation of a new program. The process can be time-consuming, but ultimately it is worth the cost and aggravation.

There are other terms and definitions that you need to be familiar with as you put the review and developmental process into perspective. For instance, illegal acts perpetrated in a business environment are more often than not characterized as other than white-collar crime. Sometimes we see white-collar crime described as business crime, occupational crime, corporate crime, economic crime, financial crime, and fraud. The media are great at creating catch phrases intended to describe a certain type of conduct and to capture therein the essence of the incident.

Many of the aforementioned examples originated under just such circumstances. And while they may legitimately serve a certain purpose, the terms are often vague. From that ambiguity they can and do create confusion in the minds of some people as to what they mean. They also lack a legal definition by which to frame them. All crimes are defined by law, whether they are federal, state, county, or municipal in origin.

The term "white-collar crime" itself can and does create confusion. Many individuals think white-color crime describes a specific crime. That is not the case. It is not a crime unto itself, although it is often so identified. And while it is not a specific crime as defined by law, the definition includes the criteria that must be met for a specific crime to be identified as a white-collar crime.

The U.S. Department of Justice defines white-collar crime as:

> …illegal acts characterized by guile, deceit, and concealment and not dependent upon the application of physical force or violence or threats thereof. They may be committed by individuals acting independently or by those who are part of a well-planned conspiracy. The objective may be to obtain money, property, or services; to avoid the payment of a loss of money, property, or services; or to secure business or personal advantage.

The term "white-collar crime" was first used in the late 1930s; it was coined by a criminologist of that era who studied corporate crime. During that period, executives typically wore white shirts and rank-in-file workers wore blue. Thus, crimes committed by executives became identified as white-collar crime and those by workers as blue-collar. Today, that generalization is no longer completely valid, but it is still used. While many production workers still do not wear white shirts in an executive mode, there is a large segment of rank-in-file workers who do. Technology has changed our working environments and, for many of us, the way we dress as well. Relaxed dress codes in some organizations today have resulted in pullover shirts and jeans as acceptable executive attire.

The key point is that white-collar crime is no longer the exclusive domain of the executive suite. By definition anyone can commit a white-collar crime, not just executives. The same definition is equally valid in a governmental or institutional context. But the problem is not limited to crime. Unethical and irresponsible employee behavior has created its own legacy of abuse. Societal attitudes toward work, individual accountability, responsibility, and morals have also changed.

Chuck Colson and Jack Eckerd, in their book *Why America Doesn't Work*, urge Americans to return to the "good old American work ethic." They believe that America needs an infusion of the "timeless values that our country was built on, such as hard work, thrift and integrity." They make a compelling case that it is through the restoration of those values that we can halt the decline of America into "the mire of shoddy workmanship, a predatory mentality, and self-defeating counterfeit values." Colson and Eckerd quote Peter Drucker: "The honest work of yesterday has lost its social status, its social esteem."

One might ask, "If fraud and corruption are so destructive and costly, why does the subject not receive more attention?" The reasons of "why" are many. Some of them deal with the attitudes, practices, and perceptions of those individuals who manage our businesses, governmental entities, and institutions. The attitudes, practices, and perceptions of the public, law enforcement agencies, and internal and public auditors influence some. One key influence, if not the dominant factor in all venues, is that crime is often viewed in a limited context. Attention of the media is very often focused on those incidents that are viewed as requiring priority attention.

Incidents involving acts or threats of violence require immediate attention. Burglary, robbery, and certain categories of overt theft require similar attention; they are commonly identified as "street crimes." Street crimes are primary factors that influence the prevailing view of crime. In each instance the offender is perceived as a danger to the victim and/or community. In each the victim knows he has suffered a loss; each act fits into a familiar category of criminal behavior. Instances of white-collar crime are often not so easily defined or discovered, and therein lies a caveat, even though dollar losses due to white-collar crime exceed by many times those attributable to so-called street crimes.

With street crimes law enforcement officials and prosecutors can easily confirm if a crime has occurred and if the evidence makes it prosecutable. In most instances the more serious the injury the greater the probability of prosecution if the perpetrator is apprehended. Upon conviction of such a crime the probability of incarceration is increased. Conversely, white-collar crime incidents do not require immediate attention in most instances, are not easily identified as a crime and are costly to investigate and complicated to prosecute.

With white-collar crime cases, there is no victim in classic terms to which people can relate. Additionally, fraud is often far more complicated than street crime. And there are many other factors that bear on the issue. The paramount factor is that fraud is always hidden. When fraud is present, it is often very difficult to determine its extent. Another key factor is that victims don't always cooperate with investigators. There are other definitions that will be helpful to know. For instance, the definition of fraud. *Gifi's Law Dictionary* defines fraud as:

> Intentional deception resulting in injury to another...It embraces all the multifarious means which human ingenuity can devise to get an advantage over another. It includes all surprise, trick, cunning, dissembling and unfair ways by which another is cheated.

Section 280.01.1 of the Institute's *Standards for the Professional Practice of Internal Auditing* states,

> Fraud encompasses an array of irregularities and illegal acts characterized by intentional deception. It can be perpetrated for the benefit of or to the detriment of the organization.

The U.S. Supreme Court has ruled that for the commission of an act to be defined as fraudulent the following legal elements are required:

- A false and material misrepresentation is made.
- The party making the representation knows it is false.
- The misrepresentation is intended to be relied upon.
- The victim relies on the misrepresentation.
- The victim is damaged as a consequence.

By definition fraud cases are devoid of threats, physical violence, and injury; this automatically alters the view of urgency and victimization. The entire perception of victimization is further complicated by the fact that in fraud cases alternative civil remedies are available in place of criminal prosecution. The victims can be individuals, businesses, governmental entities, or some other type of organization.

It is because of the aforementioned reasons that criminal prosecution of fraud is in some instances deferred to civil court for resolution. A key reason is that the burden of proof is not as stringent in civil matters as in criminal cases, making the alternative attractive. Furthermore, in these cases the perpetrator is not always viewed as a criminal — and therein lies another caveat.

In the real world management is often reluctant to acknowledge the problem. Public accountants generally limit their concerns of fraud to financial statements. Internal auditors may have direct responsibilities for discovery and prevention of fraud, but often they are not trained to find it. Many internal auditors find the area of fraud politically risky and avoid it if possible. Fraud is criminal and too confrontational and accusatory for most internal audit groups. However, the American Institute of Certified Public Accountants (AICPA) in its *Statement on Auditing Standards (SAS) No. 82, Consideration of Fraud in a Financial Statement Audit and SAS No. 52, Illegal Acts by Clients,* places a different burden on outside auditors.

Generally, corporate security personnel, when they exist in an organization, are the practitioners with shared responsibility for detection and investigation of fraud and other criminal acts involving crimes against property. Moreover, internal security personnel often possess both the desire and know-how to successfully manage the investigation of fraud along with specialized police, certified fraud examiners, highly trained private investigators, and some internal and external auditors. Losses attributable to fraud are estimated to be two to three times greater than so-called street crime; some estimators estimate fraud losses are ten times greater than losses from the latter.

We may have reached the point in the state of fraud and corruption where a degree of expectancy and a level of acceptability exist. The latter connection is often evident when a sophisticated fraud scheme is pulled off wherein large sums of money are stolen, no one is hurt, and a corporation is the only apparent victim or when a politician is involved.

For some individuals there may even be a certain level of vicarious identification with and admiration of the perpetrator who "beats the system" — and "makes the big score." After all, big corporations can afford it, the loss is covered by insurance, and corporations rip everyone off anyway. Who cares? Or so the justification goes. It is for these reasons that management must move proactively to reverse or, at a minimum, neutralize the negative attitudes, practices, and perceptions that overtly or tacitly encourage the seeding and growth of abusive employees.

If you are developing a compliance program that is intended to meet *Chapter Eight* criteria, here are a few definitions of terms you'll need to know:*

An effective program to prevent and detect violations of law means a program that has been reasonably designed, implemented, and enforced to be generally effective in preventing and detecting criminal conduct. Failure to prevent or detect the instant offense, by itself, does not mean that the program was not effective. The hallmark of an effective program to prevent and detect violations of law is that the organization exercised due diligence

* Entire Definitions of terms quoted from U.S. Sentencing Commission Guidelines Manual, Chapter Eight, Sentencing of Organizations, November 1, 2000, pp. 406–409.

in seeking to prevent and detect criminal conduct by its employee and other agents. Due diligence requires at a minimum that the organization must have taken the following types of steps:

The organization must have established compliance standards and procedures to be followed by its employees and other agents that are reasonably capable of reducing the prospect of criminal conduct.

Specific individual(s) within high-level personnel of the organization must have been assigned overall responsibility to oversee compliance with such standards and procedures.

The organization must have used due care not to delegate substantial discretionary authority to individuals whom the organization know, or should have known through the exercise of due diligence, had a propensity to engage in illegal activities.

The organization must have taken steps to effectively communicate its standards and procedures to all employees and other agents, e.g., by requiring participation in training program or by disseminating publications that explain in a practical manner what is required.

The organization must have taken reasonable steps to achieve compliance with its standards, e.g., by utilizing monitoring and auditing systems reasonably designed to detect criminal conduct by its employees and other agents and by having in place and publicizing a reporting system whereby employees and other agents could report criminal conduct by others within the organization without fear of retribution.

The standards must have been consistently enforced through appropriate disciplinary mechanisms, including, as appropriate, discipline of individuals responsible for the failure to detect an offense. Adequate discipline of individuals responsible for an offense is a necessary component of enforcement; however, the form of discipline that is appropriate is case specific.

After an offense has been detected, the organization must have taken all reasonable steps to respond appropriately to the offense and to prevent further similar offenses – including any necessary modifications to its program to prevent and detect violations of law.

The precise actions necessary for an effective program to prevent and detect violations of law depend upon a number of factors. Among the relevant factors are:

Size of the organization – The requisite degree of formality of a program to prevent and detect violations of law varies with the size of the organization: the larger the organization, the more formal the program typically should be. A larger organization generally should have established written policies defining the standards and procedures to be followed by its employees and other agents.

Likelihood that certain offenses might occur because of the nature of its business – If because of the nature of an organization's business there is a substantial risk that certain types of offenses may occur, management must have taken steps to prevent and detect those types of offenses. For example, if an organization handles toxic substances, it must have established standards and procedures designed to ensure that those substances are properly handled at all times. If an organization employs sales personnel who have flexibility in setting prices, it must have established standards and procedures designed to prevent and detect price-fixing. If an organization employs sales personnel who have flexibility to represent the material characteristics of a product, it must have established standards and procedures designed to prevent fraud.

Prior history of the organization – An organization's prior history may indicate types of offenses that it should have taken actions to prevent. Recurrence of misconduct similar to that which an organization has previously committed casts doubt on whether it took all reasonable steps to prevent such misconduct. An organization's failure to incorporate and follow applicable industry practice or the standards called for by any applicable governmental regulation weighs against a finding of an effective program to prevent and detect violations of law.

High-level personnel of the organization means individuals who have substantial control over the organization or who have a substantial role in the making of policy within the organization. The term includes a director; an executive officer; an individual in charge of a major business or functional unit of the organization, such as sales, administration, or finance; and an individual with a substantial ownership interest.

Substantial authority personnel means individuals who within the scope of their authority exercise a substantial measure of discretion in action on behalf of an organization. The term includes high-level personnel, individuals who exercise substantial supervisory authority (e.g., a plant manager, a sales manager), and any other individuals who, although not a part of an organization's management, nevertheless exercise substantial discretion when acting within the scope of their authority (e.g., an individual with authority in an organization to negotiate or set price levels or an individual authorized to negotiate or approve significant contracts). Whether an individual falls within this category must be determined on a case-by-case basis.

Agent means any individual, including a director, an officer, an employee, or an independent contractor, authorized to act on behalf of the organization.

An individual *condoned* an offense if the individual knew of the offense and did not take reasonable steps to prevent or terminate the offense.

Similar misconduct means prior conduct that is similar in nature to the conduct underlying the instant offense, without regard to whether or not such conduct violated the same statutory provision.

Prior criminal adjudication means conviction by trial, plea of guilty (including an *Alford* plea), or plea of *nolo contendere*.

Pecuniary gain is derived from 18 U.S.C.§ 3571(d) and means the additional before-tax profit to the defendant resulting from the relevant conduct of the offense. Gain can result from either additional revenue or cost savings.

Pecuniary loss is derived from 18 U.S.C.§ 3571(d) and is equivalent to the term 'Loss' as used in *Chapter Two* (Offense Conduct).

An individual was willfully ignorant of the offense if the individual did not investigate the possible occurrence of unlawful conduct despite knowledge of circumstances that would lead a reasonable person to investigate whether unlawful conduct had occurred.

1.3 Man and Society

During the course and scope of man's evolution, he has created benchmarks of conduct that guide and influence the course of human existence and interaction. Some standards take the form of laws. Many exist in our religious and philosophical foundations. Some are purely social in nature and govern conduct on that level. All are fundamentally important to the orderly functioning of a society, its commerce, and lives of individual citizens. In the absence of laws and moral codes, there is anarchy.

The development of a moral base is fundamentally significant to a society and its people. In the absence of such a base one finds corruption, both in nations and individuals. The degree of corruption found, in both instances, is proportional to the level of any breakdowns in or absence of a moral base. American ethical and moral codes are rooted in Judeo-Christian teachings.

Much of the strength of the American people has come from our character base and concepts of right and wrong, our ethics, integrity, individuality, and willingness to accept responsibility for our actions and outcomes. Our self-respect, and the respect we give our fellow man, has also contributed to the virtue of our country. It is this aspect of our national makeup that has also contributed so much to the uniqueness of American business and organizational structures in the world. Our moral standards are the foundation of our system of values. To permit the weakening, erosion, or destruction of this foundation is to weaken, erode, or destroy the individual American, the American business community, our institutions, and America.

There are advocates who argue that we must change, as individuals and as a country, if we are to grow and survive. This is true. We must grow and improve. Change is a growth imperative, both quantitatively and qualitatively. This rule applies to individuals and nations states alike. If, however, the search for change is quantitatively oriented to the detriment of quality, then an imbalance is created that can be destructive.

It is when we sacrifice quality that we create perhaps the most notable imbalance of all. It is the quality of our progress that decides the quality of our lives. This admonition applies equally to the nation's business organizations, societal institutions, and individuals. When the pursuit of quality becomes less important, all else does as well. The explanation for that corollary is simple: quality is a reflection of character.

1.4 Occupational Crimes and Abusive Behaviors

Here are some examples of wrongful employee behaviors for which your organization is at risk. Such conduct has an infinite assortment of identifiers. One is literally limited only by one's own intelligence, motivation, fear of detection, opportunity, and imagination in the commission of abusive behavior.

The following examples identify some behaviors to prevent and, failing that, to detect, identify, punish, and then reverse. These examples are only a partial listing. The sampling is random with no order of importance implied or intended. This risk is no small vulnerability. As with other lists in this manual, add examples unique to your own organization.

- Unethical business practices
- Financial, consumer, and vendor fraud

- Inventory thefts
- Equipment thefts
- Embezzlement
- Accepting or offering kickbacks
- Conflicts of interest
- Sale, possession, or use of illegal drugs
- On-the-job alcohol abuse
- Workers' compensation fraud
- Unauthorized use of personnel, equipment, and materials
- Burglary
- Trespassing
- Health insurance fraud
- Forgery
- Accepting or offering unauthorized discounts
- Accepting unauthorized gratuities
- Vandalism
- Falsification of records
- Ghost employees
- Work stoppages or slowdowns
- Industrial espionage
- Abuse of discount privileges
- Under-ringing sales
- Theft of cash
- Sabotage
- Cheating or abusing employees, customers, or vendors
- Price-fixing
- Sexual harassment
- Possession of dangerous weapons
- Soliciting or accepting gifts
- Sick-leave abuse
- Theft of time
- Sale of proprietary information
- Commercial bribery
- Insider trading
- Lying, distortions, misrepresentations, and manipulations
- Environmental crimes
- Software piracy
- Exploitation of corporate opportunity
- Arson
- Understatement of sales
- Overstatement of expenses or deferral

- Inflation of accruals
- Booking orders as advanced sales
- Creating fake inventories
- Padding inventory after physical count
- Falsification of purchase orders
- Billing for services not yet rendered
- Consignments listed as sales
- Double billing
- Credit card fraud
- Check fraud
- Fictitious vendors
- Diversion of sales
- Bid rigging
- Expense account abuse
- Abuse of travel and entertainment
- Mail fraud
- Wire fraud
- Securities fraud
- Money laundering
- Political corruption
- Antitrust violations
- Credit fraud
- Contract fraud

While some level of abusive employee behavior exists in every organization, keep in mind that each organization is unique. What exists as an exposure for abusive behavior in one environment may not exist in another. To be effective in evaluating the risks of the occurrence of any one or some combination of the above-noted abuses one has to make an evaluation based on organizational makeup and a known or suspected history of abuses.

In Chapter 2, The Cost, space is devoted to the importance of records in determining historical information. Information is needed to evaluate what has occurred, where it occurred, when, how, and why it occurred, by whom the behavior was committed, and the amount and type of any damage. This type of data can make an important contribution to the quality and accuracy of any loss evaluation, the design of a preventive response, and for forecasting future trouble spots.

1.5 Planning

Development of an employee security-awareness program or a *Chapter Eight* compliance program, or one that combines both types, requires planning — thorough planning if the program is to be effective in the long term. The same rule applies if you are updating or changing an existing program. Planning is critical to success in either instance. If you are an inexperienced planner, the book will assist in getting you over many of the obstacles that may be encountered. If you are an old pro, you will already be familiar with what is needed. Whatever the case, the importance of planning cannot be overemphasized. The quality of your final product will be a direct reflection of the amount of time and effort put into planning and drafting your program. Who was it that said, "Failing to plan is planning to fail?"

1.6 The Threat among Us

Pearl River, NY: a former vice president of corporate communications for the Orange & Rockland Utilities and his wife pled guilty to the theft of $199,000 from the utility through the use of fictitious billings from phantom companies set up by them. The wife worked as an assistant in the same office as her husband. A former vice president for the same department had pled guilty earlier in another incident.

Every for-profit, nonprofit, or not-for-profit organization in this country regardless of its size or legal form, product or service sold, manufactured, or delivered is now being, has been, or will be victimized by some level of management or employee exploitative behavior. The same applies equally to government and other social institutions. If that were not enough, some of our organizations are victimizing their employees and many of the rest of us as well. The predatory mentality is not a one-way street. Employees do not have a monopoly on abusive conduct; customers and clients are also guilty of the same behaviors.

IBM and the FBI publicly disclosed that they had been conducting a sting operation designed to uncover theft and fraud in the computer giant. Losses were estimated in the hundreds of millions of dollars. The investigation disclosed both insider and outsider involvement. Losses resulted from mismanagement, theft, and warranty fraud.

Who is acting out, and where is it being perpetrated? Abusive acts are committed by people at all levels, from those who breathe the heady air of corporate boardrooms and executive suites to those who function in the stale air of the assembly line and on the warehouse loading dock. Dishonesty can stretch from the top of the organization to the bottom and all that lies between; there are no automatic exclusions for job titles or workstations, job assignments, or tenure. Governmental and institutional organizations mirror that behavior as well. From the highest elected and appointed officials in American government to local politicians, too many have shared behavior that is the moral equivalent of dirt — corruption, lies, and fraud.

> Miami, FL: a former Assistant U.S. Attorney pled guilty in a federal court to money laundering and perjury. The $42,133 involved allegedly came from a drug dealer.

How pervasive is the problem of employee misconduct?

- The U.S. Department of Commerce estimates that approximately one third of all employees steal from their employers, and annualized losses from embezzlement could be as high as $40 billion.
- The Bureau of National Affairs estimates losses from embezzlement alone could hit $15 to $25 billion annually.
- Large-scale anonymous surveys conducted by Reid Psychological Systems, a Chicago-based honesty-testing firm, found the following percentages of employees admitted stealing from their employers:
  - Manufacturing, 26%
  - Hospitals, 32.2%
  - Retail, 41.8%
- Surveys conducted by The Stanton Corporation, a Charlotte, North Carolina honesty-testing firm, found that 32% of 100,000 applicants questioned admitted stealing from a past employer. The thefts reported ranged in value from $25 to $1500. Stanton concluded that both the percentages admitting involvement and the admitted amounts are substantially low.
- A recent 3-year study on employee theft conducted by the University of Minnesota's Sociology Department found:
  - One third of employees admitted stealing from their employer.
  - 60% of employees admitted to the commission of abusive acts.
  - 80% of all workers steal when no active deterrent is in place.

The study was conducted by Richard C. Hollinger of the University of Florida and John P. Clark of the University of Minnesota under a grant from the U.S. Department of Justice and its National Institute of Justice. Three industries were studied: retail, manufacturing, and hospitals; 9000 employees answered anonymous questionnaires. This study is detailed in the book titled *Theft by Employees*, published by Lexington Books, Lexington, MA.

- In the mid 1990s the accounting firm of KPMG Peat, Marwick released the results of a survey of 2000 of the largest U.S. businesses on the prevalence of business fraud; 330 companies, or 17% completed the survey questionnaire. The results showed that more than 40,000 individual acts of fraud were committed against those organizations included in the survey. Take a look at what they found:
  - 75% of those surveyed reported being damaged by internal fraud.
  - 25% reported annual losses of $1 million.
  - 70% believed that business-related fraud was getting worse.
  - 80% believed increasing levels of fraud were due to harsh economic conditions.
  - 75% attributed the increase to declining moral values.
  - Over half failed to take proper precautions to stop the problem.
  - Warning signals of potential fraud were typically ignored.
  - Responders reported losses in excess of $250 million.
- Also in the mid 1990s Ernst & Young conducted a nationwide survey of 800 chief information officers. Ernst & Young is a consulting firm that audits the information systems and security services of business. The results:
  - Several responders reported losses of over $1 million in a single incident.
  - 90% considered employees as threats.
  - Cost is often more than $100,000 per incident.
- The 4th Annual Report on Employee Theft in the Supermarket Industry conducted by London House and the Food Marketing Institute revealed that 44% of supermarket employees admitted to acts of theft. Admissions and estimates of individual thefts ranged from $26 to $26,000 annually.
- The U.S. General Accounting Office estimates the annual losses from white-collar crime sustained by American business and governmental entities to be $100 billion.
- In the late 1990s a survey of 1324 randomly selected executives, managers, and workers conducted by the Ethics Officer Association, the American Society of Chartered Life Underwriters and Chartered Financial Consultants produced a 236-page report. Respondents were asked to list violations attributable to work-related "pressure" (pressure arising from such things as long hours, unrealistic sales quotas, fear of job loss, workload, poor leadership,

balancing work demands and family responsibilities, and personal debt). Among the results:

- 48% admitted to unethical or illegal acts in the past year.
- 57% felt greater pressure to be unethical than in the past 5 years.
- 40% said pressures to commit unethical acts had gotten worse in the last year.
- 20% of mid-level managers reported high-level pressure to act unethically or illegally.
- 5.4% of senior executives had considered suicide over the last year.
- 2.4% of workers had considered suicide over the last year.

If these studies are accurate, today's business owners and managers face a significant challenge if they expect to run ethical and profitable business operations. Therein may lie the caveat. Can a company be ethically managed and profitable in a contemporary context? And if that caveat exists for business, does it apply equally to government?

Losses attributed to individual or collusive abusive acts range from nickel-and-dime amounts to millions of dollars per incident. The losses per incident or the accumulative effect on individual companies can be, and in many instances are, staggering. Out-of-pocket costs are many times only part of the predicament faced by management. As injurious as those costs can be, consequential damages arising from employee misconduct can and do in some instances exceed the direct out-of-pocket costs. More on the subject of consequential damage in Chapter 2: The Cost.

> The Inspector General's Office of the United States Department of Housing and Urban Development reported in 1993 that real estate speculators, mortgage company officials, multifamily property owners, and others misused or stole more than $200 million from the agency and 375 people were convicted of fraud, theft, and other crimes. Investigators recovered only $88.7 million of the losses. Total losses are not known. One highly placed HUD official was charged with 12 felony counts involving lying to Congress, conspiracy, and accepting an illegal gratuity. That person was convicted and sentenced to 21 months in prison.

Disturbingly, among employee abusers are individuals who view themselves and their actions in the abuse of customers and vendors as satisfying actual or perceived business objectives. Then there are those individuals who, for whatever reason, are simply ripping off the company, its stockholders, their co-workers, customers, and vendors. In either situation, the company is the loser.

Abusive behavior is fueled in both instances when management is passive about or encourages dishonest, illegal, or unethical behavior that furthers corporate objectives. Furthermore, abusers are most active when the expectation of detection is low and when management is perceived as uncaring or unconcerned. If not prevented or detected, employee excesses can and will become a black hole of lost profits, higher costs, and greater operating inefficiencies.

Management sets the ethical tone for the organizations they manage. Management's attitudes and practices establish the caliber of management oversight. Organizations that fail to heed the warnings and to initiate an appropriate well-measured response are destined to experience the realities of those failures.

1.7 Past Focus

In the past, most security literature focused on theft and the techniques to prevent and detect it. Much of that treatment concentrated on rank-and-file staff or production workers and the nonemployee threat. Management at all levels was largely portrayed as trusted and above suspicion.

Although implicit, not much was said about unethical and irresponsible management behavior and its effect on an organization, the environment, or our economic system. Unethical and irresponsible business practices existed but were played down. Management was sacrosanct and above suspicion. Management's actions in pursuit of perceived business interests were righteous and good for the company and the country. Business is still good for the individual company and the country, but management and their actions are no longer sacrosanct, trusted, or above suspicion.

> The former chief financial officer for the pharmacy firm Phar-Mor pled guilty for his part in a $1 billion fraud and embezzlement scheme perpetrated against the company. He was sentenced to prison.

That has all changed now. Pervasive business, government fraud, and mismanagement have eroded a nation's trust and respect for both institutions and the individuals responsible for their management. Suspicion and mistrust now dominate the minds of most Americans when considering the past records of business and government. We must wonder if we have hit bottom or if the decline will continue?

Occurrences of the last 20 years disclose many of the practical and logical fallacies of misplaced trust. Criminal, unethical, and irresponsible business practices were exposed in varying degrees throughout the 1980s, 1990s, and into 2000. Disclosures and investigations are as contemporary as the time and date you are reading this material. Business and government and its management have all figuratively "taken a bullet in the chest." Is this a case of suicide? Is "the party is over?" The balloons have been popped.

> New York, NY: The former chief executive officer of the investment banking firm Keefe Bruyette & Woods was convicted on one count of conspiracy and five counts of insider trading in federal court. A New Jersey businessman was convicted of one count of conspiracy and three counts of insider trading. The CEO allegedly tipped off a female porn actress, who then tipped off the New Jersey man about the pending merger of five regional banks. Both men were friends of the actress. Both men were married. The actress was charged with insider trading but fled to avoid prosecution.

1.7.1   Fortune 500

It has been estimated that as many as two thirds of the companies making up the Fortune 500 have been implicated in some type of illegal activity in the last 2 decades. Allegedly, that activity occurred with varying degrees of executive management knowledge, complicity, or direct involvement. The same scenario was acted out on a smaller scale within many less well-known companies. Those in the Fortune 500 group are icons of the American free enterprise system and have consequently received most of the attention.

> Norman Jaspan, President of Jaspan Associates in New York, estimates a greater than 50% chance of significant dishonesty in any firm and a 75% chance of harmful malpractice sufficient to impair a company's profit structure.

Most of those business organizations implicated in illegal activities have suffered financial losses and the embarrassment of damaged reputations. Some will never recover their former public and financial stature. Others will take years to rebuild, if they can do it all. Some are now bankrupt, in Chapter Eleven bankruptcy, or out of business. Involved management, in many instances, has been replaced or shuttled to the dark recesses of the basement. Former executives and their corporations are awaiting trial on criminal charges, while others stand convicted. Civil actions are pending in federal and state courts that will take years to grind through the legal system in search of a resolution.

In all instances, stockholders, involved management, noninvolved management, employees, customers, and suppliers have suffered. Efforts are now under way by those organizations that survived to polish their images and restore lost stockholder, employee, and consumer confidence. Meeting that objective will be no easy task. Trust, once violated, is difficult to restore.

1.7.2   Federal Bureau of Investigation

The investigation of white-collar crime is one of the national priorities of the Federal Bureau of Investigation (FBI). FBI jurisdiction in white-collar crime matters is derived from laws enacted by the U.S. Congress. Some of these laws cover government fraud, environmental crimes, public corruption, and financial crimes. Each of these areas is critical to public confidence and trust in the institutions of government and private enterprise. Local and state law-enforcement authorities are now also focusing on many of the same crimes but within a more limited jurisdiction.

Statistics (U.S. Department of Justice, Federal Bureau of Investigation, White Collar Crime Program, Statistical Report, June 1993) indicate that the FBI's white-collar-crime program utilized approximately 27% of the Bureau's direct agent workyears and achieved 37% of the total convictions and pretrial diversions of the entire FBI. The Feds have been busy. Due to budgetary constraints the Bureau cannot possibly address all white-collar crime investigations within their jurisdictions. To ensure the most productive use of these limited resources the FBI encourages joint white-collar crime investigations with other law-enforcement and regulatory agencies at the local, state, and federal levels.

According to the FBI 1993 report their white-collar-crime program recently recorded in excess of 2798 convictions or pretrial diversions. Fines in excess of $943+ million were levied. Recoveries and restitutions in over $787+ million were made. The FBI prevented more than $453+ million in losses, seized in excess of $84.5+ million in cash and assets, and received forfeitures for more than $2 billion. White-collar crime is responsible for the loss of billions of dollars annually to government, business, and the American people.

1.7.3   National Story

Thanks to media reports the American people have been inundated with a dirty behind-the-scenes look at a national tragedy. It's a pathetic tale of trust abused and violated and of personal greed and excesses. The American people have witnessed a business and institutional exposé that has disclosed fraud, theft, and other abusive acts committed by executives in high-level management, trust, and fiduciary positions. Lies, deceit, ruthless manipulations, guile, arrogance, avarice, and contempt exemplify the behavior of executives implicated in wrongdoing. Even FBI executives have had a shadow of distrust cast over them for the management and accuracy of the post-incident reporting of the Waco and Ruby Ridge incidents and allegations of malpractice in their crime lab, incompetency, and treason, among others. American citizens have been killed by government agents. The credibility of the FBI has been called into question. Doubts have been raised. Can anyone or any organization be trusted?

The display of executive excesses has shocked the conscience of anyone with any ethical concerns and has threatened the very foundations of business and governmental trust and respect. It is dishonesty in the extreme, a circumstance that undermines all it touches. One has to wonder if the term "business ethics" is an oxymoron.

The "buzzword" is corruption. It seems that every institution we trusted, respected, or held in high esteem has felt the sting of corruption. Some may have been diminished by corrupt behavior and their leadership subject to declining respect and suspicion, including the Office of the President of the United States.

> Indiana: Urologist charged by U.S. Attorney for bilking insurers out of $40,000 to $70,000 for drugs. A pharmaceutical company in Massachusetts gave the doctor drugs free of charge over a 3-year period. The urologist pled guilty. Doctors in seven states are under investigation for similar fraudulent billings.

Americans have been hammered by corruption scandals that ranges from Wall Street to our churches, national and local governments, and all that lies in the middle. Many of our police officers, doctors, lawyers, judges, clergy, and yes, even an Indian Chief (Peter MacDonald, former Chairman of the Navajo Nation, was convicted by a Tribal Court of bribery, but later pardoned by the Navajo Nation Council) have or are alleged to have succumbed to corruption. Maybe we have been overwhelmed by it all.

Are Americans awash with feelings of helplessness? Has the individual American been numbed and desensitized into passive apathy by the magnitude of it all? If the answer is "yes," and the likelihood that are that is what has occurred, then the logical question is, can the decline be reversed? The answer to the second question is also "yes." For us to effect a change, however, we must first recognize and acknowledge the pervasiveness of the problem and then move to rectify it. Until we deal with truth there will only be self-deceit, and we will continue to fall victim to our denials. That change will not occur without great personal courage, commitment, and effort.

The sad truth is that Americans are witnessing the erosion of their ethical and moral foundations. No individual or family has escaped untouched. Each of us pays a price in emotional terms and in dollars, each of us is at risk, each of us is victimized in a direct or indirect manner. Recognition of this fact has shocked us to the very core of our national being; we have been stunned by it all, and in varying degrees we have been immobilized. This is not the way it is supposed to be. This is America. We lead the world. We stand for right, not wrong. What is happening to us? Where will all this decay and corruption lead? Will it ever end?

Americans are baffled, confused, and frustrated because every aspect of our lives is now affected by corruption. We ask, what has happened to our country? Our lives have become very complex. We ask, is black no longer black? Is white no longer white? Is right no longer right? Is wrong no longer wrong? What is black? What is white? What is right? What is wrong? Are there only grays? Is everything we do just a situational exercise?

What is the current politically correct term to use, thing to do, or interpretation to be made of any given situation? Who or what interest group defines correctness? What is the agenda of that person or organization? How will we be attacked, embroiled in litigation, criticized, or vilified for being out of step with the agenda? How will the spindoctors in our government, institutions, and businesses attempt to change the meaning of any given situation? Can we trust the media? What new words and definitions will be created to enhance the spin? Can we believe anything said, seen, or written by any source, official or otherwise? What language are we now using? Who understands what is being said? Does any word or past definition still mean the same thing it did last week? How are we to communicate with each other in meaningful terms? We find that there is now a rationalization or justification to excuse any act or behavior, no matter how extreme — even murder. What is going on? What is the definition of "is"?

The American people have felt the personal and national degradation of a nation besieged by corruptive allegations. Lies, distortions, half-truths, and adulteration of our language are now standard fare. Today, individuals in leadership positions in our country, who represent every strata of our society, face allegations of corruption or convictions for criminal activity. There are those individuals who have attained the highest levels of trust and respect who now stand accused or convicted of the most abusive behavior proscribed by law.

Who will be the role models of the future? If there is no condemnation of corruption, then the answer to the question is that the liars, the greedy, the cheats, and the thieves of today will be the role models of tomorrow. Who will our children emulate? What are we becoming as individuals and as a nation? The answer is yet to be determined.

Are Americans intoxicated on a diet of self and national deceit? It seems we are. If not, how does one explain the current state of corruption in our country? Any person with a clear head and a well-founded perspective of the past must be concerned about the future. Through all this Americans have seen themselves diminished as individuals, as a people, and as a nation. For all our greatness there are many dismal commentaries of the day. The blows inflicted through trust abused, corruption, and mismanagement have staggered Americans.

1.8   Tomorrow

What does the future hold for us? As we enter the 21st century we face a decade of moral challenges. If we do not meet those challenges, the very foundations of American society will be threatened. You do not have to look far to find precedent for this concern. History is replete with examples of the carnage resulting from the self-consuming excesses of individuals and nations. One of the logical questions that arises from this knowledge is whether or not the greatest experience in self-government and free enterprise the world has ever known is destined to self-destruct, consumed by its own excesses? The answer lies somewhere in the future. As unthinkable as the prospect of such a loss is to contemplate, it is nevertheless possible.

In their book titled *The Day America Told the Truth: What People Really Believe about Everything that Really Matters*, Prentice-Hall Press, 1991, James Patterson and Peter Kim polled 200 Americans at 50 representative locations nationwide. Poll respondents were guaranteed anonymity and completed questionnaires containing 1800 questions that were completed in private.

Their base survey was supplemented by a follow-up survey Patterson and Kim conducted involving 3700 other Americans who completed a shortened version under the same conditions. Both surveys were conducted simultaneously across the country during a 1-week period in 1990. Interestingly, one of the conclusions drawn from the data collected in the surveys is that "Americans are making up their own rules, laws, and moral codes." And as Americans move toward the next century it is these attitudes that will threaten a return to the days of the wild, wild West.

Among the findings of the survey are these statistics:

- Only 13% of Americans still believe in all ten of the Bible's commandments.
- Nine out of ten Americans lie on a regular basis.
- 61% admitted to lying regularly to their boss.
- 69% admitted to lying to a lover.
- 59% admitted to lying to a child.
- 86% admitted to lying to a parent.
- 75% admitted to lying to a friend.

Overall, the report concluded, "There is absolutely no moral consensus at all in the 1990s," as there was in the 1950s and 1960s. The survey concludes that Americans believe their political, religious, and business leaders have failed them.

In a 1993 study conducted by the U.S. Department of Education (Tamara, H., 90 million can barely read, write, *U.S.A. Today*, September 9, 1993), National Center for Education Statistics it was revealed that 90 million American adults, almost half of U.S. adult population, are nearly functionally illiterate; 25% of the 90 million are immigrants who may just be learning English. Alarmingly, the study disclosed that between 49 and 58% of high school graduates perform in the lowest levels of literacy. Disappointing, you say. Well, would you believe that 15 to 19% of college graduates and 9% of graduate students did as poorly? They did.

At a time when we should be preparing ourselves for future technological demands and levels of sophistication heretofore unknown, half of our adults are functionally illiterate. Ethical, moral, and more esoteric questions and concerns will probably escape these individuals. If you cannot read, think, or comprehend other than the most simple tasks and concepts, how will you grasp the meaning of liberty, individual responsibility, accountability, property rights, or the rule of law? Right and wrong translates to the growl in your stomach, shelter, or warmth for your back.

What does all this forecast for the future of America? Trouble! No moral consensus, pervasive ignorance, a lack of confidence in our leaders and institutions, high crime, drug abuse, and low personal and national self-esteem. What a combination. All of which breeds a predatory mindset and the rationalizations and justifications one needs to excuse any conduct.

1.8.1 Management's Contribution

"Simple right and wrong issues? Right? Every adult knows right from wrong. Right? As the manager, I know what to do and how to handle these types of situations and problems. I have confidence in my employees. They know right from wrong. I cannot take valuable time to do the job parents and the schools should have done. That task is not one of my jobs. I have sales, marketing, supply, legal, personnel, customer complaints, production, credit, accounting, and operations problems to worry about, and now you want me to worry about everyone's morals and ethics, too? Get real!"

"I have a job to do and ethics are not a top priority. Profits are my concern. The bottom line. If there is a problem with ethics, I did not create it. I am just trying to survive. I deal with the world as it is, not the way it should be. This is the 21st century. Just take a hard look at senior management in this company, and then ask me about ethics. That is the real world to me, not some esoteric nonsense. I have to feed and house my family. Back off and get real."

Do this manager's rationalizations and justifications sound familiar? Have you met any managers like the one the above statement characterizes? Does the statement reflect your own opinion on the subject? Does the opinion characterize those of your company's upper management or those of any of your peers? Is this opinion one that is an accurate reflection of most managers in your organization? If you answered yes to any of these questions, then you have cause for concern.

Why? Because the manager whose attitudes are characterized in the foregoing statement should examine his underlying motives to determine if those attitudes are not just an excuse for not acting appropriately. Read the statement again. Go on, do it! While you are at it take a hard look at the attitudes his expressions represent. Do they sound like excuses for just not doing the job right?

The belief system of a manager, the values he holds, and the assumptions he makes all have a direct influence on the quality of and the manner in which he manages. His attitude and management style are a definite reflection of whether he is a person of substance and character or only a shallow pretense of those desirable qualities. The organization will always reflect the character of management.

There are those who would argue that dishonesty starts at the top and spirals downward. Moral and ethical corruption in the lower ranks is often typified by management's questionable-to-illegal business practices, permissiveness, double standards, abuse, and neglect. If there was ever any doubt as to the validity of that argument, it has surely been laid to rest by now. Everyone understands behavior — even children. We all take leads from behavior to varying degrees.

Regrettably, management must assume a large part of the responsibility, if not all the blame, for the current state of business abuses and many abusive employee attitudes. Too many people in positions of management trust have violated or are violating that trust and have become active players in the organizational abuse game.

Far too many executives are fueling the growth of abusive employee behavior at all levels of corporate America. Management commits more fraud, steals more, and does so in larger amounts than rank-and-file employees ever did. That is saying a lot, because the dollar losses attributed to the rank-and-file employee are substantial. The combined totals are staggering.

1.8.2   Ignored and Covered Up

Many abusive acts are never discovered. Of those that are discovered, many are ignored, covered up, or glossed over for various reasons by management, subordinates, or both. There are reasons for this type of response. All are judgment calls, dominated by self-interest considerations. It is, therefore, apparent that ethical compromises are part of many of those decisions.

Why would either or both groups ignore or cover up abusive behavior? The answer to that question will have as many facets as there are miscreants. Generally, it occurs because of legal, social, management, operating, and political issues. Issues that arise from such behavior can be extremely complex for both management and the rank-and-file employees.

A lack of moral and ethical direction exists on both levels that severely compounds and contributes to the scope of the problem. It is for these reasons, among others, that the problem and the resulting damages can be and many times are obscured and exacerbated. The result is a bad situation made worse in a maze of competing business, legal, professional, and personal interests. These competing interests can threaten the very existence of an organization.

1.8.3   Actions

Has business become an informal criminal brotherhood? Has our ethical decline become socially accepted or just a current phenomenon that will pass? Where have the individual and collective courage and integrity that we pay homage to as a nation and as individuals disappeared? More hypocrisy? Is the pride gone? Did it ever exist? Is the American business community morally and ethically bankrupt? The answer is a clear and compelling "no!" There is, however, cause for concern. Business leadership and institutional management must recognize the threat that abusive behavior poses and then deal with it effectively.

Employee security-awareness, loss-prevention, or compliance programs are a cost-effective and viable approach to resolving or mitigating the problem. Such programs can provide ethical frameworks that strengthen moral codes, the business organization, and the individual. The ethical or moral base of any society will deteriorate when allowed to erode.

Management sets policies, procedures, and standards of performance through written and spoken words and personal actions. In so doing, management sets the moral and ethical parameters of the organization. There is, however, another dimension to this responsibility. The damages incurred and resulting from abusive management practices go far beyond the frauds that are individually perpetrated or the goods that are stolen. Bad management practices and personal examples undermine and erode the efficiency and integrity of the entire organization. All stakeholders are negatively impacted.

What management does is far more influential than what management says, because behavior is the only thing that is understood at all levels of an organization. Failure of management to recognize this fact is demonstrably stupid. The "don't do as I do, do as I say" approach to management is fundamentally flawed.

In defense of management, there are many other considerations that play on, influence, and impact the problem of abusive employee behavior. Even the most ethically managed businesses must function within the larger contemporary societal and cultural environment that is in a constant state of change and whose influences swing like the proverbial pendulum. The negative forces acting on these environments can be changed when recognized and when the will exists to reverse the trend. Recognition, unfortunately, usually follows a disaster.

Many negative influences impact behavior. Human resources are produced in and drawn from environments that are, in many instances, less than desirable. So neither business nor its management can be charged with responsibility for all the problems of our society. Business practices alone have not caused the moral decline of an entire society, but they must certainly share the guilt.

1.8.4 Excuses and Rationalizations

It is in vogue to offer sociological excuses and rationalizations for all kinds of behavior, particularly criminal, unethical, or irresponsible behavior. This practice results in tacit approval and the legitimation of that behavior. Sociological excuses provide the abusive person with a basis for the psychological rationalization and justification of his acts. Consequently, there is a diminution of individual responsibility and accountability for those actions and the negatives resulting therefrom. This is particularly significant when society is considered responsible for all the wrongs committed by an individual, because the person is then absolved of guilt. Societal guilt is no one's guilt.

If, in fact, society is indebted to those who turn to criminal, dishonest, unethical, and irresponsible pursuits because of what it has not done for them, then to repay the criminals among us the victims of their excesses are little more than an installment reimbursement of that debt. Let us not ask what people have or have not done for themselves. Those types of questions hold people accountable and, therefore, make them uncomfortable!

The fact of the matter is that the choice to commit an abusive act is just that, a choice; a decision (assuming mental capacity) is made by an individual acting on his or her own behalf or by an individual or group of individuals acting on behalf of a business or other organization. Therefore, the first level of accountability lies with the individual.

The basic rule is simple: good choices equal good consequences and bad choices equal poor consequences. In either instance, the individual makes a choice and accordingly produces or sets in motion the forces that will produce a consequence. The consequences may be positive or negative. The effect of the consequences may be limited to the individual, or it may involve many others.

The effect may occur instantly or at some future point in time. The result may be imperceptible at the one extreme, while producing a personal, corporate, or governmental disaster at the other; nonetheless, there will be a consequence. Knowing this rule encumbers the decision-maker with the personal responsibility to make his decisions very carefully.

An individual is responsible and must be held accountable for his decisions, actions, and the resulting consequences. Remove or diminish those three factors with sociological excuses, rationalizations, and justifications, and one sets up the infrastructure for failure, within society at large, a specific business or other organization.

The author once knew the chief executive officer (CEO) of a major corporation who had a simple way of characterizing the management under whose auspices fraud and abusive behavior occurred without management's discovery of that conduct. As far as that CEO was concerned, the manager was either stupid, incompetent, or a thief himself until investigation proved otherwise.

It was the CEO's opinion that when this type of behavior occurs the manager either knows or should know what is occurring under him and, therefore, be held accountable. This CEO is a tough taskmaster who demands the highest standards of honesty and ethics from his managers.

A tough standard to meet indeed. Notwithstanding that fact, this was the standard to which management was held when misconduct was discovered and reported by a third party. If the manager discovered the misconduct, or if it was discovered by someone under his authority, then the manager was considered diligent in discharging his responsibilities. Obviously, this is a very stressful situation to be in when an investigation is initiated. If the investigation proved that the nature of the incident was such that it was unreasonable to expect management to know of the behavior, and if the manager was not implicated, then he was retained.

Conversely, if the manager was implicated, should have known or lied about, attempted to cover up, distort, or misrepresent the incident, minimized the problem, or impeded or otherwise interfered with the company investigation, he was subject to termination. Corrupt, unethical, irresponsible, deceptive, lying, cheating, devious, deceitful, egocentric, inept, or inattentive managers lost their jobs. Most of the managers terminated were poor performers with character flaws. Some were people who simply lost sight of the importance the CEO placed on job performance and on protecting the assets of the corporation and those of his employees.

This is an example of a CEO who understood that corrupt, inefficient, or incompetent management had to be replaced. The tactic was a great motivator of management. While sometimes stressful, management did keep a very watchful eye on its personnel and ensured strict compliance with company policies and procedures. The company was an industry leader and financially successful.

1.8.5   Business Interest

Business functions in and is a microcosm of the society in which it exists. Notwithstanding that fact, business can still provide positive leadership in recognizing and dealing with societal problems. This is particularly true with a problem as pervasive and destructive as corruption. This problem is altering the face of our society because American business does not function in a vacuum.

In his book *The Practice of Management* (Drucker, P.F., Harper & Row, New York, 1982), Peter Drucker describes the commercial enterprise as being "three-dimensional." Drucker was the first to define a business entity as (and I paraphrase): first, intended to produce a profit; second, as a "human and societal organization," and third, as a "social institution" that plays a major role in "society" and is influenced "by the public interest."

Drucker argues that a commercial enterprise is the cornerstone of a capitalist system. It is a wealth-generating mechanism. It is his opinion that business and its management fundamentally contribute not only to the financial wealth of the supporting society, but to the very emotional health and welfare of every individual who functions therein. Business is no less a social institution than are our schools, churches, and government, he argues. Business must function, therefore, in the public interest.

Business corruption, as any other, is not in the interest of the American economic system, free enterprise in general, and American society sin particular. Corruption is a destroyer. It is, therefore, the responsibility of business executives to take those measures necessary to insure that the integrity of our economic system is not called into question or disrepute by their actions or those of their subordinates. Our economic system must prevail, grow, and prosper to provide the wherewithal to accommodate societal needs. If America's commercial enterprises are substantially corrupt, then the American economic system and American society are at risk for failure because a large percentage of the American people may be corrupt.

American business does not operate in a vacuum, with its interests separate and distinct from the remainder of society. The interests of business are so interwoven with those of American society that they are literally inseparable. Each exists to serve the other. Each exists to perpetuate the other. Each exists to enrich the other. Each must have the other to exist.

1.8.6 Management Attitudes and Practices

This text is not specifically written as a treatment of business administration. However, no discussion, of abusive employee problems can be considered complete without some examination and analysis of management, their contemporary attitudes and practices, and how those behaviors impact the problem.

What management does or does not do and what it has or has not done in terms of its leadership, attitudes, and practices are discussed in the paragraphs that follow. It is interesting to note that those who investigate organizational misconduct consistently encounter one or more of a core group of five management attitudes and practices. This core sampling of attitudes and practices has been identified as significantly influencing the presence and level of abusive conduct and are indicative of

- The level of management or subordinate tacit or direct involvement in the commission of abusive conduct
- Length of time the abusive conduct has been ongoing
- Why employees who had knowledge or reasonable suspicion of wrongdoing did not expose it

In the following review these five common management attitudes and practices are scrutinized for their relevancy to the abusive employee problem. Management, unfortunately, oftentimes fails to recognize these factors or if recognition occurs, chooses to overlook them. These five core attitudes and practices can be contributors to the existence of an abusive employee problem in any organization. It is in management's interest to study them well. The author has named some; you may want to add your own.

Management's attitudes and practices:

- Misdirected emphasis
- Lack of management position
- Unavailability
- Economic coercion
- Merger disaffection

Some combination or all five of the above listed factors are often found on post-incident investigation of abuse-incurred losses or in the commission of occupational crime. When these factors are recognized, acknowledged, and addressed by management and efforts are made to eliminate their negative effects, the potential for loss is substantially reduced. The probability of early detection of abusive behavior is also increased and the overall effectiveness of the organization is improved.

The explanation for the positive result is simple: you obtain a more ethical, perceptive, responsive, concerned, empathetic, and competently managed organization. Employees will respond on a reciprocal basis. To get respect you have to give it; rank provides authority, but it does not automatically provide co-worker or subordinate confidence, trust, or respect; these must be earned. It seems that this fundamental truism is generally known but many times ignored in our personal and business relationships.

1.8.7 Misdirected Emphasis

The emphasis of most loss-prevention efforts is directed toward the rank-and-file employee. Recognition of management's role in and contribution to the problem is often obscured or covered up, if not completely ignored. This misdirection occurs either intentionally or unintentionally, but exists nonetheless — and not without negative consequences.

Why does this type of misdirected emphasis contribute to abusive behavior? One reason is because employees at every level recognize the class distinction" inherent therein and they resent it. This practice not only fails to recognize the scope of the exposure, insofar as management is concerned, but it also generates negative feelings and attitudes on the part of employees.

These negative feelings and attitudes are in many cases ultimately directed toward the company through the commission of abusive acts. Of course, these negatives are not always avoidable, but they could be minimized with management's recognition of the problems this practice generates and by modifying their technique.

Exposure and the actual problem of abusive business behavior involve all classes of employees, regardless of position, status, or length of service. Accepting this reality is oftentimes difficult for some managers, even in the face of compelling evidence to the contrary. Management personnel far too frequently overlook the fact that they are employees of their respective organizations. Management should not have exempt status or be treated as if they are immune from indictment when guilty of engaging in abusive behavior.

Management's role in the commission of abuses is far greater than that of subordinates. This occurs because of the differences in management's opportunities and their influence on others. If not dishonest themselves, management's attitudes and actions still create a cause-and-effect subordinate behavior. It is interesting to note that management seems to acknowledge this fact when it is applied to every other aspect of management except ethics, honesty, and integrity.

The bottom line is that the actions of both management and the rank-and-file employee impact the organization, so the negatives associated with abusive business behavior must be treated as a total exposure. Management cannot be excluded from personal accountability in the loss-prevention process. The privileges and perks of rank may apply in other areas, but not this one.

Keep in mind that many individuals who are driven by ego and exhibit a ruthless lust for status, power, and control are high-level executives or positioning to get there. These very ingredients can, by definition, be excessive and are in many instances indicative of severe personal insecurities and low self-esteem. This combination can be very potent when the executive is also amoral.

Often described as driven, ruthless, and manipulative, this type of individual can be found in boardrooms as well as subordinate positions. He is always destructive. If in business, his operation may be profitable in the short term but generally, he is not a sustainer. His credibility is always at issue. His tactics are often brutal. He never lasts long. In the short term he gives the appearance of success. He is often replaced with the same type of person. The quick fix is needed. The cycle resumes.

A company-wide exposure dictates a company-wide solution, one that is applied at all levels and to all personnel. Any employee security-awareness, loss-prevention, and compliance program that emphasizes the rank-and-file employee is destined to failure or, at best, marginal success. The emphasis of these programs should not be misdirected.

1.8.8 Lack of Management Position

While many managers do not encourage criminal, unethical, or irresponsible practices, they do not always discourage them, either. Unfortunately, certain managers display an unusually high tolerance for such practices. When employees receive tacit or actual approval to engage in abusive practices on behalf of the company, a climate for the exploitation of the company itself has also been created; "the blind eye is an approving eye."

When permitted to exist, the connection described above generates a double-edged sword. Think about it for a moment; this is quintessential common sense. If the employee is encouraged to swing the sword on behalf of the firm, then he will surely use it against the firm to further his own personal interests. The failure of management to discourage abusive behavior effectively sends the wrong message to its employees, customers, and vendors. Remember that behavior reflects what is believed.

To be effective, management must take a stalwart internal and public position against abusive behavior. That position must be backed up with security policies, procedures, and education programs that etch the standard into the minds and practices of all employees, regardless of position. These policies should set in place those mechanisms that will prevent, deter, detect, and discipline such behavior.

Seasoned managers know that no company policy on its own ever prevented a loss. Discerning managers, however, also know that policies can effectively communicate an organization's value system and security priorities to employees. Written security policies, ethics and integrity statements, and procedures remove ambiguity. They clarify which behaviors are inappropriate and, therefore, unacceptable. When properly communicated to employees, their existence can remove the "I didn't know" excuse.

Management that fails to go on record against abusive behavior, does not audit, supervise, and control this aspect of doing business, and fails to take appropriate action against abusers is effectively communicating its value system to all with whom it maintains a relationship. A man's character will reveal itself no matter the veils of self and public deceit. This rule applies to business or other organizations as well. Who you are and what you stand for either individually or as an organization will be revealed.

1.8.9   No One to Tell It to

Most companies do not have a formalized system or procedures in place that would either advocate or allow an interested employee to report known or suspected abusive acts to anyone other than his immediate supervisor or manager. This deficiency can bring about an abuse-incurred catastrophe. Many firms operate with the expectation that some level of management will recognize a problem and proceed to correct it. If management fails to see a problem, then it is expected that some employee, customer, or vendor will expose the wrong and report it to the appropriate level of management. This approach can be called "passive detection." The assumptions of this expectation are burdened with logical fallacies. The approach is also loaded with unrealistic expectations of how both management and subordinates will act in matters involving a known or suspected abusive co-worker's or manager's behavior.

Let us look at this practice a little closer and consider some of its logical inherent fallacies. The first inequity with the practice is that it assumes management's honesty, ethics, intent, integrity, duty, and commitment to the company. This is a chancy assumption. Second, it assumes management has the inclination and ability to discover abusive behavior and will then have the will, desire, self-confidence, and necessary courage to act appropriately in those situations. This is particularly true if it involves high-level management.

This practice further assumes that local management and higher-ups will not cover up the problem while trying to protect their own self-interests. The practice also assumes that management and the company will have a sufficient level of employee, customer, and vendor confidence, trust, and respect that someone will report the wrongdoing to management. The final downfall of passive detection is the assumption that such reporting will occur either out of concern for the company or to curry favor.

The practice of passive detection is not without some degree of credibility. Reports of wrongdoing are made, but they occur infrequently. The reality of the situation is that the practice receives far too much credit for effectiveness.

The deficiencies of this practice are particularly evident when contrasted with those organizations where abusive behavior is prohibited, where exposure of such behavior is encouraged, where multilevel alternatives exist to other than site management as a means of reporting abusive incidents, and where those alternatives are well advertised.

The practice of passive detection functions in an apathetic quagmire of inefficiencies when it comes to the reporting of abusive employee behavior. Oftentimes management will keep the practice in place out of ignorance or because it serves some other purpose. In fact, reliance on this approach actually discourages the exposure of abusive behavior, particularly those abuses committed by management. Belief in the passive detection of wrongdoing can actually lull management into a false sense of security, or it can be used to create a ready-made cop-out when a problem rushes out to greet you.

If getting people to report abusive employee behavior is to happen, a well-developed and publicized alternative program and method of reporting such behavior must be available. Requiring direct employee contact with management when reporting wrongful conduct gravely limits effectiveness in this regard. An alternative program should encourage the participation of all employee levels, including management, customers, vendors, and neighbors, where appropriate.

This alternative approach would set in place the mechanisms for either public or anonymous reporting of incidents. The respondent would select the method he desires. Reports could be made either directly to the corporate security department or to an outside third party designated for that purpose. Any information received would then go directly to the executive offices for routing, follow-up instructions, or disposition.

Requiring mandatory direct reporting of abusive behavior to local management can be tantamount to a lethal injection that will kill any substantive input, thereby undermining the effectiveness of an organization's loss-prevention efforts. The fear of management or a co-worker taking some type of retaliatory action against the individual employee or other person who exposes the wrongdoing neutralizes this approach in many instances.

Because of societal conditioning, organizational culture, lack of personal confidence, fear, peer pressures, and other reasons, employees, customers, vendors, and neighbors are extremely reluctant to report known, much less suspected, abusive acts. Even with management support, encouragement, and guarantees of anonymity or confidentiality, most people are reluctant to get involved. Force these sources to local management and the best and most knowledgeable sources of information may be silenced. Employee, customer, and vendor participation in the loss-prevention process is a vital element in the early detection of abusive acts. Cut off, restrict, or stifle the input and cooperation of this group and you have set up the framework for a rip-off.

Why are employees silenced? The reason is simple: they are scared. They are split, torn, if you will, between doing what they know is right and facing an uncertain situation. This uncertainty is derived from the individual not knowing the kind of response or the level of support he will receive from management when information regarding abusive co-worker or management conduct is presented. In the worst-case scenario the potential respondent may know what to expect from management: the matter will be ignored or mismanaged in some manner, including by retaliatory action. Personal fears are thus validated and silence is induced.

In addition, if there is a low level of confidence, trust, or respect for management, you can be certain that the company is being victimized at all levels within the organization. In the latter scenario management can expect little or no support from employees, customers, or vendors, unless and until those negative perceptions and expectations of management behavior are reversed.

This is just another reason why alternative methods for reporting abusive acts must be in place and their use by employees encouraged and properly managed. Without management's encouragement and support for loss-prevention programs and the reporting of abusive behavior, it becomes easy for employees to ignore all wrongdoing. If that occurs, they will retreat into a shell of apathetic silence — management-induced silence.

No matter what a company does, it will never achieve 100% participation and program buy-in by either management or rank-and-file employees. We all know that. We also know that anything less than a 100% effort by top management to achieve the highest level of participation will generate only the lowest levels of support and, therefore, a failed program. In reality, a half-hearted loss-prevention program is just another irresponsible act, resulting in a loss to the company. Therefore, management should not initiate an employee security-awareness or compliance program without a total commitment to the success of the program.

1.8.10   Economic Coercion

This factor may be the most powerful and influential of the five addressed in this subsection. This element is seen particularly in instances of fear-induced participation in abusive behavior or silence.

People will — out of fear:

- Directly participate in the commission of abusive behavior
- Stand passively by while the wrongful act is being committed
- Retreat into silence

Fear can be both a powerful motivator to action or an immobilizer. Flight, fight, or do nothing. It seems that our proclivity to lobotomize, denigrate, and otherwise attempt to destroy anyone who goes against the cultural norms of the organization results in the immobilization of most employees. Few organizations have individuals with the self-confidence to buck the system. Conform at all costs; deviate and suffer the consequences.

One's instinct to survive and avoid pain controls decision-making. Economic coercion creates fear of losing a job, a promotion, a pay raise, criticism, retaliatory action, or some other real or imagined adverse result. With these kinds of incentives it is easy to see why people opt to do nothing. In far too many situations economic coercion is the intimidator's favorite tool. The threat of "I'll fire you" is more often than not a crippler rather than a positive motivator.

Use of economic coercion is a classic management technique, whether or not it is identified as such. Management, however, has no monopoly on its use; co-workers also use the technique. In both instances, it may be used with positive effect to inspire individuals to reach their highest personal achievements. It may also be used detrimentally in the degradation of a fellow human being. In the latter instance coercion is a simultaneous illustration and example of man's excesses and frailties. In its application it can become an extreme management, supervision, or co-worker technique that is ruthless, manipulative, and exploitative of one of man's most basic fears: economic survival.

Man requires food to nourish him, a roof to protect him from the elements, clothes for his back, and medical and dental care; man also needs self-esteem and some semblance of dignity. Complicate this situation by adding a family, and you have one vulnerable individual: a person who is very susceptible to any stress that threatens (or even gives the appearance of threatening) his livelihood. Economic coercion can induce actual participation or tacit involvement in criminal activity. If indirect or tacit involvement, then silence. Masters of the game use it with the subtleties and sophistication of a psychiatrist, at one extreme, or the brutality of an ax murderer at the other.

The use of economic coercion is an old tactic. All of us have experienced it in both its positive and negative context. We have all made use of it in past personal and business relationships. It is a perfectly legitimate tool if used with ethical intent to motivate positive behavior. It is also the tool of the exploiter. Customers and vendors also understand its implications and uses. It is a powerful force for good and evil.

Depending on one's age, education, job skills, length of service, family circumstances, mental and physical health (or that of loved ones), financial commitments, financial health, self-confidence, self-esteem, moral, ethical, and character considerations, etc., we are all susceptible to some degree to the fears and consequences induced through economic coercion. Those fears evoke powerful incentives for self-preservation and can work for or against a business, government, or institution.

Management that exploits employees through abusive use of this game alienates everyone. When sanctioned, its use seeds and generates rationalizations and justifications that will be used by employees, customers, and vendors to exploit the organization. Fear can motivate abusive behavior or induce silence. In the corporate environment apathy is its mildest by-product. Use of this technique in a negative context is tantamount to playing Russian roulette with an organization.

1.8.11   Merger Disaffection

Corporate mergers are the contemporary darlings of boardrooms and Wall Street. One negative by-product often found in mergers is employee disaffection, which can have a significant adverse influence on abusive internal behavior. It appears that management, for whatever reasons, fails to take this fact into account when planning its takeover strategies. This results in a negative repercussion on the profitability of the organization — an impact that can take years to overcome.

There are two basic schools of thought on how to manage personnel and other changes that may be necessary in a takeover. One approach is for management to move immediately and decisively to make as many changes resulting from the acquisition as fits their management style and operating strategies. The other approach is to move incrementally in effecting changes.

One side argues that it is best to get any planned or needed changes over with as soon as possible. This position argues that it must eat the losses and start to rebuild. The second alternative prefers to take a slower approach to initiating change. This approach views the threats, possible damages, and lost profits as confinable.

There are sound arguments for both approaches. Some combination of the two may offer the best solution to minimizing the negatives of merger-disaffection-induced costs and losses, although either one of the approaches may be appropriate in any given set of circumstances. Balance in the use of either strategy is probably the most logical and effective approach.

The point is, choose the approach to be used thoughtfully and very carefully to avoid or minimize damages. It seems logical that management take the time to learn the culture, its people, and the management and operating practices of the acquisition prior to taking any decisive action, particularly if those actions may have a potentially disruptive influence on the organization and its profitability. No "ready, fire, aim" decisions. Incremental does not imply dragging out the required and necessary changes over an extended period. If the changes are made too slowly, although incrementally, they prolong the disruption.

Many disruptive events occur during a merger, and they all impact people and therefore the cost-effectiveness, production, efficiencies, and profitability of the respective organizations. Abrupt, nonincremental changes in management style and operating philosophies have the potential to produce severe disaffection of many employees — and usually do. Reorganizations can have negative impacts such as:

- Wholesale terminations
- Forced retirements
- Reassignment of duties and responsibilities
- Wage and salary reductions
- Changes in job titles and operating authority
- Changes in pension, vacation, and health plans
- Rampant disaffection of the workforce

Each of the above-listed items can generate grievous problems arising from disaffected employees at all levels of the organization. During a takeover, any ownership mentality, work ethic, or loyalty that existed on the part of employees can be destroyed. Furthermore, such action sets up justifications and rationalizations for abusive behavior on the part of those who are retained.

Management that is insensitive to merger disaffection is more likely to create disloyalty and insecurity among its new employees. Certainly, however, there are situations wherein drastic adjustment actions are justified. For example, the target of the takeover is ineptly managed or riddled with abusive behavior. That situation necessitates drastic action to correct the problem.

Care and discretion are dictated, however, even in the worst-case scenario, if damage is to be kept to the absolute minimum.

1.9 Crime Causation and the Criminal Personality

Why do some individuals commit crimes and others do not? What goes wrong? How, when, where? What causes some people to engage in criminal, antisocial, and anti-organizational behavior? If you examine the literature on the subject you will find competing theories that attempt to answer those questions. You will find research on the individual miscreant, physiological, psychological, environmental, societal, and organizational influences that offer explanations as to cause. Consensus is found in some areas and not in others. No single theory can explain the variety of complex forms of abusive behavior exhibited by people.

Socioeconomic, cultural, educational, intelligence, and motivational differences in individuals are very diverse, so the complete answer as to cause continues to elude us. Some researchers argue that different types of crimes require different theories of causation. The person who commits a violent crime is different than the white-collar thief. Some theorists argue that theories can be clustered, thereby producing a white-collar criminal who would commit murder.

In the review that ensues, a synopsis of some of those theories from both a historical and contemporary perspective is provided. The quest for answers originated in Europe and the United States in the nineteenth century. It was in the 1930s that the focus on corporate (white-collar) crime and abuse was first defined and serious inquiry begun as to causes. The search continues on both fronts to this day. The provided input is intended to give the broad view needed to gain insight into the evolutionary development of these theories as well as into the theories themselves.

1.9.1 The Classical School

We begin with the Classical School of Criminology. The Classical School of Criminology began in Europe and was very influential in both the eighteenth and nineteenth centuries, and it is a school that still influences our thinking today. The Classicists defined crime in terms of existing criminal law. They believed that man possessed the ability to think, had a free will, and thus, had the ability to choose his conduct and to act appropriately or inappropriately. They also believed that man knew when he was encroaching on the rights of others, and when a man broke the law, he did so willingly. It is thought that in so doing, he places his own interests ahead of the rights of others. Punishment then should be dispensed proportionally based upon the type and severity of the crime; the victim's interests were of paramount consideration. Punishment was viewed as a deterrent.

1.9.2   The Positivists

The contrarians of the day were the Positivists, a group of Italian criminologists who coined the term and viewed "criminal law as a changing social institution and crime as a product of individual disposition and environmental forces" (Radzinowicz, L., *In Search of Criminality*, Harvard University Press, Cambridge, MA, 1961, p. 3). They did not believe in the concept of free will and moral responsibility. The Positivists "sought to establish social responsibility rather than criminal liability" (Yochelson, S. and Samenow, S., *The Criminal Personality, I. A Profile for Change*, Jason Aronson, New York, 1976, p. 66). It was in part their influence that began to alter the legal and social framework in which crime and criminal acts were perceived.

Legal systems of the period began to look upon criminal conduct as partially influenced by social phenomena. It was during this time that the movement toward a greater awareness and a more scientific approach to the investigation of crime and those who commit it was spawned. Researchers began to question the thesis that all criminals were responsible for their behavior.

In 1843 in the United States the M'naghten rule mandated that assignment of responsibility for the commission of a criminal act required that the individual had to know the difference between right and wrong. Over the years court decisions have expanded and refined M'naghten and others relevant to the issue. In general, if criminal conduct is the proven result of mental illness, or the miscreant is mentally incapable of understanding the wrongfulness of this act or conforming to the requirements of the law, he will not be held accountable.

Three states have abolished insanity as an independent, exculpatory defense in criminal cases. Those states are Montana, Idaho, and Utah. Montana was the first state, in 1979, to abolish the insanity defense from its criminal code. The other two states soon followed. In a 1994 Montana assault case, allegedly involving a deranged man, the U.S. Supreme Court refused to review the constitutionality of that state's abolishment of the insanity defense. This action strongly suggests that the Court at that time did not believe that the insanity defense was a constitutional requirement.

In 1985, then U.S. Supreme Court Justice William Rehnquist was of the opinion that it is "highly doubtful that it [the Constitution] requires a state to make available an insanity defense to a criminal defendant" (Biskupic, J., Court: Insanity defense not a right, *Washington Post*, March 29, 1994, p. A03).

Other Justices have expressed similar opinions, although to date the Supreme Court has not ruled on the issue.

During and after the nineteenth century, the interest of various scientific disciplines shifted from the pure legal implications of crime to a desire to determine its causes, to answer the question "why?"

An Italian physician, and Positivist, Dr. Cesare Lombroso (1835–1909), developed an early physiological explanation of criminal behavior. He published his theory in a study entitled "The Criminal Man." During the autopsy of a convicted criminal Lombroso discovered what he believed to be a number of physical abnormalities. Based on that autopsy and thousands of others, he developed the theory that criminals were in fact reversions to a primitive form of human species.

Lombroso believed that genetics caused some men to be born criminals. As the result of his research, he presupposed that criminal types could be identified by a number of physical characteristics. Some of those characteristics were identified as facial asymmetry, eye defects, ear peculiarities, excessively long arms, the shape of the skull, and other physical characteristics he described as abnormal.

Lombroso's postulations came under critical review. An English researcher by the name of Charles Goring did a study in 1913 of 3000 convicts and published the results in his work, titled *The English Convict: A Statistical Study.* The Goring exercise disclosed that Lombroso's so-called physical anomalies were no more common in criminals than in noncriminals. Lombroso's physiological criteria for identifying a criminal were discredited and ultimately fell from use.

As is often the case, other biological theories that were supposed to explain criminal behavior have been developed. Goring and others of the day concurred that criminality did have hereditary roots but that mental deficiency played a far more important role in explaining criminal behavior. The thesis of inferiority in criminals persists to this day.

1.9.3 Psychoanalytic Theory

In the psychological vein two major explanations are offered as causative of criminal behavior: the psychoanalytic theory and the learning theory. Psychoanalytic theorists argue that criminal behavior occurs because the miscreants are "sick" or "maladjusted." The theory acknowledges that the environment of the individual criminal may be a contributing factor in the commission of criminal conduct, but it is not always a primary source. This theory has some credibility in some instances. The caveat is that while mental disorders may contribute to some criminality, it is not proven as universally causative.

1.9.3.1   The Learning Theory

The learning theory links the causes of criminal conduct to the environment of the individual. It finds its origins in the operant conditioning theory. Those who subscribe to this theory believe that an individual will act in a manner that his environment rewards or reinforces. Behavior is thus influenced by a system of rewards and punishment. If criminality is rewarded, the individual will be dishonest. If honesty and integrity are rewarded, then honesty and integrity will be the norm. If one or the other of these examples is punished, then the likelihood of a recurrence is reduced. Because the rewards of criminal behavior may be substantial, each time it is rewarded the likelihood of it being repeated is increased. Rewards can come in many forms.

1.9.3.2   The Id and Superego

Dr. Sigmund Freud postulated that malfunctions in two areas of a person's development might be causative of criminal behavior. They were identified as the id and the superego. Freud explained that the id was the part of the human personality that strives to fulfill an individual's basic needs and desires. If an individual fails to control the id, then the commission of crime can become an easy way to satisfy those needs and desires.

On the other hand, the superego works to keep the individual from committing abusive behavior. Freud theorized that the person who commits such acts does so because of an underdeveloped superego. According to the theory, this deficiency occurs because of a lack of parental development and socialization. Individuals so afflicted feel no guilt or remorse concerning criminal behavior. They will exploit opportunity where it is found.

1.9.3.3   The Sociological Theory

Sociological theory on the causation of criminal behavior basically holds that the individual is the victim of adverse environmental and social conditions. Antisocial conduct is often viewed as adaptive responses to environmental pressures. A broken home, alcoholic or abusive parent, poverty, and other adverse societal influences are often cited as causative.

This theory is currently in vogue. It essentially holds that a person is not always responsible for his behavior. It also fails to acknowledge and take into consideration the fact that individuals are exposed to a large variety of positive influences from an assortment of sources, regardless of their environment. The sociological theory negates the individual's ability and responsibility to make choices that influence the consequences of his actions, whether those choices result in positive or negative outcomes. It does not explain why multiple siblings in a common household do not all turn out bad or good.

1.9.3.4 Differential Association Theory

Edwin H. Sutherland, Ph.D., developed his differential association theory wherein he explains criminal behavior as a learned behavior and not inherited. Sutherland believed that criminal behavior is learned by interaction with other people through verbal communication and example. One must be taught the techniques, motives, drives, rationalizations, and attitudes that manifest criminal conduct. According to Sutherland, the individual miscreant must accumulate enough information, feelings, and rationalizations to justify committing a criminal act.

Sociological and Sutherland's theories have been broadly challenged on a number of grounds. One obvious criticism is that if the theory were correct, then we would all be criminals or honest in any given environment. It does not explain the origin of criminality. It had to exist before it could be learned by someone else. If that is the case, why did someone commit the first criminal act?

1.9.3.5 Moral Explanations

Then there are the moral explanations for the causes of crime. The central thesis here is that honesty is a moral behavior. Criminal conduct is, therefore, morally dishonest. This explanation attempts to answer the questions of whether or not honesty is a general trait of the human personality and whether people can be totally honest or dishonest.

Some researchers argue that moral behavior is situationally specific. This explanation attempts to explain the reasons people act dishonestly in one situation and the opposite in others. They postulate that an individual can be taught to be honest or dishonest, that we act in the manner in which we have been taught to respond in any given situation. Honesty or dishonesty is situational and based on how it has been defined for the individual. In some situations we will be honest; in others, dishonesty is the mode of conduct. Accordingly, whether an individual will lie, cheat, or commit a crime is strictly situational.

There are, however, those advocates who argue that once an individual develops the trait of honesty, he will remain honest under all situations regardless of the pressure. The person who vacillates will behave dishonestly when it is to his advantage to do so. Therefore, for some of us honesty is etched in stone, while for others it is a situational exercise.

1.9.3.6 Errors-in-Thinking Theory

Samuel Yochelson, M.D., Ph.D., and Stanton E. Samenow, Ph.D., in their acclaimed three-volume work entitled *The Criminal Personality*, set forth the results of their own study into the causes of criminal behavior. Their 15 years of research, intensive hands-on therapy experience, and important follow-up studies decimated the thesis that criminal conduct is the result of early emotional or socioeconomic deprivation.

Their study established that the same errors in thinking and thought patterns were found "among ghetto-raised blacks and suburban whites, among grade-school dropouts and college graduates" who evidenced criminal personalities. They could find "no causal connection between the way the criminal thinks and acts and the circumstances of his life." Based on their research and the conclusions drawn, sociological and psychological theories of crime causation were abandoned by them. "The use of such time-honored concepts has hardly altered the national crime picture." They focused on the "thinking and action patterns" of the criminal and found the elements of control and choice in that process. They ascribe criminality to errors in the thinking of the individual.

Well, there you have it, a synoptic overview of the various theories on the causes of criminal behavior. And while we do not have a definitive, one-stop-explains-all answer, some of this research has credibility. You will have to reach your own conclusions as to what makes sense.

1.9.3.7   *Knowledge*

We do know that insofar as organizational behavior is concerned, the presence or absence of certain elements or actions and management practices and attitudes can and do contribute to an abusive employee problem in any given organization. One or perhaps some combination of the theories we reviewed is also contributory.

As is obvious from the previous paragraphs, whether an employee is abusive or not, or to what degree, is influenced by many factors. Motives and causes are not always easy to discern. When identified, they usually appear in clusters, combinations of factors present in the organizational environment, within the mind and attitudes of the individual, and from external influences as well.

The absence of or a weakly developed and poorly defined moral or character base in the individual miscreant is often found to be influential in the commission of abusive behavior. As will be recognized in the following critique, there are other contributors as well. It is when these basic contributors exist and mesh with the individual employee that the organization is at greatest risk of exploitation.

You have probably already concluded that no single factor or condition causes a person to commit a wrongful act. We also know that hardened criminals are not the only ones to engage in wrongful conduct. Research into the personalities of those individuals who act out has shown that the miscreant's profile is more often than not comparable to that of the average man.

What, then, in all this confusion, is the most reliable predictor of an individual's propensity to abusive behavior? After all is said and done, you will find that the absence of personal integrity is probably the greatest single determiner in the commission of wrongful conduct. Low integrity is the fundamental component to search for when attempting to identify and predict the potential for future misconduct by current employees and prospective employees. To reduce or eliminate abusive behavior you must find and hire, those individuals who possess high moral values, i.e., integrity.

Finding individuals with the desired values is no easy task. In fact, it is a very difficult job. Essentially, until better methods are developed you are limited by the quality of your own judgment and by the results of background investigations and psychological tests. The lie detector is out as a pre-employment resource except in certain exempt classifications of employees.

1.9.3.8   Actions and Attitudes

The factors and attitudes researchers say contribute most to the presence of abusive employee behavior have been divided into the following six categories:

1. Character factors
2. Need, greed, and personal excess factors
3. Psychological factors
4. Opportunity factors
5. Attitudinal indicators
6. Rationalization and justification indicators

Each of these categories is characterized by the absence (or presence) of certain factors and attitudes that are outlined below. The categories are presented in numerical order, with the contributing factors under the appropriate heading. Each of these contributing factors is presented in its shortest form to make the point briefly. Generally, when these factors are present, they occur in combinations and clusters. This fact does not preclude a single factor's influence as the sole motivation in the commission of a wrongful act.

1. Character factors:
   Integrity
   Ethics
   Morals
   Honesty
   Veracity

2. Need, greed, and personal excess factors:
   "Wheeler-dealer" mentality
   Drug or alcohol abuse
   Excessive gambling
   Extramarital affairs
   Excessive debt
   Financial losses
   Blackmail
   "Keeping up with the Joneses" mentality
   Severe personal or family illness
   Inadequate income
   Excessive divorce settlement
   Stock market speculation
   Low moral values
   Desire to beat the system
   Criminal background
   Poor credit rating
   Personal bankruptcy
3. Psychological factors:
   Lack of or poor emotional stability
   Rationalization of wrongful behavior
   Poor human resource practices and attitudes
   Lack of respect for or dislike of individual management or management practices
   Peer pressure
   Individual low self-esteem
   Poor management practices
   Job frustrations
   Sociopathology
   Neurotics
   Pathological personality
   Psychopathic tendencies
   Disaffection
   Lack of security policies and direction
   Lack of company concern
   Actual or perceived lack of management concern or follow-up in instances of known or suspected abusive behavior
   Actual or perceived lack of ethical business practices
   Actual or perceived, unfair, indecisive, inconsistent, or double standard in discipline
   Poor supervision
   Lack of incident investigation and reporting

Little or no fear of detection
Failed management oversight
Company-generated unrealistic performance objectives
Undefined honesty and dishonesty expectations
Lack of maturity
Frequent job changes
Overqualification for job
Lack of promotion, or job stagnation
Unstable behavior
Poor job performance
Falsified employment application
Frequent changes of residence
Loss of standing and power
Favoritism shown in raises and promotions
Unrealistic corporate profit goals
Pay incommensurate with skills or abilities
Double standards

4. Opportunity factors:
Lack of, ineffective, or inadequate accounting controls
Lack of, ineffective, or inadequate inventory controls
Lack of, ineffective, or inadequate audit controls and procedures
Lack of, ineffective, or inadequate supervision
Lack of, ineffective, or inadequate financial auditing and controls
Lack of, ineffective, or inadequate investigation
Little or no fear of detection
Lack of, ineffective, or inadequate management practices
Lack of employee trust in management
Little or no fear of punishment if detected
Lack of, ineffective, or inadequate individual accountability
Actual or perceived tolerance of unethical behavior
Lack of employee loyalty and ownership mentality
High personnel turnover at all levels
Corrupt management

5. Attitudinal indicators:
"Don't do as I do, do as I say."
"We seldom take a real inventory, and when we do the manager lies about it."
"If they don't care, then neither do I."
"Even if I told my boss, he wouldn't do anything about it."
"If I told who was stealing, I'd be the only one penalized."
"The boss knows what's going on. He must be involved."
"It's their problem, not mine. They don't care, neither do I."

"The jerk from auditing is so stupid and lazy he couldn't find a problem if it was right in front of him. All he wants to know is 'does it balance?' He doesn't care where the numbers come from."

"The security people are too stupid, lazy, and fat to ever catch me."

"They don't care if my personal things get stolen. When they care, I'll care."

"I've got to make a profit, and I don't care how I make it."

"The biggest liar I know is my boss."

"My boss is ruthless and amoral."

"If my boss is not cheating and lying, he isn't happy."

"I never accept responsibility for a screw-up. Blame it on a subordinate."

"Management doesn't care who they hire."

"You can't trust management."

"Never apologize; it's a sign of weakness."

"If I told, they would tell everyone it was me."

"There's no one in the company to talk to about crime."

"I don't know what the company wants or expects me to do about co-workers who steal, lie, and cheat. You know if they don't care about us low-level types they sure don't give a damn about what management does."

"This company has no pride."

"The manager will just ignore it or cover it up."

"You can't trust the manager, and there's no one else to talk to. So forget it."

"If I tell, the manager will fire me."

"Management will make you the scapegoat."

6. Rationalization and justification indicators:

"The company has plenty of money and resources."

"They owe me."

"Everybody does it."

"Nobody cares."

"Management sure gets theirs."

"This whole company is crooked."

"Even if they catch me, they won't do anything about it."

"They can't report me because I know too much."

"It's the way things are done here."

"The company won't miss it."

"I'm overworked and underpaid."

"The union will protect me."

"I've got to steal the company to get fired."

"The benefits are lousy."

"The manager takes more than I ever will."

"The company never does anything for me."

"I'm going to get mine. Everyone else is getting theirs."

"Management cheats the customers, so it must be all right to steal."

"They're too stupid to catch me."

"Look, everyone lies. You have to lie to survive. No one tells the truth anymore."

"Nobody wants to work anymore."

"No one checks, 'cause no one cares."

"The company cheated me. They owe me."

"The company beat me out of my incentive pay."

"Honesty is the best policy, business is business."

"I'm just borrowing the money; I'll pay it back later."

"No one cares about me, and I don't care about anyone else."

"Paybacks are hell."

"The union will protect me."

"My union owns the politicians."

The presence and clustering of these factors provide a potent source for abusive behavior and are present, to some degree, in every organization and in the mind of every person. The degree to which a company is vulnerable is determined by the presence of some combination of the above factors or others, the quality of management oversight, and the company's internal controls. Knowing that, a company can put in place specific countermeasures that will reduce or eliminate many of those factors and thus reduce the risk.

1.9.4 Countermeasures

The design, implementation, and maintenance of effective countermeasures will be no easy assignment. Systems and procedures can be complex. If in-house resources are not fully up to the chore, do not hesitate to outsource the task. Countermeasures are far too important to your organization to take the short route during the developmental process. In addition, many internal and external forces at work will influence your efforts. Some of those forces try to undermine the most appropriate efforts of management. Others offer positive reinforcement and leadership. You must remain ever vigilant because the undermining will occur, from within and outside the organization.

Certain efforts at subversion will originate with management, others will come at diverse intersections downline. Sources of adverse pressure must be pinpointed and negated when possible. Do not forget to acknowledge, recognize, and encourage those employees who are wellsprings of positive input and whose actions strengthen management's approach. You are going to need all the support and encouragement you can get if the program is to be successful.

Security policies and procedures must be carefully crafted and fairly enforced with disciplinary action initiated against those employees who fail to comply with them. Double standards in the use of disciplinary measures must also be eliminated if confidence and trust are to be established and precedent set with management. Fairness and a reasoned balance must be achieved.

1.9.4.1 Mindset

There is a mindset, however, that must be recognized and dealt with when pursuing a successful loss-prevention or compliance program. This mindset refers to "the ends justify the means" philosophy of some people. Personal excesses and greed typify some lives. In the business setting they are often our employees, friends, and co-workers. They are the employees whose total focus is on themselves, the acquisition of material possessions, power, control, and status — not to mention the method of acquisition. Damn the potential negative consequences to the enterprise, to their co-workers, or to themselves. Behavior is typified by the "I want it, I need it, and I must have it now" mentality that dominates their lives, thoughts, and actions. These are employees who will lie, manipulate, exploit, cheat, victimize, steal, and perpetrate fraud in a feeding frenzy of greed-inspired selfishness. They are, of course, dangerous. Their actions are destructive to themselves, their families, and the organizational and societal framework in which they satisfy those excesses.

The world described above is a phony one. But it is real to them. It is their world, a universe that is devoid of personal substance and individual character. It is the world of people who are amoral, ruthless, and devoid of ethical concerns. It is a world of pretense and appearances, a universe that justifies any action, if that action perpetuates and satisfies the personal interests of the individual. As you will learn in the ensuing paragraphs, in far too many business organizations this mindset may be either tacitly or overtly encouraged or even rewarded. The lesson here is that the behavior rewarded in the organization will be the behavior that will endure.

1.10 Ethical Considerations

The ethical base of the American business community appears to be eroding. It is declining when both domestic and foreign challenges to our economy require the very best within us. If this perception is reality, then one must ask, "Why?" The "why" may be influenced by the fact that ethical and moral conduct is frequently penalized, while the opposite is rewarded.

In the early 1990s the results of a study that addressed ethics in the workplace were released. 1000 graduates of the Columbia Business School in New York participated in the study. The respondents were all business professionals who graduated between 1953 and 1987, and they comprised a diverse cross-section of American industries and occupations. The study found:

- 40% of the participants were implicitly or explicitly rewarded for taking some type of unethical action that benefited their employer. The unethical behavior reported ranged from insider trading, solicitation of bribes, and income-tax-evasion to the marketing of unsafe products.
- 31% of those who were asked to commit some unethical act and refused to do so on ethical grounds reported receiving some type of punitive action from their employer.
- Over 40% said their employers or superiors stood to gain more from the behavior than they did.
- Less than 25% felt they would gain professionally for unethical acts.

Abusive employee behavior is not exclusively the by-product of second-rate or unethical management practices. Where serious workplace abuse is found, it is typified time and again by corrupt management.

Incompetence oftentimes plays a role in the presence and level of abuse in an organization, but it is not necessarily the lone ingredient. Many intelligent, well-educated, talented, and capable managers have fallen victim to greed, personal excesses, or other psychological motivators. Yet when you discover incompetence coupled with other individual contributors, you find the perfect scenario for disaster.

The ethical underpinning of any organization is set at the top, not at the bottom. The top people, starting with senior management down, set both the policies and the personal examples that influence the ethical and moral base of the entire organization. This is no small responsibility, but it is often ignored, underemphasized, or overlooked by top management.

It is management's responsibility to create a corporate culture based on ethics and integrity rather than one based on permissiveness and apathy. When that high-standard culture does not exist, a climate for abusive behavior has been created. Effective loss prevention will begin when all levels of management view themselves as ethical role models for their subordinates as well as their peers. When this latter standard is achieved substantially diminished levels of abusive conduct will be seen.

The author has personally witnessed the ethical metamorphosis that can occur within a business organization with a change in executive leadership. In one instance one individual made a radical difference in how business was conducted. The prior chief executive had created an environment in which anything went if it contributed to the bottom line and his wealth enhancement. Distortions and misrepresentations of sales and inventories were only two of the many activities that were not only permitted, but also encouraged. He was ultimately terminated.

Post-termination investigation disclosed gross conflicts of interest and exploitation of business opportunity. An entire operating division within the company had to be eliminated at a cost of millions of dollars and over 100 jobs. The division manager had been in collusion with the chief executive. The new CEO moved immediately and aggressively to establish new ethical standards for the company.

In the months that followed numerous other corporate and division level executives had to hit the streets. A massive and costly cleanup of the entire company followed. The former CEO had nearly put the company into bankruptcy, and this was no mom-and-pop operation. This was a market player with sales in excess of $300 million at its peak, 2000 plus employees, and four operating divisions. It took 3 years of investigation and costly litigation to clean up the mess.

The corporate culture and environment the miscreant chief executive functioned in were not unethical insofar as the parent company was concerned either. The former CEO of the parent organization, along with his senior executive in one state and several close associates, executed a fraud scam involving the sale and leaseback of nine key properties to a real-estate general partnership; a fraud investigation disclosed the deal and the principals. Subsequent legal action resulted in total recision and cost reimbursement.

With the recision a full recovery of $9 million was made and title of the property returned to the parent company. Once the company regained control of these properties they were subsequently sold as part of the massive downsizing and liquidation of assets necessary to save the company. Even now executive leadership in this company still suffers from the legacy of lost confidence, trust, and respect among its employees. The negative impact is still a drain on productivity, morale, and the bottom line.

Ethics are the moral and pragmatic lifeblood of every organization. Ethical failures demean the individual responsible and damage the organization. One has to wonder if the erosion of business ethics is just another short-lived compromise or a legacy built on the admixture of greed? As we enter the decade of 2000, the answer to that question will reveal itself.

1.11 Conclusion

In this section many of the elements that impact the existence and extent of the abusive-employee problem have been considered. We have taken a historical look at the corruption of the last decade and now know that corruption has reached into the executive suites of many of our most respected and trusted businesses and institutions. Abusive behavior has been defined and specific examples provided. The problem was reviewed from both practical and philosophical perspectives. There was discussion on the "whys" of abusive behavior, and six contributing factors were outlined. Management's contribution to the problem was discussed in detail, as were five of management's specific failures that contribute significantly to abusive behavior. The importance of ethics was also given considerable attention. It is now understood that employees have strong emotional incentives to stand on the sidelines and either ignore or participate in the abusive behavior occurring around them.

The point is that management has the power, the rational self-interest, and the profit incentive to effect a positive change in its respective organizations. An employee security-awareness or compliance program provides a means to effect that change in a cost-effective and efficient way. Profit in a governmental or institutional context can be translated into the level of a community's confidence, trust, and respect for that entity. The key question is, Does management in either a public or private environment have the will to change the way it is? It should now be clear that:

- Corruptive influences are a threat to our economic viability and survival.
- Abusive behavior is complex and extensive.
- Abusive behavior negatively influences every aspect of an organization.
- Abusive behavior negatively influences commercial practices.
- Abusive behavior is triggered by complex human and organizational factors.
- Poor management attitudes and practices are major contributors to abusive behavior.
- There is evidence of deterioration in societal ethics.
- Loss-prevention programs that emphasize rank-and-file employees send ambiguous ethical signals from management.
- Most organizations offer limited options for reporting abuses.
- The psychological impact of economic coercion can produce many negative by-products within an organization.

- Failure to recognize employee disaffection and to respond appropriately during mergers, restructuring, and downsizing can be destructive to an organization's culture and profitability.
- Some management attitudes and practices make it easy for the concerned employee to remain passively silent to abusive internal conduct, providing the not-so-concerned employee with both the opportunity and the rationalization for wrongdoing.

This discussion hopefully has stimulated many questions in the mind of the reader. If nothing else, one should be motivated to question the validity of the author's opinions on the subject. But then, other questions will arise in that debate. For instance:

- Has there been a shift in societal morals and ethics?
- Have the definitions of "right" and "wrong" become blurred by a combination of personal, organizational, societal, and business pressures?
- Is management providing ethical and moral leadership?
- Does the organization have written ethical standards?
- Does policy provide a written 'Code of Conduct'?
- Is policy compliance required at all levels of the organization?
- What kind of ethical standard is set or implied by management's actions and the demands of subordinates or suppliers?
- Are unethical practices rewarded, tacitly approved, or discouraged?
- Do management's attitudes and practices convey the message that when achieving organizational and personal goals, the means justify the ends?
- Is unethical behavior rewarded? If yes, how? Tacitly or overtly?
- Is ethical behavior punished? If yes, how? Tacitly or overtly?
- Are sound management practices lacking in the hiring of new employees, orientation programs, disciplinary procedures, security policies, employee security-awareness and loss-prevention programs, internal controls, incident investigation, records management, and audit procedures?

These and many other questions must be asked and the answers evaluated. Just asking questions is insufficient. Questions must have a purpose. What do you want to accomplish? You define the purpose. You then weigh, analyze, and evaluate the answers. You will get the picture. Your purpose may be to:

- Expose and identify the contributing causes of a problem
- Verify that a problem does not exist and identify the reasons why

- Identify specific policy weaknesses
- Identify weaknesses in systems and procedures
- Identify weaknesses in internal controls
- Quantify the actual and perceived character and integrity of management
- Determine if organizational culture contributes to ethical practices or otherwise
- Determine if organizational practices are considered ethical or unethical
- Assess the reputation and standing of the organization in business, professional, and governmental venues
- Determine damages

Once the questions are asked and the answers analyzed, the internal and public perception of the organization will emerge. The expectation is that the output will be positive. If the view is not where it should be, then the change process should begin. The ability to influence, guide, implement, and monitor change will ultimately be limited to constraints imposed by or the level of commitment of executive management and the organizational culture.

If you are the chief executive officer or chief operating officer, then the commitment will be your own. If there are internal abusive or ethical conduct concerns, then you have a management attitude and practice problem. Management creates the culture. Management has created or permits a wrongful employee problem to exist if one is present. Management must fix it. Even if you are the most senior executive in your organization, making changes, as you already know, is no simple or easy task. This is particularly true in large organizations with multiple layers of management, turfs, and bureaucracy to work with — and through.

Abusive internal behavior is no longer an insignificant annoyance that requires only superficial management notice. In the world of commerce, this is one business problem that can no longer be viewed as "just another cost of doing business," with those costs passed on to the consumer through increased prices.

In noncommercial environments there are costs as well. In that venue the cost is often manifested in the loss of public confidence, trust, and respect. All costs, regardless of where they are incurred, are passed on to the consumer or taxpayer in one form or another. The potential negative consequences are very real: loss of public participation and revenues. Government and institutional abuses have fostered revolutions; businesses can be and are forced into bankruptcy. Leaders, in either instance, may be subject to criminal and civil penalties.

Corporate security professionals, law enforcement officers, certified fraud examiners, forensic and investigative accountants, and outside and internal auditors can all attest to the criminal and civil complexities and bracketed costs generated by internal abusers. These professionals have calculated and itemized the costs and tabulated the lost profits. They have seen careers plummet, lives ruined, and personal damages soar. All of which are by-products of unethical, illegal, and irresponsible behavior. Sadly, much of the undesirable behavior (criminal or otherwise) has been committed by those individuals in positions of leadership and trust, the very people whose responsibility it is to prevent, deter, detect, and punish such conduct.

Hopefully, assisted by what you will learn in this book and other sources, you will be inspired to take positive action that will prevent, deter, or detect abusive behavior within your organization. If the information in this chapter did not convince you of the significance of such an undertaking, the data in the next section on costs surely will.

If you have an ethics and compliance program in place, employees are more likely to report problems and are more likely to stay within the company.

W. Michael Hoffman
Bentley College, Center for Business Ethics
May 2000

The Cost 2

Objective: Provide an overview of the costs of occupational crime and abusive employee behavior and its impact on business, government, societal institutions, the American economy, the individual American, and the American experience.

2.1 Overview

In this chapter many of the costs spawned by occupational crime and abusive employee behavior are reviewed along with the importance of incident documentation, data collection, analysis, and accurate determination of cost. In this review you will examine costs and their accounting from a general perspective including:

- Direct and indirect impact on the bottom line
- Negative tangible and intangible personal cost
- Importance of accurate record keeping
- Security as a business function
- How to calculate losses
- Overall negative economic impact
- The negative impact on personal and public confidence, trust, and respect

What is the bottom line on the cost of abusive employee behavior in our country? No one knows for certain. The best information available is estimates. Accounting for and reporting these costs merit considerable improvement. Even in public- or private-sector organizations with solid accounting practices in place few statistics regarding employee misconduct are kept much less publicly reported. Public entities seldom report the cost of internal abusive conduct unless it is in connection with the results of an investigation. As with the private sector, most public-sector organizations are conscious of potential negative effects on public and consumer attitudes when such behavior is disclosed.

Estimates of employee abuse-incurred costs are the best we have, and of course the accuracy and value of estimates are always subject to review. The information and sources listed herein are provided with the aforementioned understanding. A synopsis of some of those estimates and their sources follows.

- *The National Business Crime Information Network* has estimated that $200 billion is lost annually to cash and merchandise thefts committed by employees of American businesses.
- According to *Robert Half International*, employees steal an estimated $170 billion of their employer's time annually.
- The *U.S. Department of Justice* estimates that 30% of all annual business failures are the result of abusive internal behavior. Companies with $10 million or less in sales are primarily represented in this estimate.
- The *Federal Deposit Insurance Corporation and the General Accounting Office* estimate that 50% of all bank failures are due to abusive internal behavior. The average annual bank loss from embezzlement or fraud is approximately $42,000; 83% of all bank losses are due to abusive employee behavior.
- The *North American Securities Administrators Association* estimates individual investors lose in excess of $400 million in financial planning frauds annually.
- The *American Trucking Association* estimates that approximately 70% of cargo thefts are the result of abusive employee conduct.
- The *National Underwriters Association* estimates that insurance fraud costs $15 billion annually. This loss adds up to 25% to the cost of policy premiums that the consumer pays.
- The *National Health Care Anti-Fraud Association* estimates 3 to 10% of insurance claims are fraudulent. Losses range somewhere between $30 and $80 billion annually. These losses are paid by the individual policyholder or, if Medicare or Medicaid billings, by the American taxpayer.
- The *National Retail Federation* estimates retailers lose over $5 billion to shoplifters annually and another $7.5 billion to employee theft. These are combined losses of $1 trillion plus in annual sales.
- The *Hallcrest Report II: Private Security Trends (1970 to 2000)*, funded by the National Institute of Justice and published by Butterworth-Heinemann Publishers, Stoneham, MA, estimated the cost of economic crime in 1990 at approximately $114 billion. The report states,

".... at 2% or more of the gross national product, economic crime is out of control and on the rise."

- *Report to the Nation on Occupational Fraud and Abuse,* a 2.5-year study conducted by the Association of Certified Fraud Examiners was released in 1996. In the study 2608 certified fraud examiners provided information on actual fraud and abuse cases occurring over the last 10 years that totaled $15 billion. Those cases ranged from $22 to $2.5 billion and represented 12 different major industry groups, including government.

Among the conclusions reported:
  - Fraud and abuse cost U.S. organizations more than $400 billion annually.
  - Fraud and abuse cost employers an average of $9 a day per employee.
  - The average organization loses about 6% of its total annual income to fraud and employee abuse.
  - The median loss per case caused by males is about $185,000; by females, about $48,000.
  - The typical perpetrator is a college-educated white male.
  - Losses caused by management were four times those by the rank-and-file employee.
  - Median losses caused by executives were 16 times those of subordinates.

- *Michigan State University Study of Cybercrime*: a mail survey of corporate security directors of 500 major corporations was conducted by criminal justice professor David Carter in 1995; 150 directors responded.

Of the responders:
  - 98.7% acknowledged that their companies had been victimized by computer-related crimes.
  - 43.3% had been had 25 times.

The most common abuses reported were:
  - Credit card fraud, 96.6%
  - Telecommunications fraud, 96.6%
  - Employee personal use of company computers, 96.0%
  - Unauthorized access to confidential files, 95.1%
  - Cellular phone fraud, 94.5%
  - Unlawful copying of software, 91.2%

The survey found that staff and contract workers commit most computer crimes.

- A *1997 workplace pressure survey conducted by the Ethics Officer Association and the American Society of Chartered Life Underwriters and*

Chartered Financial Consultants randomly selected 1324 employees including management of multiple industries.

Results:

- 48% admitted to commission of unethical or illegal acts.
- Pressure was identified as the leading cause of unethical behavior by employees.
- 2.4% of all workers and 3.2% of senior executives had considered suicide.
- John Curtis, CEO of Luby's Cafeteria, cut his throat in 1997 when corporate earnings dropped 10%.
- 56% of workers feel some pressure to act unethically or illegally on the job.
- 17% feel a high level of on-the-job pressure to act unethically or illegally.
- 20% of mid-level managers reported a high level of pressure to act unethically or illegally.
- 74% of men and 78% of women feel families are neglected because of pressure.
- 73% say ethical violations can be deterred through improved communications.
- 71% say serious commitment of management is needed if the issue is to be addressed.

Factors that may cause employees to act unethically or illegally include:

- Trying to balance job and family pressures
- Inadequate management
- Lack of management support
- Poor leadership
- Pressure to meet sales or profit goals
- Too much work and too many hours
- Internal politics
- Personal financial pressures
- Alcohol and drug abuse

The following questions and answers will help put the issue into perspective:

1. Are the employees of America's commercial, governmental, and institutional organizations really as abusive as estimates indicate?

   Answer: Many are. No one knows what percentage of any workforce is abusive in any given environment. If the estimates we have are accurate, then one can only conclude that organizational abuse is epidemic in all venues. That is not to state or imply that all employees are corrupt or abusive of their employer; they are not. Generally, individual employees are hard-working, honest, ethical, and sincerely carry out their assigned duties to the best of their abilities and in a conscientious manner, all in the best interests of their employers. They are concerned about their careers, families, and country. But there is always a certain percentage of individuals, in and out of the workplace, who constitute a threat to the well-being of those with whom they live and work.

2. Do the American people share the problem?

   Answer: Yes! Everyone in America shares the problem and the costly consequences.

3. How widespread is abusive employee conduct?

   Answer: Wrongful employee conduct is inclusive. It appears that every organization, regardless of its purpose or intent, whether commercial, social, governmental, or religious, is touched by and shares the problem.

4. What factors contribute to or cause the existence and growth of abusive employee behavior?

   Answer: Many factors contribute to the existence and growth of this problem. A decline in societal and individual moral standards, ethics, and managerial leadership is a primary contributor.

5. Can an abusive employee problem be corrected?

   Answer: The problem can be diminished but never completely eliminated. While the prognosis for the future can be encouraging, many troubling overtones remain that must be addressed if there is to be a favorable impact.

6. Whose responsibility is it to correct this problem?

   Answer: Yours! That also includes the leadership of every business or other organization in this country. Each must make his respective contribution to identifying and reversing abusive internal conduct. Taxpayers and consumers pay for all fraud and theft committed in America. It makes no difference by whom or where the misconduct is committed; the American taxpayer and consumer pick up the tab for the loss. These losses come right out of your pocket and that of your neighbors through increased taxes and costs of goods and services.

2.2 Discussion

Presuming that the estimates of costs given above are accurate and that our ethical and moral foundations are indeed in decline, how then can the problem of escalating abusive employee conduct be reversed? The answer is as simple as it is complex. As far as business is concerned, the managers of our commercial enterprises must, by their own examples, leadership, integrity, and ethics, set the highest standards of personal conduct and then demand the same of their subordinates. Subordinates must demand the same from their leaders, co-workers, and themselves. Those individuals who manage other societal or governmental organizations must meet the same criteria.

As a matter of policy and national commitment, we must set about cultivating an innovative breed of executives who will manage our commercial, governmental, and social institutions. If the current trends of abusive internal conduct are to be reversed, a metamorphosis in executive leadership must occur. A new class of managerial and executive leadership must be developed. America needs a new cadre of men and women whose sense of ethics, honesty, and integrity is uncompromising.

America requires a new standard by which to measure managerial excellence. The old approach of profit at any cost is destructive in both a material and psychological way. Profit can be made ethically. Greed is wrecking the environment, the marketplace, consumer confidence, and American self-respect. Americans need a new pride in integrity. The core curriculum for this requisite transformation must come from within.

Executive management sets the criteria for employee conduct through the force of its own character, whether that conduct is ethical or unethical, honest or dishonest, legal or illegal. For the most part employees will follow management's example. Executive corruption is emulated throughout an organization. The incidence of lower-tier corruption is, therefore, a valid indicator of upper-level mismanagement or corruption.

2.2.1 Internal Threat

Internal threat is present in every commercial enterprise and social institution known to man. None is exempt. Each is now affected, from mom-and-pop enterprises, to the multinationals and from churches to government. The greatest risk to the stability of an organization is generated from corrupt internal sources and not from external ones. That is not to deny or minimize the danger posed to an organization by external sources. The latter threat is clear and present, but it is oftentimes easier to fortify against the outside threat than it is the one from within.

The internal threat can be more sophisticated, often ambiguous, and more difficult to identify, quantify, and protect against. The dimensions of the outside threat are often easier to recognize than the internal peril — burglary, theft, natural disasters, fire, and arson, for example. Countermeasures intended to offset recognized outside threats are often easier to identify and implement than those directed from within. Internal fraud is not as easy to find or prevent. Thus, in some organizations the threat from within goes unacknowledged, unrecognized, and the potential for occurrence is underestimated. When and where the latter occurs, the internal threat may flower into a full-blown disease capable of ravaging an organization.

Many organizations have felt the financial sting and experienced the bewildering aftermath of public and internal exposure of abusive employee conduct. Notwithstanding the management embarrassment and resulting disgrace, abusive employee acts are an undeviating drain on and threat to organizational efficiencies, employee confidence, public opinion, and profits.

One gets the impression that America is undergoing a catharsis; it seems we are searching for a sense of what we really are, both as a nation and as individual Americans. Dishonesty in business, government, and our social institutions is undermining all we perceived ourselves to be, including the underpinnings of our republic and our capitalist economic system. The price of fraud and greed is indeed exorbitant.

2.2.2 The Bottom Line

What has been going on in business, government, and other areas of our society in the last decades? One is loathe to say "business as usual," because of the rampant fraud and mismanagement that has occurred. If what has been occurring in many of America's respected business and societal institutions is characterized as "normal and customary," then you would have to say that fraud and mismanagement are "business as usual." From the estimates of the economic damage attributable to abusive employee conduct, the argument will surely be made, if not a proved, that fraud, theft, mismanagement, and failed executive leadership are normal business practices in contemporary American society.

A blanket indictment of all businesses and institutions would be wrong and equally unfair. The record, however, reflects a deplorable state of affairs. The economic cost and the more oblique damage to American self-respect are reaching alarming proportions.

Governmental-, institutional-, and business-related misconduct is not limited to management employees. Thousands of abusive acts are committed daily by those in nonmanagement positions, but the misconduct of management does more damage to an organization than that of the rank-and-file employee. The reason for the difference is that management has more status, authority, and opportunity.

The focus herein, therefore, is on management misconduct and how such misbehavior influences the rest of the whole. The cumulative trauma that failed leadership and management misconduct have inflicted on the American psyche, image, and self-respect has yet to be fully determined. Such conduct has, and will continue to have, a profound negative effect on the American people, country, and economic system, even in the face of all the growth and profit positives.

A litany of America's largest, most successful companies and, therefore, presumably the best of business and industry have felt the sting of illegal acts, questionable ethical decisions, and poor management practices. Management sets the moral and ethical tone under which an organization functions. Management is often responsible and should be held accountable for the state of abusive business and institutional behavior in their respective organizations.

If abusive or corruptive behavior exists in an organization, it may be there because management has chosen to permit it. Abusive behavior will cease or be substantially reduced when management chooses to oppose it. In management's actions and attitudes one can find the factors that contribute to the existence of the problem — as well as the solution. Organizational culture is a reflection of management. Management is responsible for what the organization represents, what the organization is, and what the organization ultimately becomes. The quality of management is reflected throughout an organization.

2.2.3   Corruption

The following is a synopsis of the scope and magnitude of corruption from six different perspectives:

- General business
- Government and business
- Wall Street
- Organized labor
- Religion
- Federal courts

The cases summarized below facilitate the clarification of management's influence and contribution to the problem of abusive employee conduct. The same factors influence the ethical decay of American business and our societal institutions. The negative implications of abusive employee conduct for every sector and component of American life are obvious and compelling. There should be little doubt that the time is right for a sober reassessment of past management attitudes and practices and how they impact this serious predicament.

The number of cases illustrated below is limited due to space constraints. Both criminal and civil actions are used. There are many thousands of examples that one could choose to illustrate a specific or general point related to misconduct of any type. Federal and state cases are cited and are a matter of public record. The cases chosen focus on management misconduct and failed leadership. All exemplify conduct that undermines organizational success and employee and public confidence, trust, and respect.

For each of the incidents cited to occur, management's direct knowledge, tacit approval, participation, failed oversight, or incompetence was required. Each situation is an indictment of management attitudes and practices. Each case is an individual testament to the unscrupulous influences that exist in contemporary America. Each occurrence is an example of failed trust and legal, ethical, and fiduciary responsibilities. Each is a spike driven into the heart of the American psyche and the soul of the American experience. Each is an example of the corrupting of America.

2.2.3.1 *General Business*

- *BeechNut Nutrition Corporation*: pled guilty to 215 felony counts and paid a $2.2 million fine. Alleged to have sold phony apple juice for babies. Millions of dollars lost in slumping sales. Two executives fined and sent to prison.
- *Eastman Kodak*: charged with alleged illegal disposal of hazardous waste. Fined $2.5 million.
- *Panasonic*: charged with allegedly masterminding a nationwide price-fixing scheme. Company agreed to reimburse 665,000 American customers $16 million in rebates.
- *Hertz*: charged with defrauding 110,000 customers and some insurance companies. Hertz allegedly billed inflated or fake collision-repair costs. Pled guilty. Fined $6.8 million. Ordered to refund $13.7 million to wronged parties.
- *Value Rent-A-Car*: charged in a 32-count indictment alleging the company overcharged customers for car repairs and the bugging of Mitsubishi's offices. Mitsubishi had purchased the car rental company. The criminal action grew out of a $31 million lawsuit filed by Mitsubishi against its former owners. The Cohen family of Palm Beach County, Florida had previously owned the company. The father Sidney and sons Jeffrey and Steven pled guilty to racketeering charges in 1994. The senior Cohen was sentenced to 3 years of federal probation. Jeffrey and his brother Steven each received 2- and 5-year sentences, respec-

tively, to be served in a federal prison. The court ordered a $2 million fine. The family allegedly owed $14 million in taxes and penalties.

- *General Development Corporation*: charged in a 16-count indictment. Pled guilty to conspiracy in defrauding thousands of Florida homeowners. Fined $500,000 and agreed to restitution of $80 to $100 million.
- *Sundstrand Corp.*: aerospace firm pled guilty to four counts of conspiracy and fraud. Another case of billing fraud. Fines, repayments, and damages equaled $115 million.
- *Prudential Securities*: accused by the U.S. Securities and Exchange Commission and various state regulatory agencies of offering unsophisticated investors limited partnership deals in real estate and energy development in the 10-year period between 1980 and 1990. Allegedly, Prudential failed to disclose the risks inherent in such investments. Nationwide, 384,000 individuals invested in the deals. The company settled by paying fines of $26 million to state regulators, $10 million to the Securities and Exchange Commission, and $5 million to the National Association of Securities Dealers. Plus, the company set up a nationwide claims fund starting at $330 million to compensate investors for losses sustained in the deals.
- *Miles, Inc.*: the country's leading maker of the kitchen staple, SOS steel wool soap pads, pled guilty to price-fixing charges in an action brought by the Justice Department. Miles and Dial Corp., the maker of Brillo brand pads, allegedly agreed to coordinate price increases and discounts. Dial cooperated with the investigation and was exempted from prosecution. Miles was fined $4.5 million.
- *Sears, Roebuck and Company*: settled charges alleging that the company had cheated customers through shoddy or unnecessary work in its auto repair shops. Original charges were brought by the California Department of Consumer Affairs and then picked up by other states. Sears estimated that 933,00 transactions were affected. It will cost the company $15 million to settle all claims.
- *Metropolitan Life Insurance Co.*: sales of life insurance policies promoted as savings and investment plans misled customers and were judged as improper by state regulators in late 1993. The plans were not forthrightly labeled as life insurance. Met Life dismissed or forced into retirement seven executives, among them its highest-paid salesman. The company agreed to offer refunds to 30,000 to 45,000 customers. Settlements are expected to reach between $20 and $30 million.

2.2.3.2   RICO

The 1970 Racketeer Influenced and Corrupt Organization Act (RICO) allows prosecutors to charge organizations with crimes and to seize their assets upon conviction. This act was primarily created for and used against organized crime interests until the 1980s. During the 1980s the law's use was expanded and used successfully by law-enforcement officials against drug smugglers and allied interests.

The 1980s also saw this law used (with success equal to that achieved against organized crime and the drug lords) against businesses engaged in criminal enterprise. Sanctions mandated by the law are tough. The Act requires that firms convicted under its provisions must forfeit profits and/or property gained in the commission of a crime. Treble damages can be awarded to successful plaintiffs.

Approximately 100 criminal cases and 1000 civil lawsuits are filed each year under RICO. Many millions of dollars in fines, damages, and other penalties are assessed. Use of this law against corrupt businesses has definitely gotten the attention of the nation's business managers and their lobbyists.

2.2.3.3   Government and Business

Efforts to combat corrupt breaches of public trust by federal, state, and local officials and their private-sector counterparts have met with some success. Limited law-enforcement resources place constraints that impact the type and number of investigations.

Three categories of public corruption are primarily investigated by the Federal Bureau of Investigation (FBI):

1. Contract Corruption
   - This may occur between a public official and a businessman whose company furnishes products or services to a city, county, state, territorial, or federal governmental body. In this type of case, either the government employee demands a kickback in exchange for awarding a contract or a representative of the business offers a bribe to insure they receive the contract.
   - An FBI investigation into corrupt purchasing practices in a county in Mississippi resulted in the conviction of 48 county supervisors and six vendors.
2. Regulatory Corruption
   - This occurs with the payment of bribes to public officials in exchange for their official actions or lack thereof involving licensing, zoning, or other regulatory actions.

- A recent investigation by federal agents of the New York City Health Department disclosed inspectors were extorting money from restaurant owners throughout the city in exchange for allowing the restaurants to remain open; 46 people were charged.

3. Legislative Corruption
    - This occurs when local, state, territorial, and federal legislators receive something of value in exchange for official acts with respect to legislation or other matters that the body can affect. Illegal payoffs can take the form of cash, campaign contributions, promises of future employment, or a future business advantage.
    - The President Pro-Tem of a State Senate demanded a $50,000 payoff to ensure the passage of legislation that would legalize horse racing in his state. The victim cooperated with the FBI. The Senator was convicted and sentenced to 9 years in federal prison.

Case Examples

- *Washington, D.C.*: former U.S. Representative Dan Rostenkowski (D) pled guilty to two counts of mail fraud and was sentenced to 17 months in federal prison and ordered to pay a $100,000 fine. Originally charged with 17 counts of criminal violations that included hiring no-show employees, taking kickbacks from workers, embezzling from the House Post Office, and conversion of public monies to his personal use. Allegedly, the abuses exceeded $600,000. Rostenkowski adds his name to the roster of congressmen who have gone to prison for corruption. He was once one of the most powerful men in Congress as Chairman of the Ways and Means Committee.
- *Oklahoma*: Governor David Walters was indicted on eight felonies including conspiracy, perjury, and accepting more money in campaign funds than state law allowed. More than a dozen people linked to the Governor were also charged. A plea bargain was cut wherein Walters was permitted to plead guilty to one misdemeanor count, pay a $1000 fine, pay $135,000 to the state ethics commission, and serve 1 year of unsupervised probation. The plea was worked out by the State Attorney General, a Walters appointment and old friend.
- *California*: U.S. Congressman Walter Tucker, III (D) was convicted in federal court of seven counts of extortion and two counts of tax evasion for accepting bribes while Mayor of Compton, California. He was charged in connection with a vote-selling deal on a proposed $250 million waste-to-energy project. Tucker is a nondenominational minister.
- *Virginia*: Former State Senator Robert Russell, Jr. was convicted of embezzlement. Russell was the treasurer of Richmond Velo Sports and

co-founder of the nonprofit organization. Velo was set up to benefit the Signet Cycling Team. State Police investigators discovered $13,650 in checks written to cash from the Velo accounts that were deposited in the Senator's personal bank account. The jury recommended 5 years probation. Russell now has the distinction of being the first senator in modern Virginia history to be convicted of a felony.

- *Louisiana*: Four-term former Governor of Louisiana, Edwin Edwards and his son Stephen, a State Senator, were convicted in federal court of fraud and racketeering charges in connection with allegations of casino license bribery in New Orleans.

More than 100 members of the Reagan Administration were accused of impropriety or corruption during his term of office. Many of those individuals now stand convicted of criminal wrongdoing or have worked out plea bargains in their respective cases. Some served time in prison and paid fines; others paid fines and were placed on probation. This level of corruption occurred during the administration of the most popular American president in decades. The saga of President Richard Nixon and the illegal excesses exposed in the Watergate scandal also speak with alarming clarity to the issue of public corruption. And then there is President William Jefferson Clinton and his administration; that's another book.

Excesses, corruption, greed, mismanagement, and a partnership of criminality, however, seem to typify every aspect and level of government's association with business. As the saying goes, power corrupts?

What about the Congress of the United States? When sex, lies, and allegations of misplaced trust are thrown into any analysis of the U.S. Congress, it becomes moot to elaborate further in making the point. What's the net result of this defilement of our political and economic systems? In addition to the staggering costs, it is the direct and implicit threat to the stability and future of those very systems and, ergo, our future as a nation. The actions of myriad elected officials have undermined the confidence, trust, respect, and pride Americans have long felt in the free enterprise system and in our precious representative republic.

As disturbing as it is to contemplate, many Americans now hold the Congress of the United States (and government in general) in contempt. Trust has been betrayed — and thus lost. That trust must be restored if confidence is to be restored. The restoration process, if ever initiated, will be no elementary task.

A few examples of federal corruption are:

- The 1980s crisis in the Savings and Loan Industry:

- This industry was plagued with allegations of rampant and pervasive fraud, mismanagement, and failed regulatory oversight. Losses are estimated to range from $150 billion to $500 billion over a 30-year period. That's correct, "b" as in billions. The frightening part is that the $500 billion figure may be too conservative.
- How did all this happen? There are many reasons. Listed below are a few of the allegations cast about: easy credit, poor regulatory oversight, funding of highly speculative projects, developers involved with thrift owners and managers, federal insurance-protected depositors (who had a false sense of security), greed, stupidity, criminal acts involving kickbacks, phony sales, and false financial reporting.
  Estimated cost: up to $500 billion.
- Pentagon procurement scandals:
  - This is another marriage of government and business plagued by allegations of fraud and mismanagement; from little Wedtech to some of the companies who make up the crown jewels of the military-industrial complex, allegations of bribery, fraudulent sale of defective products, falsification of test data, mischarging on labor, defective pricing in negotiated contracts, corruption in contracting, and the sale of confidential information set the scene for this one. Furthermore, there is equipment that does not function to specifications and allegations of lies, cover-ups, rampant deceit, and failed regulatory oversight.
    Estimated cost: $3 billion.
- The scandal in Housing and Urban Development:
  - Another government and business liaison plagued by allegations of fraud, mismanagement, and failed regulatory oversight. In this one, add political influence pedaling and waste. As this text was being written, there were an estimated 630 criminal inquiries under way.
  - Estimated cost: $7–8 billion.
- The nuclear weapons plant cleanup scandal:
  - Here is another government and business mess typified by allegations of fraud, mismanagement, and failed regulatory oversight. This scenario is also yet to be fully written. Look for the next installment in this continuing saga; previews are now playing in your local media. The full-blown dramatic presentation is to be made in a serial format to avoid a disastrous public reaction.
    Estimated cost: $130 to 150 billion.
- The scandal in the system for Farm Credit:

- Another potential debacle characterized by allegations of fraud, mismanagement, and failed regulatory oversight. This situation has not received much attention to date, but it's a biggie, politically explosive because this one goes to the heart of the heartland — the farmers.

  Estimated cost: $5 billion.
- The Medicare and Medicaid fraud scandal:
  - This is a major area of concern and abuse because it is a system fraught with allegations of fraud, mismanagement, and failed regulatory oversight. Medicare is the fastest-growing federal spending program and the fourth largest program, ranking behind only defense, social security, and interest on the national debt. In the year 2000 approximately 45 million Americans received benefits. Substantial criminal investigative effort has been undertaken.
  - Estimated cost: Over $10 billion.

2.2.3.4 *Large Numbers*

The low-end total of these estimates is $315 billion, and the high end is $676 billion. These estimates from the government's own accountants relate to only six areas of concern. The frightening thing is that there are many other cases of a similar nature that have not been publicly exposed or reported. Add in the estimated cost attributable to these other categories, and the numbers are beyond the comprehension capabilities of the majority of Americans.

All of the noted costs are going to be paid by the American taxpayer and consumer. When one adds to this calamitous situation the current price tag for satisfying the national debt, the magnitude of the problem numbs the minds of the most sophisticated financial thinkers, even with contemporary projected budget surpluses factored in. On the high-end of these estimates you're talking over $4 trillion of debt.

The level of contemporary allegations and evidence of monumental fraud, mismanagement, and failed regulatory oversight, and individual and corporate greed is mind-boggling to contemplate. It is evident that a binge of greed-motivated excesses is being satiated at incalculable cost to the American people, and the American experience.

For numerous individuals in trusted positions in both business and government, the decision as to whether to remain a spectator or a participant in the exploitation game is simply one of a benefit-to-risk analysis. The benefits can be immense, and more often than not, the risk of detection can be minimal.

In the 1990s, at least on the federal level, there was evidence of more aggressive investigation and prosecution of miscreants. In some cases the sanctions imposed have been substantial. A few states are beginning to follow the federal example — or is it vice versa? What does 2002 and beyond hold for America?

2.2.3.5 Negative Impacts

Economic crimes are crimes against every American and are just as or more damaging as those committed by the street criminal. The weapons of destruction are different in the commission of economic crimes — no guns, knifes, or explosives. The economic criminal uses guile, fraud, misrepresentations, and lies coupled oftentimes with computers or paper and pencil.

The destructive scope also changes on an economic level. Hundreds, thousands, or millions of people can be affected. Another difference is that the victim may never see his assailant. The damage in terms of the personal negative consequences is often no less and, in many instances, far greater than "crimes against property or person" if life, limb, or sight is not lost. In many instances the only difference between the economic crime and the crime against the person or property is the legal definition of the crime; life, limb, and eyesight can still be lost in both. Medical and defective products frauds, for example, can result from all three. Life savings can be lost in financial frauds involving a large class of victims spread over many states.

The difference is that the assailants in economic cases are found in the executive suites and boardrooms of corporate America. No burglar prying open a locked door. No dark alleys involved. No knife fights in a sleazy bar. No terror-filled moments while a cat burglar ransacks your apartment and then rapes your wife. No car windows knocked out while stopped at a traffic light and a gun shoved into your face demanding your vehicle and wallet. No drugged-up armed robber with a shotgun robs you of the night's receipts, and no television cameras or probing reporters intruding into private sorrow. No cop cars shown in the background of the local TV evening news, with flashing lights and crackling radios. No blood or bodies of victims covered with sheets behind a police line.

There are other differences as well. Economic criminals often wear fine tailored suits, live in the best neighborhoods, drive the finest cars, eat in the best restaurants, are members of the important clubs, play golf on the most private courses, party on their yachts, and rub shoulders with the social and political elite. Their faces are seldom seen in print or TV, except as it benefits them from a public-relations standpoint. But they are no less criminals than those who attack you or a family member with a gun or knife, and they deserve to be treated on the same level, treated with the same fear and contempt, the same disrespect, harsh criminal penalties, and fines.

The individual assailant may injure one person or many people if the crime is serial in nature. Economic crimes have the capability of wiping out thousands of jobs and even companies. On an international level such destruction would be considered terrorism. For instance, there are environmental crimes that cause loss of life or debilitating damage, corporate fraud in design or manufacture that causes death or debilitating damage, government fraud of an economic nature that causes loss of life or personal damage, etc.

Economic crime and fraud should no longer be viewed and treated as lesser crimes; they are crimes against a person or property. The sanctions imposed by law and the penalty must fit the crime. The only way America is going to change the face of economic crime is to make the personal penalties so severe and the financial costs so devastating that the potential loss will outweigh the probable gain.

What do all this corruption and mismanagement make America? Is America becoming a nation of greedy, unethical, lazy, stupid, and incompetent morons who are content with mediocrity, as some detractors would allege? The preponderance of the evidence says "no," but the manifestations of the problem say "yes." And while this depiction is extreme, there does exist that thin thread of truth that sets up the inference, the questions, and, therefore, the doubt.

2.2.3.6   Wall Street

- Drexel Burnham Lambert, Inc.:
  - Scandals are nothing new to Wall Street. The episode involving Drexel, however, rocked the financial canyons of New York and small-town America alike. In December 1989 Drexel admitted its guilt in a securities-fraud scheme. The firm had been charged with six felony counts, including mail, wire fraud, and other violations of security laws involving insider trading. Drexel's plea included a $650 million settlement, half the money to be set aside to compensate wronged stockholders and companies. The indictment is estimated to have cost Drexel $1.5 billion in lost sales.
  - Drexel gained fame and became a power in the securities business as an investment bank that traded heavily in the "junk bond" market. Michael Milken, who headed the California office of Drexel, pled guilty to six felony counts and agreed to pay $600 million in fines and restitution. In connection with his plea, Milken was sentenced to serve 10 years in a federal prison. He began serving that sentence on Sunday, March 3, 1991 but served only a

brief fraction of the time. Drexel sued Milken, asking billions in
back pay, legal fees, and assorted damages.

- Milken had faced 98 counts of racketeering and fraud charges prior
  to striking the plea deal. He and others associated with Drexel are
  alleged by the federal government to have "devised and carried out
  a fraudulent scheme involving insider trading, stock manipulations,
  and fraud on their clients." Milken, after facing prostate cancer, has
  become a high-profile spokesman for cancer research and education.
- A friend and confidant of Milken was Ivan Boesky. Boesky pled
  guilty in 1987 to one count of lying to federal authorities. He was
  sentenced to 3 years in prison. Boesky served a little over 2 years
  and was released in April 1990. As part of the plea, Boesky agreed
  to and paid $100 million in penalties.
- Boesky cooperated with federal authorities in a sweeping investigation of Wall Street that produced the now famous insider-trading
  scandals and evidence of other gross irregularities. It was this investigation that led to the indictment of Drexel.
- The two instances outlined above represent abusive behavior problems facing Wall Street. These cases were chosen because of their
  notoriety and because they typify the scams and criminal excesses
  found on Wall Street.

In the 1990s two major scandals involved financial interests. Salomon
Brothers, Inc. faced allegations concerning the alleged cornering of U.S.
auctions of Treasury Notes. The Bank of Credit and Commerce International
failed after the international news media exposed allegations of money laundering and arms smuggling. Fraud and corruption continue to be alleged in
financial markets as you read these words.

Listing all the cases known or currently under investigation by federal
and state authorities would be impossible. The number of incidents is too
great to list in a forum this small. One thing is irrefutable — as you read this
paragraph fraud is being perpetrated, mismanagement is occurring, and
regulatory oversight is failing on Wall Street, in government, in our social
institutions, and in commerce.

2.2.3.7 *Organized Labor*

- *Teamsters Union*:
  - During the 1980s the Department of Justice moved against alleged
    criminal abuse in organized labor. Individuals and labor organi-
    zations were indicted and convicted. During the decade, approxi-
    mately 25 alleged mobsters were arrested, tried, and convicted of

crimes allegedly related to Teamster Union activities. Inquiry revealed that three of the last Teamster presidents have been sent to prison. As part of this effort the Department of Justice filed suit against the Teamsters Union, alleging that the union was a puppet of the Mafia. Teamster management has denied the allegations. Ron Carey, Teamster President during the 1998 national elections, was removed from office amid allegations of improper use of Teamster membership dues for campaign contributions. The son of the still missing former Teamster Union President Jimmy Hoffa has replaced Carey.

- Teamster President Jackie Presser died July 9, 1988 while awaiting trial on federal racketeering and embezzlement charges. Among the allegations were charges that Presser paid $700,000 in union funds to mob-related "ghost employees" who never worked for the union. Still outstanding are allegations concerning the Teamsters and 20 murders allegedly related to mob activities. Needless to say, many past and current activities of the Teamsters Union remain under close federal scrutiny. There is considerably more to the organized labor story and to the alleged corruption within their ranks than can be delineated here. However, there is both good and bad in that story.

Many of the alleged violations leveled at the Teamsters Union, however, typify allegations leveled at other unions in the American labor movement, including the International Longshoremen's Union, the Laborer's International Union, and the nation's largest hotel and restaurant employee union, the Hotel Employees and Restaurant Employees International Union. Accusations have ranged from collusion with organized crime to bribery and theft of union funds.

No scrutiny of corruption would be complete without a look at religion and at least one televangelist. As with the Teamsters, the case chosen for review was selected because of its notoriety and for its illustrative value to the topic of corruption.

2.2.3.8   *Religion*

- *Jim Bakker*:
  - Jim Bakker and his PTL (Praise The Lord) Ministries were probably the most publicized case involving a cleric in the 1980s, but he was not the only one. Allegations of wrongdoing were made in many areas of the religious communities of this country. Those allegations ranged from theft and fraud to sexual misconduct. Most of

the cases were played out on state and local levels. Bakker's misconduct went national and was disposed of in federal court. The incident became just another episode that further damaged our national self-respect and diminished our confidence, trust, and respect for religious leadership and institutions.

- Jim Bakker's $172 million ministry began to crumble shortly after Jessica Hahn revealed her allegations of sexual misconduct involving him in a Florida motel. Next came the financial scandal that sealed the fate of both Bakker and the PTL. In late 1989 Bakker was convicted in a Charlotte, North Carolina Federal Court of 24 counts of fraud and conspiracy. Bakker was charged with defrauding a group of PTL members of $158 million. The conviction also involved the diversion of $3.7 million, allegedly used to maintain the extraordinary lifestyle that he and his wife, Tammy Faye, enjoyed. Upon conviction, Bakker was sentenced to 45 years in federal prison and fined $500,000. He served only a fraction of the sentence and is now back in the ministry.
- *Ellen Cooke*:
  - Ellen Cooke served as treasurer of the Episcopal Church. In 1997 Cooke admitted to embezzling more than $1.5 million from the church during her 9-year tenure at church headquarters in New York. She deposited church checks in her personal account, misused her church-authorized credit card, and topped it off by paying for her two sons' private school out of church funds. An audit disclosed $2.2 million missing. She pled guilty to federal charges and was sentenced to 5 years in prison. The money was allegedly traced to the purchase of an $850,000 farm in McLean, Virginia; a $465,000 historic estate in Montclair, New Jersey that required $300,000 in renovations; $325,000 in designer clothing, vacations, and meals; and a Tiffany necklace valued at $16,000. Her husband, who had been an Episcopal priest during her tenure, resigned.
  - Cooke alleged that she suffered from bipolar mood disorder that caused her to steal and forget what she had done. In addition to the embezzlement charges, she allegedly falsified her education, claiming a degree in economics.

2.2.3.9 *The Federal Courts*

- *Impeached Federal District Court Judges*:

- Judge Walter L. Mixson Jr., of Nevada received a 5-year sentence for allegedly lying to a federal grand jury during a bribery investigation and was subsequently impeached.
- Judge Alcee L. Hastings of Florida faced impeachment charges alleging conspiracy to accept a bribe in a 1981 criminal case, perjury, and disclosure of confidential information. Shortly after his impeachment in 1989 Mr. Hastings became a candidate for the office of Governor of the State of Florida. Hastings later withdrew from the race. He was subsequently elected to the U.S. Congress where he still serves.
- Judge Robert Collins of Louisiana was convicted in July 1991 of three counts of bribery, conspiracy, and obstruction of justice. Collins was tried and convicted in the same New Orleans courthouse in which he had served since 1978. He was alleged to have accepted half of the $100,000 that was allegedly paid to reduce the sentence of a convicted drug smuggler. He faced a maximum penalty of 25 years in federal prison and a fine of $750,000.

The cases presented here are a minuscule sample of the abusive excess being perpetrated in our country. The instances critiqued were restricted to only six categories out of many that could be developed. Toss in some additional categories typifying corruption in all aspects of American life such as lawyers, police officers, and doctors, and then include the damaging costs of drugs, alcohol, and environmental concerns, and one can see an exceptionally dismal scenario for the contemporary state of affairs — a view to the future.

2.3 Critical Problems

America is facing critical problems in so many areas that those problems may just overwhelm our ability to manage them. There is great cause for concern. The reason for this concern is simple: the quantity and scope of abusive behavior and excesses we are currently witnessing have in the past negatively altered entire civilizations. In an ancient context the fall of the Roman Empire is a prime example of self-destructive behavior. In a more contemporary mode, one has only to look at the transformations that have occurred in the world in the last 50 years and the reasons for many of those changes to gain a more contemporary perspective.

Yes, war has changed the map of the world. But what brought on those conflicts? To be sure, the desire for freedom has been a principal motivator, but freedom from what and for what purpose? On inquiry you will find, in addition to the great democratic incentives and debates, the calamitous destructiveness of public and private corruption has often provided the catalyst for the resulting change in a given society.

The German philosopher Nietzsche believed that the central moral problem of the 19th century was suicide. Camus, addressing his opinion as to the central moral issue of the 20th century, postulated that murder was its epicenter. The central moral issue of the 21st century will also find the interest of the great philosophers. Perhaps the 21st century, at least in America, will be noted for its ethical decline, corruption, and greed.

Management is beginning to understand that the security function is no longer a stepchild or a requisite evil in the business community. Security is a business function and an essential element in the success of any organization. In the absence of a professional in-house security department a precautionary mindset must be adopted to stay competitive and profitable in the 21st century.

Abusive behavior is like a cancer, a cancer that can sweep throughout a business organization, ravaging profits, morale, and productivity. It can linger over an extended period of time before the danger signals are fully recognized and acted upon, and treatment prescribed. As with cancer, attempts at curing or arresting the disease of business abuse can come too little, too late.

If one abuses oneself or permits others to, then one increases the potential for negative consequences in direct proportion thereto. While there is no sure cure for some types of cancer, one can reduce the probability of contracting the disease or insure its early detection if proper preventative approaches are used. In business, as in personal health matters, a proactive preventative response is by far the most logical, efficient, and cost-effective approach.

2.3.1   The Personal Cost

Another aspect of abusive behavior is frequently overlooked when calculating losses. That other dimension is the personal, the human carnage and devastation that can befall those individuals who are found to be directly or indirectly involved in the commission of such behavior.

Once wrongful behavior is publicly exposed, no one is exempt from the devastation that follows, be they management or subordinate. Everyone implicated in an abusive situation will be held accountable for his or her conduct in some manner and to some degree. Blame will be placed or shared somewhere, even if only on a scapegoat, as unethical as that practice may be. Typical of these situations is that fingers start pointing, cover-ups begin, and blame-shifting goes into full gear. The rats begin abandoning ship. Personal and career damage control kicks in; those less crafty and most vulnerable take the bullet.

No one knows, nor to the author's knowledge has anyone attempted to ascertain and calculate, the individual personal damage and costs resulting from the commission of abusive behavior. While many acts of abusive behavior are rewarded, all are not. Many tragic stories go untold and unreported about the personal losses and damage resulting from wrongful conduct.

If suspected, accused, or convicted of wrongful behavior, one must consider the following potentially harmful effects:

- Financial and career damage
- Divorce potential
- Damage to family relationships
- Damage to reputations and standings of individuals, professionals, and otherwise in their respective communities and among relatives, friends, and associates
- Fines, restitution, and forfeitures imposed
- Emotional and physical damage incurred while incarcerated or under protracted parole or probation conditions
- Loss of self-esteem
- Suicides
- Prison
- Questions

Does one ever recover financially or emotionally once exposed in a misconduct incident? Did the gains of misconduct outweigh the costs arising from discovery? Do the rationalizations and justifications that led to the commission of the behavior continue? Is personal responsibility for the negative consequences ever accepted by those involved? Who is to blame? How do we measure the trauma? Do they regret the behavior? Would they do it over again? If yes, then why? And if no, then why not?

Perhaps if you could ask the above questions of the individuals listed below, you would gain some insight into the concerns those questions address. One thing is certain: the negative circumstances these individuals faced are not all that unique to persons who have faced similar experiences in the past.

For example:

- *Woody Lemons*: former chairman of Vernon Savings and Loan in Texas, convicted of 13 counts of fraud involving a scheme to receive kickbacks on a real estate loan. The bank lost $18 million on the deal; Lemons was sentenced to 30 years in prison.

- *Lee Alexander*: convicted of extorting over $1.2 million from city contractors. Alexander was the Mayor of Syracuse and the former head of the U.S. Conference of Mayors.
- *Paul A. Bilzerian*: convicted of violating U.S. securities laws; sentenced to 4 years in prison; fined $1.5 million.
- *Leona Helmsley*: convicted of income-tax evasion; sentenced to 4 years in prison; fined $7.1 million; sent to prison.
- *Nicholas Mavroules*: U.S. Congressman from Massachusetts. Indicted on 17 counts, including RICO, bribery, and tax violations. Pled guilty to several of the counts charged.
- *Deborah Gore Dean*: former highly placed executive with the U.S. Housing and Urban Development Department. Dean was convicted on 12 felony counts of defrauding the government, taking a payoff, and lying to Congress. Maximum possible sentence is 57 years in prison. She was accused of funneling $66 million of taxpayer money to selected developers who received preferential treatment.
- *Carl William Peach*: former manufacturing director for United Technologies at their Zanesville, Ohio, plant pled guilty to one count of mail fraud. He had originally been charged with 16 counts of mail fraud. Peach allegedly embezzled money and received kickbacks. He was sentenced to 1 year in prison and ordered to pay $301,561 in restitution.
- *Mark L. Nathanson*: former Coastal Commissioner for the state of California. A Beverly Hills real-estate broker, Nathanson admitted soliciting almost $1 million in bribes from individuals seeking approval and issuance of building permits. He pled guilty to two counts of racketeering and tax fraud; sentenced to 4 years and 9 months in federal prison. Nathanson claims he lost his wife, family, and business investments and ruined his life.
- *Paul Mozer*: Former highly placed trader with Salomon Brothers, Inc., pled guilty to two counts of lying to the Federal Reserve Bank of New York in the submission of eight false bids totaling $13.5 billion in seven Treasury Bond auctions from 1989 to 1991. He was sentenced to federal prison and fined $30,000. The United States Securities and Exchange Commission subsequently sued Mozer. In 1994 he agreed to settle the suit and pay a $1.1 million fine. Part of that agreement was a permanent ban from the securities industry.
- *Alex Daoud*: former Mayor of Miami Beach, Florida, pled guilty to federal charges of tax evasion and accepting a bribe. He had been charged with two dozen counts including attempting to obstruct a grand jury investigation. He was fined a total of $85,000 and sentenced

to 63 months in federal prison. Daoud, an attorney, was disbarred; he lost his wife and home.

- *William Webster*: former Missouri State Attorney General pled guilty to federal charges of conspiracy and misapplication of state funds. Webster and others allegedly solicited campaign contributions by promising rewards from the state's Second Injury Fund. This fund is administered by the Attorney General's office and is part of the state's workers' compensation program. He faced a maximum of 15 years in prison, a $500,000 fine, and disbarment as an attorney.
- *David Paul*: convicted in a Miami, Florida Federal District Court of 97 counts of bank and securities fraud. He is alleged to have pilfered $3.2 million from CenTrust Bank in Miami where he served as chairman. Paul has been ordered to pay a civil penalty of $841,750. The bank lost $1.7 billion in 1990 when it failed. He was sentenced to 11 years in prison and ordered to pay $65 million: $60 million in restitution and a $5 million fine. *Donald K. Anderson*, a CenTrust vice president under Paul, pled guilty to conspiracy.
- *Cesar Odio*: former city manager of Miami, Florida pled guilty to reduced charges of obstructing justice. Odio had been charged with accepting kickbacks. He was sentenced to 1 year in prison and 2 years probation. Odio was caught in a FBI investigation into official corruption in the city called "Operation Greenpalm." Commissioner Millar Dawkins was caught in the same investigation along with city hall lobbyist Jorge de Cardenas. Dawkins was sentenced to 27 months in prison after pleading guilty to bribery and conspiracy charges. Cardenas pled guilty to obstruction of justice.
- *Mark Whitacre*: former president of the Bioproducts Division of Archer Daniels Midlland Company, pled guilty to defrauding the company of approximately $9 million. Whitacre used an elaborate scheme involving foreign bank accounts to perpetrate his fraud. He cooperated with the federal government in the investigation of alleged price fixing of agricultural commodities by ADM and thus received a recommendation from federal prosecutors for a light sentence.
- *Michael Kahoe*: 26-year veteran of the Federal Bureau of Investigation and former chief of the Bureau's Violent Crimes Section, sentenced to 18 months in federal prison. Kahoe pled guilty to obstruction of justice. The charges grew out of the shooting incident at Ruby Ridge, Idaho involving Randy Weaver and the deaths of his wife and son. Kahoe allegedly destroyed a key report that criticized the role of the FBI in the incident, thereby attempting to cover up the Bureau's involvement. Sentenced to 2 years in prison with 2 years of probation upon release; fined $4000.

The cases cited represent only a minuscule sample of the thousands of instances of criminal behavior committed on a daily basis for which prosecution is undertaken; criminal behavior, for which people are investigated, charged, tried, and convicted. Coupled with this fact are those thousands of individuals who are not criminally charged with an offense, but who are investigated, discharged, or civilly sued by their employer or other injured parties for criminal conduct or other abusive acts.

It is doubtful that any one of the above-noted individuals will ever publicly answer the types of questions that were posed. Any conclusions that are drawn, absent their specific individual input regarding those questions would, of course, be speculative and will accordingly be avoided herein. Despite that, it appears the negative personal and financial consequences each of the noted individuals incurred were substantial.

Being personally investigated, charged with, tried for, and ultimately convicted of a crime can be an expensive affair. If a conviction is appealed, the cost in personal and financial terms is even greater. The above-listed examples and the many thousands of others not noted leave no doubt that the price of corruption can be very high, at least for a few individuals. It is in these instances that the old adage "crime does not pay" is surely true; too bad it is not universally true.

2.3.1.1 Suicide

Facing personal embarrassment, prison terms, fines, devastated family relationships, reputation damage, and the financial ruin that often accompany criminal investigations, trials, and convictions can overwhelm some individuals. Just facing the allegations of criminal misconduct and the corresponding investigations and public exposure can be sufficient in and of themselves to create appalling consequences for some of those individuals so accused, and those consequences may involve paying the ultimate price.

The public record reflects that a few individuals facing allegations similar to those described in the previous paragraph are motivated to commit deadly acts of desperation. There are those few tragic instances of individuals who choose to end their lives during the investigation or post-trial process. What do the circumstances of their deaths tell us about personal costs? Below is a representative sample of individuals who have taken their lives.

- *Donald Manes* was under investigation for allegedly taking kickbacks from his city's Parking Violations Bureau. Mr. Manes was the president of his Borough in Queens, New York and its Democratic Party boss. Manes ended his life by thrusting a kitchen knife into his chest.
- *Allen Rosin* was a Circuit Court Judge of Chicago County, Illinois. When rumors and allegations that he would be indicted for accepting

bribes began circulating in his community, Judge Rosin shot himself in the head with a single shot from a .38 caliber revolver. The incident occurred on Father's Day. Rosen chose a well-known downtown health club as the location to end his life. Found with the judge was his Purple Heart, a Father's Day card, and family photos.

- *R. Budd Dwyer* was the Pennsylvania State Treasurer. Mr. Dwyer was convicted in a kickback scheme and sentenced to 55 years in prison. Dwyer shot himself in the mouth with a single shot from a .357 magnum pistol. The incident occurred at the close of a press conference he had called and television news crews filmed the shooting.
- *Nicholas Bissel*, a former Somerset County Prosecutor in Newark, New Jersey, took his own life with a gunshot to the head. While a U.S. Marshal was attempting to talk Bissel out of his hotel room in Laughlin, Nevada, he placed a gun in his mouth and pulled the trigger. Bissel had been convicted of 30 counts of fraud, tax evasion, obstruction of justice, abuse of power, and perjury. He was 49 years old. Federal prosecutors recommended a 10-year prison term. The former official had been described as a flamboyant person who sought media attention. He left a wife, two teenage daughters, and a 76-year-old mother.

Motivated by similar circumstance, others have elected to take the same journey as the individuals noted above. All left grieving families and numerous unanswered questions. One can only speculate as to how the stories of these tragic circumstances would have changed had the principals chosen more ethical courses of action in the conduct of their lives.

2.3.1.2 Calculating the Cost in Dollars

Cost accounting is nothing new to business. Many sophisticated systems are in place and serve business efficiently. Cost accounting in the area of business abuse, however, may be deficient. This is a situation that needs to be improved if management is to reach a full understanding of the actual or potential degradation of profits and organizational behavior resulting from such behavior.

This neglect primarily occurs for two very basic reasons: first, management fails to recognize the total negative significance of abusive behavior on profits and organizational behavior, and second, it is management's practice to transfer losses to the consumer through increased prices. Both of these reasons are unsatisfactory if the goal is to successfully manage a profitable business in the long term.

Management must reassess conventional attitudes and practices related to the concept of employee misconduct and the negative impact of such conduct on the organization. Accurate accounting of abuse-incurred losses is essential if this problem is to be placed in a realistic perspective. Accurate information combined with management knowledge and experience is the foundation on which sound business decisions are made.

Management makes business decisions based upon information; numbers, accounting, market surveys, and forecasting are the business cornerstones of decision-making. If the extent and ramifications of abusive employee conduct are not measured, known, and understood, then an appropriate response cannot be formulated. Systems must be in place that will allow the collection and analysis of abuse-related data. It is only through this process that management can identify and address the abusive-employee issue and thereby keep the problem and any response in perspective.

As you proceed through this subsection it will become clear that determining abuse-incurred costs is not an exact science, and unfortunately for many managers, interest in determining those costs is not always as high as it should be.

For the reasons previously stated, most business organizations languish in apathy and ambivalence, not really knowing and perhaps not caring much about the problems arising out of abusive employee behavior or the costs resulting therefrom, that is, until the organization is challenged, possibly staggered, into reality. Something about a major loss somehow has an exceptionally sobering influence on a business, government, or other organization.

Other reasons prejudice this situation. Identifying, quantifying, and keeping track of the costs arising out of employee misconduct are in the infancy stage of need recognition. Just as cost accounting and the more contemporary managerial accounting went through recognition-of-need phases in the evolution to their present-day development, so must accounting associated with abusive employee behavior.

The evolution of cost and managerial accounting was the greatest influence for change in the post-Industrial Revolution era. So, one can rightly say that cost accounting as it is known today is essentially a 20th-century creation, with managerial accounting developing in the 1960s. Both methods of accounting are designed and intended to aid and facilitate management in the analysis of costs important to managerial decision-making. Both systems provide information necessary to informed decision-making and, ergo, the quality of those decisions. Both systems, while distinct disciplines in many respects, provide data for analysis that can be utilized to meet changing business circumstances.

Abusive employee behavior is one of those changing business problems. Therefore, the manner and degree to which such behavior negatively impacts the organization demand to be assessed with the same precision and accuracy developed in the more established accounting systems.

As was the circumstance in the two disciplines previously cited, recognition of need will eventually motivate the development of systems to account for costs created by employee misconduct. Until then, accounting for losses incurred through abusive employee behavior will be a neglected area of cost and managerial accounting. The problem, therefore, is becoming increasingly worse and the solutions far more complex.

The rumblings of change, however, are perceptible on the business horizon. Need recognition is becoming more and more a reality for many managers. Systems designed to record and analyze these unique costs are being developed by security practitioners, internal auditors, and other protection-of-assets-related practitioners. Many of the systems already developed by security professionals are very sophisticated and are used effectively by management for profit enhancement and in the overall planning and decision-making process.

Illegal, unethical, and irresponsible employee behavior must be seen as a composite picture; these behaviors make up the total. It is these behaviors that damage a business at the very core of its purpose (assuming its purpose is lawful), which is to make a profit and, in so doing, make a contribution to society as well. Abusive employee behavior can no longer be viewed just as a cost of doing business. Why not? Because the costs attributable to misconduct can get out of control. These costs, just like all costs of doing business, must be controlled if a company is to stay competitive. Abuse-incurred losses are reaching such proportions that they can no longer be just passed on to the consumer. Losses attributable to abusive behavior must be calculated in terms of both direct and consequential costs. While direct costs on a per-incident basis may or may not be significant, those losses are often the tip of the iceberg when compared with consequential costs.

Let's explore this point further by providing some examples of the two cost classifications. First, we review (1) direct costs and then take a quick look at (2) consequential costs and their influence on the total loss picture. Both aspects must be calculated in determining the true cost of damages.

1. Direct Costs
   Definition: Tangible losses or damages
   Examples:
       Cash
       Interest
       Dividends
       Capital gains
       Property whose value is determined by the cost of its acquisition
          or production
2. Consequential Costs
   Definition: Those costs occurring as a consequence of a direct loss
   Examples:
       Repair or replacement costs

Interruption of service and customer damage
Declines in productivity and morale
Added labor costs for company repairs or replacement
Damaged reputation or standing in the community
Increased cost of physical security measures, investigation, and
    prosecution
Price increases to cover costs
Lost market share
Increased insurance costs
Loss of employee confidence, trust, and respect
Reduced employee benefits
Personnel layoffs
No pay increases
Scuttled plans for expansion and related costs
Effort and cost to generate new sales to replace lost sales and
    profits
Investigative costs
Cost of recovery
Management involvement
Poor management practices
Lost bonuses
Reduced profits
Higher overhead
Diminution in the quality of service
Loss in investor equity
Legal costs

Consequential costs can be ambiguous. This kind of damage can be difficult to recognize and accurately quantify, which often makes it difficult to place a dollar value on losses attributable to this cause. Some level of consequential damage results from every direct loss. Any attempt, therefore, to accurately calculate and appraise the damage derived from wrongful behavior can become complicated. It is because of recognition and ambiguity factors that losses attributable to consequential damage often go unaccounted for or underestimated.

Notwithstanding the complications intrinsic to the calculation of this type of damage, a reasonable effort should be extended to do so and to do so as accurately as possible. In many of those instances where management fails to account for the damage resulting from consequential causes, another negative by-product is often created. That by-product is the increased potential for management to grossly underestimate the full extent of the damage incurred. When this failure happens, the quality of any damage-control countermeasures can be severely compromised. The consequence of this miscalculation often results in damage-control methods that are misdirected, fragmented, ineffective, and costly.

An inadequately managed response can result in further strife, added costs, and lost revenue. This, of course, is a very undesirable predicament that can extract a heavy toll on profits. The most productive managers are those who recognize the potential enormity of the negatives arising out of consequential costs and who move to differentiate those impacts in a manner appropriate to the exposure in an effort to minimize and control damages.

It is the perception of some security professionals that few in management recognize not only the importance of tracking abuse-incurred costs, but also the distinction and the importance of jointly calculating direct and consequential damages as well. The role that these two distinct methods of loss and damage accounting play in determining the true cost and thus the real impact of abusive employee behavior on an organization should not be ignored by management. Efforts spent to prevent and promote early discovery of a loss or reduce its impact on the bottom line constitute a far more logical, rational, cost-effective, and efficient approach than does post-incident investigation and the employment of damage-control countermeasures.

2.4   Essentials of Data Collection

If management is to know the extent of abusive behavior and the cost within their respective organizations, then data related to that subject must be collected and analyzed. If this kind of information is to be collected and analyzed, then a system must be designed and put in place that will aid in accomplishing that objective. The type of system, its purpose, scope, and administration will have to be determined. The purpose of this subsection is to provide management planners with some of the information they will need to decide on the purpose, intent, and the specifics of a data-collection system customized to meet their unique circumstances, history, risks, and exposures.

When it comes to quantifying losses, it is important for management to know not only the amount of a specific loss, but many other pieces of information as well. A data-collection system should be liberal enough in design and scope to cover the exposure, yet not so extensive as to impede its cost-effectiveness or management's efficiency in complying with it. Unwieldy accounting systems develop their own inefficiencies and costs that ultimately undermine the purpose for which they were originally created.

Merely collecting information is not enough. To be effective, the data collected must be analyzed and evaluated. Putting the information collected to appropriate use is its most important function. Having information and not using it is as unsatisfactory as improperly using what one does have. The most constructive data-collection systems are those that provide information to management that can be utilized in the improvement of employee relations, organizational cost-effectiveness, and efficiency, as well as employee security-awareness and loss-prevention efforts.

A data-collection system will usually consist of four components:

- An incident-classification system
- A method for reporting and collecting certain basic information related to an incident
- Formula for costing
- Analysis of captured input

Data collection effectiveness improves in direct proportion to the quality and completeness of the incident-classification system used and the collection of information the latter component is designed to assemble. These four components constitute the nucleus of a data-collection system.

Incident classification is nothing more than categories of behaviors or specific types of incidents that are prohibited by policy or, in the case of a crime, by law, the commission of which management wants know about. An appropriate place to start the development of an incident-classification system is with a review of the examples of abusive behavior outlined in Chapter 1: The Problem, Section 1.2.

The types and number of categories of prohibited behavior are limited only by the needs of the specific environment they are intended to serve. Corporate policy implements these specific categories and mandates reporting of known or suspected violations. This input is then collected, tabulated, analyzed, and followed up where needed.

Notification is generally made in writing in a manner prescribed by policy. Usually a form designed to collect certain basic data is completed by site management and submitted to some upper-level manager at the corporate office for processing. In larger organizations, reports are submitted to the corporate security department for review, analysis, and follow-up.

In cases where a security department exists, provisions are made for a telephone call-in of an incident's basic details, and security personnel complete the required reports. This approach improves the timeliness of incident reporting and the collection of data. Refer to Chapter 4: Support Materials for a sample incident report.

What kinds of basic information should an Incident Report collect? Below are some examples of pertinent data.

- Case or file number.
- Incident classification.
- Location occurred.
- Date and day incident occurred.
- Time incident occurred and discovered.
- Time incident reported.
- Person discovering or reporting incident.
- Location manager.
- Location, building, parking lot, district, division, and region.
- Description of property stolen, missing, or damaged (including value, age, condition, markings, serial number, model number, etc.).
- Identification of suspects (number, age, race, physical description, weapons, and vehicle tag numbers, etc.).
- Narrative description of what is known or suspected to have occurred. The narrative answers the questions of: Who? What? When?" "Where? How? and Why? to the extent known.
- Witnesses, complainants, and defendants by name, addresses, telephone numbers, etc.
- Police report case number and name of responding officer.
- Costs.

Report forms should be designed to reflect the needs and purposes of the organization. They are used to collect pertinent data in a uniform manner. This type of format is used for first or preliminary reports related to known or suspected violations of security policies. More substantive input and documentation usually follow in a more detailed investigation report. However, data on wrongful employee conduct are acquired in whatever format, and the information collected is then used for a variety of purposes. For example to:

- Assessment risks
- Establish predication for further investigation
- Design remedial action plans for specific or developing problems
- Change policies and procedures
- Report of tax-losses
- Insurance loss reporting
- Determine costs
- Facilitate further investigation

Who assigns case numbers, classifies reports, analyzes data, and determines what investigative or corrective action should be initiated? The answers to those questions and many more are determined by management. Most of these types of questions are answered in the formative stages of program development. Case numbers and classification systems are used for easy retrieval of data and for analytical purposes. Specific responsibilities and lines of authority are set forth in written policies and procedures. As a general rule, the corporate security department handles all or part of this function in larger organizations. In smaller companies some executive must be designated to perform the task. When appropriate, follow-up investigations are conducted by in-house security personnel, management, law-enforcement, contract services, or some combination thereof.

Perhaps the next two logical questions that need to be answered are, who completes the required report and to whom is the completed report distributed? The answer to both of these questions is that the protocol will vary from organization to organization. The reason is that the entire process will be designed to satisfy the needs of the particular organization. Each system should be customized to the organization.

There are some general rules of thumb that characterize the process:

- First reports of crime-related instances usually originate with supervisors or management.
- First reports of unethical or irresponsible behavior usually originate with subordinates (the rank-and-file employee), customers, or vendors.
- Those organizations with security departments may require that first reports of crime-related incidents be phoned into them immediately upon discovery. First reports, in this instance, are solicited and received from any source. Security staff complete the required written report.
- Another approach requires location management to immediately call in the first report to the security department or other designated executive and then submit a complete written report setting forth the details of the incident. E-mail or fax transmittal can be used.
- Timely reporting is extremely important in these instances and that is the purpose for the immediate notification requirement. "Immediate" is generally interpreted to mean "as soon as practical," unless there is an on-site security capability that is required to respond. Then, the time requirements change and the report is completed prior to the end of a shift.
- The majority of corporate security departments solicit, document, and act on all reports of illegal, unethical, and irresponsible employee, customer, and vendor conduct, regardless of the source or the manner in which the information is received.

First reports of security-related incidents are preliminary and summary in nature. Not all incidents reported are investigated. All incidents are reviewed and analyzed, but some incident categories are reported and maintained in a "record only" status. In other instances, further investigation is required to determine the full extent and exact nature of a particular situation. Further investigation may take the form of a full-scale inquiry or be preliminary in nature.

If an investigation is preliminary in scope, then the purpose is to collect or acquire more information. Any information that is subsequently developed is then used to determine if further inquiry is needed and if the scope of the investigation should be expanded, or if the data accumulated are sufficient to act upon.

When the information acquired or developed in the preliminary step is sufficient for the purposes of making a decision, then further inquiry is not made. If the information gathered is insufficient, or if the facts indicate some other need exists, then a full-scope investigation may be initiated. The investigative approaches illustrated are intended to gather facts to be used in determining the appropriate remedial or other course of action necessary to effectively resolve the issue or problem under consideration. More detailed information about the purpose of an investigation is found in Chapter 3: The Solution, Section 3.16 Investigations.

Another logical question is, who gets a copy of the investigation report and is informed of the results of any investigation? The answer to this question is identical to the two answered in the preceding paragraphs. That is, who gets what, where, how, and when will vary from organization to organization. As with the previous questions, some general practices are used, for instance:

1. Report distribution is influenced by the type of incident, legal implications, and the level of confidentiality required. Not all incident reports receive general distribution within the organization.
2. Usually, preliminary reports of a routine nature have general distribution within the organization (i.e., thefts, vandalism, burglary, and arson.)
3. Reports of investigations are generally treated as confidential with a very limited or a need-to-know" only distribution (i.e., legal, human resources, or top management.)

Reporting of losses, security-related incidents, and certain policy violations is an important adjunct in the overall process of loss prevention. Documented abusive conduct creates a database that can substantially contribute to prevention strategies. Additionally, the mere fact that a company documents and investigates incidents of illegal, unethical, and irresponsible conduct creates its own deterrent effect. Few employees, customers, or vendors want to become the subject of a police or security-related investigation.

This latter circumstance can and does contribute its own deterrent effect and thus augments security-awareness and loss-prevention processes. Failure to document, review, or investigate security-related incidents sends its own message — management is either indifferent to or does not disapprove of such behavior.

What are some of the many payoffs that can be expected from a well-designed, implemented, and maintained data-collection system? Such a program will allow an organization to:

- Document known or suspected abusive incidents and behavior
- Document losses, dollar amounts, and their sources
- Identify vulnerabilities
- Identify high-loss items and locations
- Identify areas where corrective action is indicated
- Pinpoint security deficiencies by location
- Pinpoint deficiencies in security policies and procedures
- Pinpoint locations with abusive behavior problems
- Determine abusive behavior patterns and trends
- Determine negative operational impact of losses and behavior
- Assess effectiveness of loss-prevention countermeasures
- Determine demand for security services
- Produce statistics for analysis
- Determine where, how, when, and by whom abusive acts are committed
- Assess investigative effectiveness
- Quantify loss-recovery efforts
- Assess effect of disciplinary actions on loss-prevention
- Provide documentation for insurance claims
- Adjust self-insurance reserves
- Compel management to assume responsibility for abuses and their prompt reporting
- Identify topics for employee training sessions

Much can be accomplished with a well-designed, implemented, and maintained data-collection system. One source of more detailed information is the book *Loss Prevention through Crime Analysis* by Francis James D'Addario, written for the National Crime Prevention Institute and published by Butterworth-Heinemann of Stoneham, Massachusetts in 1989. This text explains crime-analysis methodology in an objective, quantitative manner and as a means of collecting, cataloging, and examining crime data generated by both internal and external causes. The book demonstrates how crime analysis enhances subsequent policy decisions, allocation of resources, selection of countermeasures and hardware, training objectives for loss prevention, and thus the profitability of the organization.

With the use of a computer and a professionally designed database program, the task of collecting and analyzing important security-related information is simple and cost effective. The complication for most organizations is that the cost associated with the custom design of such a program is prohibitive; however, that problem has now been solved.

IRIMS (incident reporting and information management software) is a fully automated security management system that puts data collection and analysis at management's fingertips in an easy-to-use, menu-driven format that provides all the features of a customized system without the expense. This computer software system was developed by security professionals and is intended to serve the simplest to the most sophisticated security data-collection and applications needs. The IRIMS program gives management the broadest flexibility in the collection and analysis of security-related data.

This security software program has it all, from collecting incident-specific information by location to the documentation of loss and recovery histories. It will prepare management reports with statistical graphs and all that lies in between. The program's design allows management to administer its security and loss-prevention efforts, including employee security-awareness programs, in the most cost-effective, timely, and efficient manner. IRIMS is the product of PPM 2000, 10405 Jasper Avenue, Suite 1400, Edmonton, Alberta, Canada, T5J 3N4.

2.5 Problematic Issues

The requirements for the reporting and analysis of abusive conduct in the public and private sectors range from none to excellent; many are poor. Of those incidents that are reported, the analysis of, interest in, and capability of managing data will generally mirror the organization's reporting procedures and practices. That is, they too range from none to excellent. With the exception of those organizations that have excellent reporting and problem analysis, vital statistical information is lost or insufficiently analyzed if captured.

Further complicating information gathering is that many of the organizations that do require incident reporting either inadequately classify the type of incidents they want reported or use classifications that are too restrictive. Most companies concentrate incident-reporting requirements on illegal employee behavior. They do not recognize unethical and irresponsible conduct in those requirements. The result is missed information. If not aware, even the most competent, ethical, and interested management can be lulled into an erroneous sense of security.

For the most part, thefts or other suspected or actual misconduct perpetrated by nonemployees are reported internally and, with some exceptions, to law enforcement. On the other hand, similar acts committed by an employee are not always reported, either internally or to the authorities. Even when noticed, most known employee criminal behavior is never reported to the police. The matter is administratively handled as an internal disciplinary process.

The disturbing fact is that management will often cover up or attempt to cover up known or suspected subordinate or higher-level wrongdoing. Failing that effort, the situation may be further complicated when management attempts to cover up or minimize post-incident damage. Management may be so motivated because of self-interest or because they wish to protect the financial interests of the organization.

The explanation for this sort of management behavior is fairly simple. If a manager perceives that his career and promotional chances, pay, or other incentives can be harmed by acknowledging an incident or that such an acknowledgment will in some way negatively reflect upon his managerial competency, then the incident is more likely to go unreported or underreported.

There are, however, exceptions to these predictors of management behavior. One exception is the felonious commission of a crime against an individual, for example, an aggravated assault, wherein a deadly weapon of some type is used and serious bodily harm or death inflicted on the victim. Another example would be a grievous crime against property in which a major loss was sustained that could not be hidden, absorbed, or explained to senior management, stockholders, outside auditors, or regulators.

In either of the criminal examples cited the probability that such an incident would be reported to police authorities is high. That probability is present even if an employee is a suspect. This assessment of probabilities is most reliable when applied to the rank-and-file employee or management of low rank and can change dramatically and becomes less probable when a member of upper management is suspected.

The prevailing practice in many organizations is to selectively report property crimes to authorities. Incidents of this nature are generally only reported after a preliminary evaluation of the incident by some level of management is complete. The purpose of such an evaluation is to determine if management wants police involvement in an investigation. For the most part criminal incidents involving nonemployee suspects are reported to police authorities.

The reporting of an illegal act to the police does not automatically guarantee an organization's full cooperation in the investigation and prosecutorial process, if prosecution is initiated. In some instances, where crime reports are prematurely made to the police, executive support is not always present. There is another factor that will cause a rapid change in corporate attitudes and cooperation. That change is noticeable when a subsequent police investigation expands into other areas of the organization and opens unanticipated exposures.

If the legal process becomes difficult, management will often waffle, bow out completely, cover up, provide eyewash, or actually impede the investigative or prosecutorial process. This is another example of low management attitudes and practices can contribute substantially to an abusive employee problem and alienate the law enforcement community in the process.

The response described above will certainly be found if management (particularly if highly placed) is implicated in any criminal wrongdoing or if the scope of an investigation expands into other sensitive areas that are beyond the scope of the specific complainant or misconduct originally reported.

Most management-related criminal incidents are disposed of internally, shrouded under a cloak of secrecy. The reason for this approach is simple. Criminal incidents involving management have a tendency to generate negative press and, thus, frighten executive management. Through the press, the organization's dirty linen may be publicly exposed (including other crimes), and the potential for negative business consequences from such exposure generally outweighs any possible gains. Another consideration is that if the implicated executive is publicly exposed, he might blow the whistle on other executives and their wrongdoing.

When upper management is implicated in meaningful wrongdoing, the highest levels of the executive chain will become involved in the supervision of the case. These executives, often hidden behind the scene, will guide and direct the decision-making and disposition process. This process will, at all times, be conducted under the heavy influence of the legal and public relations departments.

The thesis of the "let the chips fall as they may" approach is that a business will be better managed, from top to bottom, if each case is investigated and those involved are held to the highest standards of conduct. If this strategy were used, it would certainly send a forceful message throughout an organization. Such an approach would tighten the legalities and ethical aspects of employee conduct. Whether abusive employee behavior is acknowledged and reported internally or to some outside authority or both and how that information is managed upon receipt are important business decisions that have many business, legal, and operating implications for management, all of which must be taken into consideration.

Noted below are examples of the types of questions that must be addressed and for which answers must be found if management's response to the abusive employee behavior problem is to accurately reflect organizational attitudes, practices, and policies.

- What employee behaviors are going to be prohibited?
- How, when, by, and to whom is prohibited conduct to be reported?
- What kinds of behavior or incidents will be reported to the police?
- What kinds of behavior or incidents will be disposed of internally?
- Who will investigate, review, and make dispositions?
- What kinds of disciplinary actions are prescribed for what conduct?
- Is the process fair?

Obviously, how these and other key questions are answered, and the issues related thereto addressed, will ultimately either contribute significantly to the presence and growth of an abusive employee problem or to the prevention, deterrence, and detection of such behavior. Whatever the ultimate outcome for any specific organization, that result will be determined by the interaction of myriad influences and factors. Not the least of which will involve:

- Management action or inaction
- Management's attitudes and practices
- The level of management's honesty, ethics, and integrity
- Management's standards of performance
- Management's policies and procedures
- The quality of management's leadership
- The character and substance of the individual manager and the collective quality of his or her peers
- The character of the organization as reflected in the quality of its employees

2.6 Conclusion

If the estimates of the cost of abusive employee behavior illustrated above are even close to being accurate, then those estimates are cause for great concern. It is not just the billions of lost dollars that are at issue here. That issue is only symptomatic of a much more substantive issue. The issue that begs to be addressed is far more basic and fundamental to both public and private interests than just that of money. It centers on morals. Illegal, unethical, and irresponsible business and government management behavior calls into question and doubt the moral fiber of an entire people. The fundamental issue that is then raised with exposure of corruptive behavior, be it business leadership or that of government, is the honesty, integrity, and ethics of individual Americans and the character of the nation.

Damage the latter and you damage the substance of this Republic. Raise doubts and concerns about our individual and national character and you undermine the most basic and fundamental aspects of the American experience. To denigrate or destroy the character of America is to denigrate and destroy the belief of the individual American in himself.

Moral issues are not resolved with just a new set of internal controls, policies, and procedures. If these issues are to be resolved, then the root causes of corrupt employee conduct must be addressed and identified, and remedial action initiated. If it has not already done so, executive management needs to reassess its operating practices, opinions, and prior positions on this subject if current trends are to be reversed.

Investigation and apprehension are important to the success of any loss-prevention efforts, but they represent only a partial solution to the overall problem of abusive employee behavior. The fear of detection and the certainty of disciplinary action go with deterrence.

Management's reluctance to adopt broad-based employee security-awareness and loss-prevention programs are often based on the following:

- Lack of a demonstrated need for such an approach (without records and analysis, the need may never be recognized).
- Inability to accurately estimate the expected return-on-investment of time and money to put such a program in place.
- Management often refuses to admit to the existence of a problem.

The central question begs an answer. Why has the emphasis of American business and its loss-prevention efforts been with external threats and so little attention, other than internal controls, paid to the threat from within? This situation has arisen for a variety of reasons:

- Many managers simply do not understand the nature of the employee threat. They view the internal threat as insignificant (managed through its internal controls) and the external threat as significant. This situation is often influenced by the fact that losses from external sources are well documented and those from internal sources are not. Those managers who have learned bitter lessons regarding the internal threat or who have read the research on their industry regarding this exposure have changed their approaches; the loss-prevention focus is directed inward to all levels within the organization. Those managers who have not yet learned or accepted contemporary realities languish in a state of self-destructive ambivalence.

- Oftentimes security practitioners are more comfortable with the external-threat approach and are, therefore, advocates of it.
- Security hardware, security guards, motor and foot patrols, CCTV, and access controls are tangible, as is the threat. The internal threat is much more subtle — and potentially more damaging.
- Management's confidence in and reliance upon existing internal controls, management practices, oversight, and audit functions mean that the internal threat appears less significant than from the external one.

Where changes are dictated, it will take personal and corporate courage to inspire those changes. The decision to initiate a search for truth, via a thorough internal review, is fraught with caveats that not only exist in a legal and managerial context, but are rooted in the psychological as well. The inherent risk to be faced in a quest of this nature is that in the course and scope of the inquiry and discovery one may uncover facts that will have a detrimental effect on management's own selfish interests, those of the organization, or both.

This situation can create conflicts and threats that will challenge personal integrity and ethics to the limits. The situation generates a desire and (reasons often perceived as compelling) to deny, distort, misrepresent, or cover up and outright lie in an effort to protect those interests. The potential losses arising out of poor decisions made in these situations occur on personal and business levels.

On a personal level the loss exceeds any monetary values; self-respect is gone. Total damage in that instance may be impossible to calculate in either emotional or monetary terms. For the commercial enterprise or institutional entity it is the loss not only of the respect and trust of employees and customers, but of money as well.

The argument is made. The die is cast. The case is made that full accounting of costs and damages attributable to both employee and nonemployee misconduct is essential, that is, if the impact of those costs on the organization is to be determined. Without systems in place to collect and analyze this data, guesswork is the process used to quantify the problem and design the response. The latter approach is hardly the foundation on which sound business decisions are made. More importantly, perhaps, is that without a sound moral and ethical foundation upon which to rely for guidance and build, our business and legal systems will deteriorate into chaos.

The Solution

3

Objective: To provide a prescriptive package of information that offers a solution to abusive employee behavior including elements that comprise an employee security-awareness compliance program.

3.1 Overview

After reading Chapters 1 and 2, you should have an understanding of the factors that influence the existence and growth of occupational crime and abusive employee behavior in an organization as well as the associated economic and psychological costs. The information in this section will further augment your knowledge of the problem and provide a prescriptive package that offers a potential solution.

The prescriptive package offered here not only assists in the prevention and deterrence of occupational crime and abusive employee behavior, but it also increases the probability of early detection of unprevented acts. The net outcomes of this approach are a reduction in losses; improved management, employee, customer, and vendor relations; decreased abuse-incurred costs; and increased profits.

If the intent is to develop a compliance program that meets the criteria set forth in *Chapter Eight*, "Sentencing of Organizations," of the *U.S. Sentencing Guidelines*, the program described herein may aid in that development. Emphasis must be directed to fulfilling Chapter Eight criteria if there is to be any creditable expectation that sanctions will be mitigated in the event of need. The employee security-awareness/compliance program discussed here may not meet each of the seven criteria in Chapter Eight to the satisfaction of U.S. Department of Justice attorneys' objective and subjective evaluations of program effectiveness should your organization ever come under scrutiny in a federal court.

Legal review of any program's design and content, regardless of its purpose or intended consequence, is highly recommended. Court rulings and changes in evaluative criteria and law may favorably or adversely impact your program, its anticipated outcomes, and effectiveness. Even if your lawyers bless the program in its entirety, there is no guarantee that it will meet the burdens or interpretations of law, or completely shield you from criminal or civil liability, or sanctions arising from or attendant thereto. For these stated reasons it is prudent that a legal review of any actual or proposed program and any changes or modifications to an existing program be conducted.

Identifying specific areas of concern, isolating those problems, and then finding the solution for each of them are part of a complex process. Notwithstanding the inherent legal implications therein, the task is complex because human and organizational cultures and behaviors are complex. Because each of us individually is unique and complex, it follows that each organization we have created and work in will mirror that uniqueness and complexity.

Because of the aforementioned factors it is understandable that in searching for and finding answers that will help resolve occupational crime and abusive employee behavior and in meeting compliance criteria, there will be no simple solutions. This should not deter management in its quest for solutions. It is during the search process that management will discover that resolving the issues and finding the answers they seek are ongoingevaluative-processes. Management must understand that the inquiry process is a quest requiring honest, introspective analysis if it is to be successful.

Since finding a starting point — much less a solution — to this crucial organizational problem can be confusing to many managers, they either never get started or they begin in a way that ensures failure, or at best only marginal success. With the information offered herein any manager can begin the process that will lead to the successful development of an employee security-awareness/compliance program and thus, the prevention, deterrence, and detection of wrongful employee behaviors.

In the paragraphs that follow a complete employee security-awareness/compliance program is outlined. Management, using this program or some modification of it, not only has a place to start but is offered a viable solution to employee misconduct. Employee security-awareness/compliance programs can be designed for and implemented in any type organization. The concepts introduced can and should be modified and customized to fit the needs, concerns, and circumstances of the entity for which it is intended.

The design, implementation, and maintenance of an employee security-awareness/compliance and loss-prevention program is not a simple task. It is a serious undertaking that requires management's best efforts to ensure success. Legal, accounting, and auditing input is required if the program is to meet loss-prevention objectives and *Chapter Eight* criteria for an effective compliance program.

The purpose of these programs is to enhance every aspect of the organization in which they are used. Those organizations with a high level of employee security awareness and concern experience less abusive behavior and are better managed and more profitable than those organizations without one, and such incentives are significant motivators.

By improving employee security awareness, management impacts and improves all aspects of loss prevention. Every existing system intended to interdict losses is enhanced: internal controls, inventory, internal and outside audits, security policies, procedures, etc. all become more effective and efficient; abusive behavior is reduced and the likelihood of detection improved. Stockholder, employee, customer, and vendor relationships are enhanced. But that's not all, the overall quality of management is also improved, the net result of which is improved service, customer or client relations, production, and profitability. In the event of a breakdown in prevention efforts that produces a worst-case scenario situation, those negative consequences can be mitigated through application of your program's mechanisms and in federal court if needed.

As management's recognition, knowledge, and understanding of the problem and inherent risks increase, so too will the quality of their efforts and the programs they put in place to deal with it. Managing and finding solutions for the abusive employee problem are part of a continuing, evolutionary process. What management does today will be done, but contemporary theories and practices in loss-control and mitigation management will probably be considered elementary in future contexts. Things will change and improvements will be made as managers develop more effective ways to deal with the challenges faced, but then that's for tomorrow. Today, management must make the most effective use of what they know, and learn from this book and other sources.

3.2 The Big Picture

Management's awareness of the potential for and actual occurrence of abusive employee behavior and their efforts to prevent, deter, detect, and manage such behavior post-incident are nothing new. Struggles in this regard are as old as business itself and well substantiated. Many business loss-prevention efforts have centered on:

- The personnel selection process
- Development and refinement of internal controls
- Internal and outside auditors
- Management oversight

Today, efforts may be insufficient to reverse the ethical erosion that has taken place (and is occurring) in an organizational context and in our daily lives. The primary indicators of this insufficiency are the current levels of abusive behavior in business, governmental, and social environments and their upward trend. The moral and ethical decline of the individual American is becoming ever more apparent. This deterioration is evidenced in every facet of our lives. More effort is now required in terms of:

- High-level management oversight
- Perceptions of and approach to the misconduct problem
- Management of existing loss-prevention systems and procedures
- Development of new controls and methods to meet changing exposures
- Enhanced pre-employment screening
- Care in delegation of discretionary authority
- Development of a broad base of employee, customer, and vendor involvement
- Development of a new emphasis on ethical behavior
- Effective communication with all levels of employees that sets an ethical standard
- Fair and consistent enforcement of performance standards
- Fair and consistent disciplinary action
- Proactive response to reporting
- Proactive response to post-incident management and prevention of recurrence

With the prevalence of abusive employee behavior we are discovering that persons predisposed to abusive or criminal behavior are no longer just outside the corporate door in the streets. "They" are now inside the corporation and our social institutions and working among us, inside the organization where "they" exploit stockholders, co-workers, customers, vendors, and, thus, the organization that sustains them.

Increased security awareness and greater employee involvement in and improvement of the loss-prevention process are becoming mandatory considerations for many organizations. How that participation is to be accomplished and how those systems are to be improved are two critical questions that in some way confront every business and institutional manager.

Achieving effective protective countermeasures will require major adjustments for some organizations in the following areas: Management practices, attitudes, and policies and operational and organizational approaches.

It appears to many security practitioners that management is fundamentally predisposed to crisis management; it has a reactive mindset that is always seen as putting out fires, but never practicing fire prevention. There are considerable data in business literature that validate this perception. Loss prevention requires a proactive mindset to be successful.

Insofar as abusive behavior is concerned, the emphasis must be on anticipating the problem and then aggressively moving to prevent unacceptable behavior before it becomes a crisis, a "don't wait to close the barn door until the cow is out" strategy. Contributing to the problem is that management typically wants to see documented evidence of losses prior to funding security countermeasures. The standard formula is:

- Show X dollars lost
- Budget Y dollars on countermeasures
- Show Z dollars saved

The described technique is representative of the classic (and partially ineffective) "let the cow out, and then close the barn door" mentality. Employee security-awareness/compliance and loss-prevention programs anticipate the problem and proactively move to "close the door" before the cow is lost. You have learned that most public and private organizations do not keep the kinds of records that reveal the extent of abusive employee behavior. The basic formula used to justify remedial action is, therefore, flawed from the outset and, so it follows, is the decision-making process and, ergo, the results. A well-developed employee security-awareness/compliance program will provide for thorough record keeping and analysis. The entire decision-making process is then qualitatively and quantitatively improved.

In a security framework there are two broad categories of abusive exposures that threaten an organization and for which countermeasures are designed. Security practitioners may define those two exposures as:

1. The internal threat
2. The external threat

This terminology makes it easy to classify countermeasures (target-hardening techniques and methods) and the specific threats those countermeasures are intended to impact. Of course, there are many derivations of the two categories. Countermeasures, in either category, are intended to protect the organization against the threat imposed from:

- An employee acting alone
- An employee acting with a co-worker
- An employee acting with a nonemployee
- A nonemployee

- An ex-employee acting with a currently employed person
- An ex-employee working alone but with insider knowledge
- An ex-employee acting with a nonemployee and using insider information.

Internal and external threats are prevented, reduced, and detected with the use of target-hardening methods and techniques that can employ procedural or physical countermeasures.

What are countermeasures? Countermeasures are those attitudes, practices, policies, procedures, audit and oversight systems, and hardware designed and intended to safeguard the integrity of an organization's assets and those of its employees. Countermeasures range from pre-employment standards and internal accounting controls to intrusion-detection systems. When countermeasures are well designed, properly implemented, and effectively managed and maintained, they effectively eliminate or reduce opportunities for the commission of wrongful conduct and magnify the risk of detection for the violator.

The terms "countermeasures" and "target-hardening" are often used interchangeably. What is meant by the term "target-hardening?" The "target" is the organization and all its assets, including employees and their personal property. "Hardening" is the incorporation of loss-prevention methodologies for the purpose of preventing or reducing losses from all threats, and providing early detection if not prevented. Typical countermeasures used to offset the internal threat include:

- Pre-employment screening
- Accounting controls
- Purchasing controls
- Inventory controls
- Internal and external audits
- Management oversight
- Security officers
- Incident investigation
- Disciplinary guidelines
- Security policies and procedures
- Corporate code of conduct
- Employment contracts
- Professional security department
- Surveillance equipment
- Sanctions against vendors who assist in or commit fraud
- Training in prevention and detection of fraud
- Employee security-awareness/compliance program

- Improved management practices and attitudes
- Required periodic position changes
- Required vacations for key personnel
- Realistic performance and production goals
- Safes
- Access controls
- Internal and external compliance audits
- Computer network and individual computer/workstation security
- Typical countermeasures used to offset external threats:
- Locks
- Lighting
- Fences
- Intrusion-detection alarms
- Closed-circuit television
- Uniformed security officers
- Mobile and foot patrols
- Access controls
- Guard dogs
- Armored car service
- Computer firewalls
- Virus detection and interruption
- Disaster recovery plans

The noted methodologies are utilized in combination for protection against external and internal threats. Expert use and application of these and other countermeasures can make unauthorized access virtually impossible without detection. When used in combination, they offer the highest degree of security and probability of prevention and detection. Some examples of procedural target-hardening methods are:

- Internal controls
- Policies and procedures
- Internal and outside audits
- Investigations
- Disciplinary actions

Countermeasures and target-hardening methods can also be described as visible and subtle. What is meant by that? Visible deterrents are those that are easily seen by casual observation as security controls. Subtle deterrents are those that are not so easily identified as security controls. Maximum deterrent effect is achieved when these two approaches are used together. Some examples of visible deterrents are:

- Locks
- Lighting
- Fences
- Intrusion detection
- Closed-circuit television
- Access controls
- ID cards
- Restricted areas
- File-cabinet controls
- Uniformed security officers
- Security policies and procedures
- Security orientations
- Security training sessions
- Educational media
- Computer security mechanisms

Examples of subtle deterrents include:

- Pre-employment screening
- New employee security orientation
- Contractor, part-time, and temporary personnel security orientation
- An employee security-awareness/compliance program
- Personal security materials and training
- All internal controls
- Internal and outside audits
- Security investigations
- Personal accountability
- Management example and practices
- Management oversight
- Ethical business practices
- Fair and impartial disciplinary actions
- Legal remedies
- Criminal prosecution

Civil prosecution, personal restitution, and bonding company recovery are good illustrations of visible and subtle deterrents. Note that "subtle" is not always so subtle. You can add some examples of your own in each category. Do not hesitate to modify any example sets provided here to suit a particular circumstance. The utilization of visible and subtle security methods must be balanced with the known needs and vulnerabilities of the organization and must also be consistent with sound business practices if management and employee acceptance and cooperation are to be achieved.

All countermeasures are vulnerable to compromise. Each has its own set of inherent weaknesses, be they procedural, physical, subtle, or visible. Hardware can effectively protect against unauthorized intrusion by a nonemployee who is not aligned with a current employee, an ex-employee, or by an ex-employee acting alone. The effectiveness of hardware can be reduced if the prospective intruder is an expert in intrusion detection and/or has insider knowledge of the system and any possible weaknesses.

The opportunity to compromise a countermeasure system or systems most often occurs when target-hardening methods, hardware, and system controls are poorly designed, installed, and maintained. The employee-aligned nonemployee or ex-employee would face the same target-hardening methods but would have an advantage because of insider knowledge. The variables listed below influence the vulnerability of a given target:

- How and the extent to which the target is hardened
- Employee honesty, integrity, and ethics
- Management practices and attitudes
- The quality, completeness, and supervision of internal controls and compliance with them
- The absence or presence of policies and procedures
- The quality, operational status, and maintenance of devices and personnel
- The employee co-conspirator' knowledge of the targeted area and level of access
- Whether the crime will be committed while the employee is on or off the job
- Whether the employee is acting in concert with another insider with knowledge greater than his own

If some or all of the above variables favor the perpetrator, then countermeasures can be controverted and a crime committed, which emphasizes the importance of target-hardening techniques and the necessity of expert design, installation, maintenance, staffing, and supervision. Countermeasure quality and integrity are critical to their success.

Management in some instances equates target-hardening applications made for external threats with protection against all threats, but this is only half of the loss-prevention formula. Most security deficiencies are not physical, and most internal vulnerabilities can be altered with little or no cost.

The point is that defending against the internal threat poses an entirely different set of exposures, circumstances, and complexities than does defending against the external threat. Do not confuse one with the other; both exposures have their specific countermeasures. If not properly planned and implemented, approaches can make adversaries of employees. All must be cost-effective. Most countermeasures, whether internally or externally specific, complement each other in the prevention of losses and in the early detection of wrongful conduct.

The utilization and application of internal or external countermeasures should be at a level consistent with sound business practices and demonstrated need. This point cannot be overstressed and must be clearly understood by the decision makers. Organizations should not be a prison, and not all employees are crooks. Fear is debilitating, and oppression stifles all it touches.

Management can measure countermeasure effectiveness using the following criteria:

- The level of employee participation in wrongful conduct
- The reduced level of abusive incidents
- The level of abusive conduct detected
- The level of employee participation in the program

Without significant employee buy-in to the need for, compliance with, and participation in the loss-prevention process, many of the countermeasures employed will be largely ineffective. Take the time to explain the program, the reasons for it, and how it benefits the individual as well as the organization.

Well-planned, implemented, and maintained countermeasures enhance employees' feelings of personal security. They also generate greater confidence and trust in the company. If properly executed, loss-prevention programs help employees view management as concerned for their welfare. Security and ethics policies or procedures should be written, advertised, and understood by those who will enforce them and those expected to comply. Communication, education, and training are essential.

Internal exploitation can be inversely proportional to existing economic conditions. When times are good, the threat can go up, and when times are bad, the internal threat can diminish. Most people think the opposite is true. They reason that when times are good, the internal threat is reduced, and when times are bad, the internal threat goes up. They believe that when times are good, there is no reason to be abusive, and when times are bad, the motivation exists. This logic is most credible when applied to the external threat. However, internally, good times and bad offer opportunities, rationalizations, and justifications for abusive conduct, but for different reasons. Let us review them.

Prosperity has its own negative by-products, for example:

- Inherent opportunities for mismanagement
- Breakdowns in policies and procedures

- Higher employee turnover
- Sloppy work practices
- General neglect
- Breakdowns in internal controls
- Lowered performance standards and practices
- Reduced employment standards and screening
- Strained or sloppy supervision
- Compromised ethics

The presence of any or all of these variables creates many opportunities for irresponsible, dishonest, and unethical behavior. When times are tough, the reverse is true in varying degrees; everything gets tight. It is during periods of economic downturns that many of the sins of prosperity are exposed. Efforts are then made to correct problems, and the focus is on surviving. This is a perfect example of crisis management and the reactive response; the more cost-effective approach is the proactive one. This is particularly true if a federal crime is committed and sanctions imposed upon conviction. In this instance the cost can be substantial in the absence of an effective compliance program that can be used to mitigate the impact.

It is more constructive to prevent the problem in the first place and minimize the damage. The reasons for this approach are simple: the damages incurred may not be easily repaired and, if fixable, may take an extended period of time to do so. Either alternative is undesirable and probably avoidable if the potential for loss under both circumstances is recognized and precautions taken in advance.

Let us not forget the hard times and thereby inadvertently underplay the inherent exposures. Hard times have their own sets of pluses and minuses. Yes, in hard times management gets tough, things are run more tightly and hopefully more operationally efficiently and cost effectively. But hard times create stress and anxiety within all levels of the workforce, from the executive suites to the production line. This kind of stress often evidences itself with an increase in internal losses. The following are examples of pressure points created during economic hard times:

- Jobs are eliminated.
- Wages are cut.
- Benefits are reduced.
- Reorganizations occur.
- Layoffs happen.
- Bonuses are cut or eliminated.
- Stock values decline.
- Stock options are reduced or eliminated.

- Perks are reduced or eliminated.
- Ethics can be compromised.

All or some combination of the above factors are present during periods of economic downturns. Each one is a danger signal that can influence and trigger psychological factors that contribute to abusive behavior. Managers will overlook these factors at their own peril!

3.3   The Key Components of Loss Prevention

Optimum loss prevention is achieved when both the negative factors noted in Chapter 1: The Problem, Section 1.5, "Management Attitudes and Practices," are eliminated with institution of the following operating guidelines:

- Management commitment to loss prevention
- Comprehensive employee security-awareness/compliance program
- Comprehensive pre-employment screening procedures and practices
- Ethical management practices
- Comprehensive ethics and security policies and procedures
- Performance evaluations that include ethical issues
- Comprehensive prepromotion screening (includes ethics evaluation)
- Comprehensive internal controls and procedures
- Comprehensive inventory controls and procedures
- Comprehensive internal audit controls and procedures
- Comprehensive financial and fraud-auditing controls
- Comprehensive computer security controls and procedures
- Professional security management and practitioners
- Positive enhancement of a security department and its functions
- Comprehensive incident investigation and analysis
- Comprehensive security-related disciplinary program
- Well-publicized system for anonymous reporting of abusive behavior
- Comprehensive application of security hardware
- Comprehensive security exit-interview program
- Comprehensive off-the-job personal security-awareness program
- Comprehensive coordination of security, personnel, auditing, and legal
- Comprehensive system that solicits loss-prevention ideas and suggestions from employees, customers, and vendors and provides incentives and recognition
- Management leadership, concern, and commitment to the growth and development of the individual employee
- Effective post-incident reporting, management, and remedial action

- Fair and consistent disciplinary processes

Security-awareness and loss-prevention efforts are inseparable. Each company may have its own components and considerations, but the ultimate objectives are the same: prevention, deterrence, and detection of wrongdoing and effective post-incident management and remedial action. Therefore, a comprehensive, company-wide systems approach is required if optimum effectiveness is to be assured.

Prior to the commission of an abusive act, the offender will consider the chances of detection and the probable punishment if caught. Therefore, the probabilities of detection and the expected punishment play important and indispensable roles in the success of the loss-prevention process. Optimum loss prevention is attained when:

- There is a high level of accountability.
- There is certainty of or a high probability of detection.
- There is certainty of disciplinary action upon detection.
- Management sets a high standard for business ethics.
- Ethical practices are part of the overall performance-evaluation process.
- Program components are audited for compliance.

Fear of detection and certainty of punishment are effective deterrents to wrongful conduct. The presence of these elements, balanced with other healthy practices, can provide management with an effective loss-prevention program. Discipline is discussed in detail in a later subsection.

Security awareness and compliance programs are the umbrella under which all loss-prevention efforts function. A comprehensive system should be designed to offset internal threat, influence attitudes, and effectively communicate management's ethical standards and practices, concerns, and caring attitude. Therefore, the ideal loss-prevention and detection process is not oppressive; generates positive responses and attitudes; provides a sense of personal safety and security; and involves employees (at every level), customers, vendors, and (where applicable) neighbors.

Many of the ingredients noted above are already in place, to some degree, in most businesses, and many of the internal controls are standard business practice. In most cases adopting or expanding these recommendations involves little to no additional cost. All involve healthy management practices and the use of low-cost educational methods and media.

To ensure that components of the security-awareness, loss-prevention, detection, and incident-management process remain relevant, cost-effective, and efficient each must be periodically reviewed and evaluated. A segment must be analyzed individually during the assessment, and any deficiencies noted must be eliminated. Every effort must be made to ensure that all security practices, hardware, policies, and procedures are reasonable and compatible with known and recognizable vulnerabilities. This consideration is very important to the success of loss-prevention efforts.

Employee security-awareness/compliance and loss-prevention programs that do not meet this criterion may be viewed by employees as oppressive. If this is the perception, then there is a high probability that the program will negatively impact morale, production, employee relations, and customer and vendor relationships. In more precise terms, inadequately designed, implemented, and maintained employee security-awareness/compliance and loss-prevention programs are costly and can be detrimental to the interests of the organization.

3.4   The Importance of Management Commitment

Management commitment is the most critically important ingredient in the establishment and maintenance of a genuinely effective employee security-awareness/compliance and loss-prevention program — whatever the components. Item two of the seven criteria set forth in *Chapter Eight* requires "oversight by high-level management," and the degree to which it is accomplished is a measurement of "effectiveness." Management commitment, in all probability, will also be a measurement of program "effectiveness" if mitigation efforts are ever initiated.

Without management support, three occurrences are likely:

- It is extraordinarily unlikely that loss-prevention efforts will be taken seriously throughout the organization.
- The program is destined to failure or, at best, marginal success.
- The compliance program may not meet the definition of "effectiveness."

Management must buy in to the need for the personal and corporate benefits that can be derived from the prevention and detection of abusive behavior. This dictates that management understand the purpose of an employee security-awareness/compliance program, its philosophy, concept, methods, materials, and techniques. It also requires that management understand the positive impact sound security practices have on the profitability of the organization and the potential for sanction mitigation. When these considerations are understood and incorporated into a shared value system, then management will be capable of providing the leadership essential for a successful security-awareness compliance program. Accomplishing this objective is no easy task, and management is often the least receptive in this regard and therefore — the hardest sell.

The only effective employee security-awareness/compliance and loss-prevention programs are those mandated from the top of the executive chain. Many managers are not interested in security or are ambivalent on the subject. It is for these reasons that top management must mandate participation and link management performance evaluations to program compliance.

Management and staff may have a tendency to ignore security procedures and deviate from sound accounting practices. This proclivity has the net effect of undermining the entire program because the practice encourages and contributes to substandard employee attitudes and practices. If an employee security-awareness/compliance program is to be successful, management must strictly adhere to all security policies, procedures, and practices. Those employees in nonmanagement positions will not accept security concepts and practices if management does not. The old "don't do as I do, do as I say" approach, although long ago proven invalid, is still with us. Prevention, deterrence, and detection of abusive behavior is brought about through a committed and determined effort on the part of management working — for the mutual benefit of all concerned.

Employee respect for a company and its management has the inherent effect of reducing the psychological justifications and rationalizations that typify occupational crime and abusive conduct. Trust and respect must be earned; they are not a given. High levels of abusive behavior are a classic indicator of how management is perceived by subordinates, and a not-so-subtle management exposé that discloses the realities of employee perceptions and, often, lack of confidence and respect.

Program management and performance accountability should be at the corporate level. A vice president or director of security is the most logical choice. The reason for this is that employees will judge the importance of the program by the level of management assigned to administer it. Whether the program is new or an upgrade of an existing one, success is influenced by the importance assigned to it by top management. This function should be a direct report to the CEO with a dotted line to the board of directors.

No compliance program can ignore the importance of conformity with the Generally Accepted Accounting Principles established by the American Institute of Certified Public Accountants. The integrity and ethics of any organization are disclosed in their financial reporting.

Every chief executive officer, chief financial officer, chief operating officer, member of the board of directors, audit committee, internal auditor, outside audit firm, or manager in any organization knows the importance of compliance with sound accounting practices. Each of the individual positions or groups noted is comprised of sophisticated and knowledgeable people who fully understand their fiduciary or professional responsibilities related to compliance with sound accounting practices and the credibility of the numbers reported. The financial well-being and integrity of the organization are reflected in its numbers. The importance of their credibility is thus validated.

While the latter statement is true in all instances, it carries particular importance if the reporting organization is publicly held. Investor trust, confidence, and respect are impacted, positively or negatively, by the numbers reported. Any fraud or inaccuracies in those numbers can severely damage individual investors and the reporting organization.

In 1985 the private, all-voluntary National Commission on Fraudulent Financial Reporting (COSO) (The Treadway Commission) was formed. The Commission's central focus is on financial reporting and on ways and means that improve that process. It is jointly sponsored by five of the largest American organizations whose purpose revolves around financial reporting, business ethics, effective internal controls, and corporate governance. Those associations are the American Institute of Certified Public Accountants, the Institute of Internal Auditors, the American Accounting Association, the Financial Executives Institute, and the National Association of Accountants. From its conception to the present day, the Commission has been made up of representatives from the New York Stock Exchange, private investment and public accounting firms, and business. For the purposes of their 1987 study, fraudulent financial reporting was defined as, "intentional or reckless conduct, whether act or omission, that results in materially misleading financial statements."

The Commission operated independently of its sponsoring organizations. They studied, identified, disclosed, and reported factors that may lead to fraudulent financial reporting. Their results were reported in the 1987 Report of the National Commission on Fraudulent Financial Reporting (The Treadway Commission). This report is a comprehensive benchmark study, the results and recommendations of which should be reviewed when management considers the design and implementation of a compliance program. The recommendation is made notwithstanding what management may feel is a high-quality existing program. The Treadway Commission Report may have influenced the U.S. Sentencing Commission regarding the need to develop *Chapter Eight* and the seven criteria to be used by the U.S. Department of Justice in evaluating the effectiveness of a compliance program in mitigation of sentencing.

On March 26, 1999 the Committee of Sponsoring Organizations of the Treadway Commission issued another study entitled "Fraudulent Financial Reporting: 1987–1997: An Analysis of U.W. Public Companies" As part of the study the Committee randomly selected 200 cases of alleged financial fraud investigated by the U.S. Securities and Exchange Commission. The 200 cases selected represented approximately two thirds of the 300 fraud investigations conducted by the agency between 1987 and 1997. This, too, is a landmark study on fraud in financial reporting and provides significant input on how these frauds are committed and by whom and the negative consequences arising from them. Among the findings: financial statement fraud techniques involved the overstatement of revenues and assets, prematurely or fictitiously recording revenues, understating allowances for receivables, overstating the value of inventory, property, plant, equipment, and other tangible assets, and recording nonexistent assets. Some other findings include:

In 83% of the cases, the CEO, the CFO or both were named as being associated with the financial statement fraud. Other individuals named included controllers, chief operating officers, other senior executives, and board members.

Most audit committees met only about once a year or the company had no audit committee while 65% of audit committee members appeared to have no significant experience or qualifications in accounting or finance.

Most of the auditors explicitly named in SEC enforcement releases were non-Big Eight/Six auditors.

Audit firms of all sizes were associated with companies committing financial statement fraud. Fifty-six percent of the companies studied were audited by Big Eight/Six auditors, 44 percent by non-Big Eight/Six.

Cumulative amounts of frauds were relatively large in light of the relatively small sizes of the companies involved. The average misstatement or misappropriation of assets was $25 million, with a median of $4.1 million. Some companies committing fraud were experiencing net losses or were close to break-even positions in periods before the fraud. Pressures of financial strain or distress may have provided incentives for fraud for some companies.*

Management that desires to develop an effective employee security-awareness/compliance program should review the results of the 1999 COSO study. This report and the original 1987 study certainly can assist in framing any assessment of an organization's vulnerabilities and any inherent risks.

Traditionally, management has assumed that everyone in the organization operates at some level of security consciousness. Any voids in this regard

* Quoted with permission of the Committee of Sponsoring Organizations of the Treadway Commission (COSO), 2002.

are to be filled in by management. It is now well established that management does not always know or understand the importance of this function and therein lies a weakness. Management too frequently operates on a reactive level. The traditional approach can become ineffective. The finest counter-measures, policies, procedures, and controls can be and are exploited on a daily basis in every organization.

The difference is that even if some abuse exists, the consequences will be far less damaging once vigilance becomes part of the organization's culture. You should not become discouraged if your efforts are not 100% effective. The search for the ultimate security-awareness/compliance and loss-prevention methodology is analogous to the search for the Holy Grail.

3.5   The Employee Security-Awareness/Compliance Program

Cultivating employee security awareness is a multidimensional educational process. Think of the employee security-awareness/compliance program as an umbrella under which the value of all loss-prevention efforts is enhanced.

The employee security-awareness/compliance program:

- Is a comprehensive ongoing communications approach
- Uses a variety of media to communicate its message
- Is a method of raising the level of employee security awareness
- Is used to emphasize the importance of security awareness (on and off the job)
- Is a means to motivate employee participation in the loss-prevention process
- Emphasizes the importance of ethical conduct to individual and organizational success
- Introduces employees to security concepts, policies, and procedures
- Encourages customer, vendor, and (where appropriate) neighbor participation in the prevention and detection of abusive behavior
- Is a method of preventing or deterring abusive behavior and, failing that, providing for the early detection and reporting of such behavior.
- Provides for strict management oversight
- Involves responsibly delegating discretionary authority
- Provides for compliance audits
- Requires incident reporting and remedial action
- Enforces standards fairly and consistently
- Has a fair and consistent disciplinary process and action plan
- Uses competent post-incident investigation

- Focuses on incident analysis as a way of preventing future recurrences

If an employee security-awareness/compliance program can hope to have any success, it must have the following eight essential components:

- Total commitment and support of management
- Comprehensive scope
- Stakeholder involvement in the loss-prevention process
- Mechanism in place for anonymous reporting of abusive behavior
- Status of an acknowledged, permanent, ongoing process
- Emphasis on management concern for the personal safety and security of employees — on and off the job
- A high probability of detecting wrongful behavior and certain punishment — regardless of the employee's status, rank, or tenure
- Incident reporting, investigation, management, and remedial action

Employee involvement in the loss-prevention process is a necessity, and the level of that involvement is a key measurement of success. If the program fails to motivate employee buy-in, as well as their personal involvement in the process, then either the wrong message is being sent or the message is being wrongly received. If this situation occurs, change the program.

3.6 Program Benefits

Outlined below is a compilation of typical benefits that can be expected from a well-designed and carefully implemented and maintained employee security-awareness/compliance program. The list provided is a comprehensive presentation that characterizes the maximum results to be expected from a program of this nature.

Each organization will experience different levels and degrees of success with their respective programs. Not all organizations using an employee security-awareness/compliance program will achieve maximum results. Some programs will fail, while others will achieve the most favorable results; most will fall somewhere in the middle. Those programs that achieve the best results are the ones that are managed best. You will determine the how and the why of your program. The benefits outlined below give management something to strive for and a standard of performance by which to evaluate their efforts. A solid and effective program:

- Reduces the number and frequency of abusive incidents and their costs
- Evokes a cost-effective proactive response

- Defines abusive behavior and delineates unacceptable behaviors
- Provides a disciplinary framework
- Sets ethical standards for the organization
- Communicates management position
- Has a consistent security message
- Motivates a high level of employee involvement
- Creates a climate of mutual concern and cooperation
- Raises security concerns and awareness on and off the job
- Provides encouragement and direction for reporting abuses
- Underscores the negative impact of abusive behavior on and off the job
- Improves employee, customer, and vendor commitment to the company
- Improves security practices and procedures
- Reduces fears and frequency of economic coercion
- Creates the impression of a company that is caring and concerned
- Improves security department image, functions, and practices
- Sets importance of loss prevention and detection of abusive conduct
- Emphasizes importance of honesty, integrity, and ethical practices
- Establishes individual accountability for actions
- Sets individual responsibility for prevention and detection
- Promotes early detection of abuses
- Reduces resistance to cooperation and apathy
- Improves record keeping and statistical base
- Improves the bottom line
- An effective compliance program can mitigate sanctions in federal court

No one can accurately predict the level of success that a specific employee security-awareness/compliance program will achieve. Each organization is unique despite the many similarities that exist in business or organizational management practices, services, or products; each will experience different results. The general rule of success, however, applies here as in any other endeavor. That rule is, the more you put into the program, the more you can expect out of it. We all know the rule, and we know what occurs when we violate it. We know that half-hearted efforts always produce half-hearted results. Govern yourself accordingly. Seriously, a program of this nature and importance deserves your best efforts; you are urged to take the time and make the effort. If you fail, you poison the program for a long time. Ensure program effectiveness.

3.7 Program Philosophy

A well-defined belief system provides the necessary confidence, direction, and framework upon which everything else can be built upon; it is the point at which all progress starts. Your belief system will set the parameters, the intent, and the foundation for any endeavor that you undertake. The development of an employee security-awareness/compliance and loss-prevention program is, therefore, no different than any other effort. Start the developmental process of the program by determining the belief system of the organization and the philosophical foundation upon which your program would be built. This philosophical base will provide a starting point. The philosophy of each program, of course, will vary depending upon the belief system of its author. A generic philosophy contains the following principles:

- Abusive employee behavior is detrimental to the interests of an organization, its employees, customers, and vendors and should be eliminated.
- The ethics, honesty, and integrity of an organization's employees are the character foundation upon which an organization is built and from which mutual confidence, trust, and respect in interpersonal relationships and in the marketplace are derived.
- Ethics, honesty, and integrity are a personal responsibility. No one can justify a dishonest, unethical, or illegal act. No one in management can compel an employee, customer, or vendor to engage in such behavior.
- All employees are responsible for maintaining high ethical and moral standards in their conduct.
- Management should provide leadership, encouragement, and policy direction in the prevention, deterrence, detection, and disciplining of abusive business behavior.
- Loss prevention is less expensive and disruptive of morale and production than is managing a problem post-incident. A proactive response is far more effective than a reactive one.
- Most employees are honest and reject abusive behavior.
- Most abusive behavior is committed by a small percentage of employees.
- Management must ensure that a well-advertised system is in place to process anonymous reporting of abusive behavior by both internal and external sources.
- Mandatory reporting of abusive behavior is required.
- Individuals guilty of abusive behavior should be dealt with decisively, fairly, and in a manner consistent with the nature of the abuse.
- Loss prevention is a shared responsibility of management and each individual employee.

- Abusive behavior potentially exists at every level of the organization. Loss-prevention efforts and security policies and procedures, therefore, apply equally to all levels of employment — without exemption.
- Management will work to eliminate all factors known to contribute to abusive internal behavior.
- Performance standards shall be reasonable. Employees will not need to resort to lying, cheating, or other unethical behavior to meet standards.
- Security should be visible enough to make it a deterrent but not oppressive in nature.
- Employee, customer, and vendor involvement in the loss-prevention process is essential.

Devote careful thought and consideration to the development of the philosophy of your program. That philosophy will be a direct reflection of who management is and what management stands for; it will reflect the character of management.

3.8 Program Goals

Listed below is a generic set of goals representative of those that characterize a typical employee security-awareness/compliance and loss-prevention program. Goals, in their simplest terms, are just statements of what you expect to accomplish with the program.

The list is an example for your review; it is thorough and states with specificity what the program is intended to accomplish. Goals must be developed that reflect the purpose and intent of the specific user. The development of program goals should not be approached on a casual basis. Think their development through and select them carefully. It is important to the success of your program that goals are well thought out because they form the foundation on which the program will find much of its strength — the basis upon which the program will ultimately be evaluated and your success measured and judged.

Program goals should provide:

- A comprehensive, proactive, corporate-wide employee security-awareness/compliance and loss-prevention program that will educate and motivate the involvement of employees, customers, vendors, and neighbors in the prevention, deterrence, reporting, and management of occupational crime and abusive behavior

- A program that will assist in reducing the nature and frequency of abusive behavior and promote the early detection of abuses not prevented
- A cost-effective and efficient method of communicating with, educating, and motivating people to be involved in the loss-prevention process
- An organizational environment created from mutual respect, trust, and cooperation
- An atmosphere that avoids the use of intrusive tactics or methods where possible
- A comprehensive set of security- and ethics-related policies and procedures
- A comprehensive approach for the reporting and investigation of security-related incidents and data collection and analysis to be used in the documentation, plotting, and trending of abusive acts
- Comprehensive educational media to communicate the organization's message on loss prevention to target groups
- A comprehensive program for anonymous reporting of misconduct
- A comprehensive off-the-job personal security-awareness and loss-prevention support program
- A comprehensive program for the administration of compliance-related discipline
- Ethics criteria that are incorporated into performance and promotional evaluations
- Management oversight of the program
- Auditing of performance standards
- Incident investigation and management
- Anonymous reporting of known or suspected incidents

The above set of generic goals should give a good idea of the scope of a program, what you will want to achieve, what is involved, and, hopefully, what will aid in the development of goals for your own organization.

3.9 The Employee Security Orientation

Once management commits to the use of a formalized employee security-awareness/compliance and loss-prevention program and its development and plans for implementation are complete, the next step is to introduce that program to the existing organization (including part-timers, temps, and contractors) and then to each subsequent new employee. This subsection critiques some of the more important aspects of planning for, creating, and effectively utilizing an employee security-awareness/compliance program orientation as an introductory vehicle for a new or an existing program.

The review is facilitated through a question-and-answer format:

1. Why is an employee security orientation important?
    *   Whether the security program is new to existing employees or being introduced to a first-time employee, the concept will be new to the individuals to whom it is introduced, and change can threaten morale, productivity, and employer–employee relationships.
    *   The participant's first exposure to the new concept will determine his perception, reception, attitude, and level of buy-in toward the organization's approach to security. It is important, therefore, that changes be introduced in the proper forum. The employee security orientation serves that purpose, assuming it is properly prepared and presented.
    *   Orientation sessions will influence the degree of success or failure of the organization's overall loss-prevention efforts. It must be effective in meeting its stated purpose and objectives.
    *   Can it be a segment of an existing orientation program, or can it stand alone?
2. What can the orientation accomplish?
    *   The employee security orientation informs employees what is expected of them and solicits their personal involvement in the loss-prevention process. It also introduces the ethical basis upon which the organization functions. It sets forth all personal requirements to minimize the possibility of any misunderstandings between the employer and the individual.
    *   It sets forth program philosophy and goals.
    *   It demonstrates respect for the individual and concern for his success within the organization.
    *   The employee security orientation is an important opportunity to have a positive influence on employee attitudes. A well-prepared and presented security orientation contributes to the cultivation of positive employee attitudes and cooperation.
    *   This is an opportunity that should not be missed or poorly done. It is during the orientation session that the organization takes on a form and personality and assumes an identity in the mind of the employee.
    *   The employee security orientation sets the ethical tone of the organization. By communicating the organization's position on security you are communicating the honesty, integrity, ethics, and

intent of the organization. Employees will know that abusive behavior is not tolerated and, upon discovery, is punished.

- An employee security orientation offers an opportunity to instill a sense of organizational pride. Most people want to be part of a quality operation. Quality organizations are administered and staffed by quality people and encourage a sense of pride in the organization and in its people.

- The employee security orientation is a fundamental part of the loss-prevention and detection process. It is also an excellent way to get employees to identify with the organization and to link the satisfaction of their personal goals with those of the organization; concern links with concern.

- An employee security orientation demonstrates concern for employees by the importance it places on off-the-job security and the support it provides on the subject. Through this approach the employee realizes a direct personal benefit and the organization derives indirect benefits; both win.

3. Isn't the employee security orientation really a sales presentation?

- Yes. The employee security orientation is as much a sales presentation as it is an introduction to an organization's ethics, security policies, and procedures. But it is not a question of just issuing instructions as much as it is gaining the confidence, trust, and respect of the employee group.

- Employee attitudes have an effect on the levels of abusive behavior in an organization because they set up the rationalizations and justifications for that behavior. Security in the organization is a reflection of those attitudes, the honesty of the individual employee, and the acceptance of personal responsibilities.

- Those employees who do not identify with or who are indifferent to the needs and problems of the organization contribute to abuse-incurred losses. Security programs will fail without employee support. It is important that most employees buy in to the necessity for, relevance, and purpose of the security program. The security orientation session can further this objective.

- Security is enhanced when the organization is perceived in a positive manner and when the employee feels that he belongs to and is a member of a special team, one that is concerned about his safety and security and that of his family as well.

4. How important is planning and preparation?

- Very important. An employee security orientation must be well planned and executed. The orientation session sets the tone for security and demonstrates the importance management places on it. Planning and preparation are critical to the success of the program.

- This program requires skill and high-quality presentation materials and technique. It must be presented in a positive and upbeat manner that projects a quality image of the organization and security.

Standardize and script the presentation.

5. When is the orientation session conducted?
   - The employee security orientation should be presented within the first week of employment. It is imperative that employees know and understand what is expected early on in the process.
   - People need and want to know the rules they are expected to live by; they want to know and must understand the need for security policies and procedures. This first introduction to security concerns is the organization's opening gambit to gain the trust and respect of the new participant.

6. To whom is the employee security orientation presented?
   - All existing employees, new hires, part-timers, temporary workers, and contractors. It is sometimes advisable to prepare and present a special security program for contractors and service-type companies who frequent the facilities as well. The latter group can be a valuable adjunct to the program as it interacts with your employees. This interaction can be beneficial from a prevention and detection standpoint.
   - Remember, the more people you successfully involve in your program, the more successful the program. The employees of contractors and service organizations will often have greater opportunities for theft than your own people and less incentive not to steal. These same individuals interact with and observe the conduct of your personnel. If wrongful behavior is committed in their presence or if they become knowledgeable of it, some of these individuals may report that conduct if they know you care and they have the means to contribute the information.

7. Is the orientation presentation made on an individual or group basis?
   - The presentation can be made on either an individual or group; depending upon the circumstances either method can be effective.

8. Who makes the presentation?
   - If a security department exists, a senior member of the security staff should make the presentation. If there is no security department, then a senior member of the personnel staff or management can handle the duties. Remember that people assign importance based on the importance assigned.

9. What is the purpose of the employee security orientation?

- Encourage communications between the organization and its employees
- Promote personal and business ethics
- Promote improved security awareness
- Insure an understanding of security policies and procedures
- Explain the reasons for (and purposes of) security policies and procedures
- Answer employee questions and address concerns
- Promote the organization's concern for employee security both on and off the job
- Promote voluntary involvement in loss prevention
- Promote the thesis of individual responsibility and accountability
- Promote team spirit and organizational pride
- Instill the importance of security policies and procedures and compliance with them
- Develop an organizational culture dedicated to honesty
- Promote a positive image of security
- Promote input, including constructive criticism of security policies and procedures
- Promote the concept of security as every employee's job

10. What specific points should be included in the orientation?
- The purpose of security
- Program philosophy and goals
- Review of specific security policies and procedures
- Review of identification card requirements
- Review of building access controls, requirements, and procedures
- Review of fire and intrusion detection systems and procedures
- Identification of authorized entrances, exits, and restricted areas
- Review of visitor controls and access procedures
- Review of locked door and cabinet policy and procedures
- Review of key controls and procedures
- Review of package inspection procedures
- Review of policy on the conduct of personal business on company time or property
- Review of emergency procedures
- Review of parking lot locations, restrictions, and vehicle security
- Participant review and signature of specified policies indicating understanding of each
- Questions and input
- Review of controls and procedures applicable to computer systems

11. What handout materials should be used?

- One each, to every participant of an employee security-aware-ness/compliance and a loss-prevention kit. This kit holds a variety of security-awareness materials, some of which are listed below. All materials used should be tied to a specific security policy (see Chapter 4: Support Materials, for specific samples).
- Copies of specified security policies.
- Copies of program philosophy and goals.
- Security-awareness/compliance pamphlet.
- "Speak Up," wallet card.
- Employee security responsibilities statement.
- Instructions for reporting abusive behavior
- Acknowledgment-of-responsibilities statement
- Original of the above statement to personnel file and copy to employee
- Each of the above items is explained and reviewed in the orien-tation session. It is important that each person understand the policies and practices of the organization on security-related issues.

12. Are there any problems you will need to watch out for?
- Yes. Policies that are not rationally and logically justified will be rejected and create more problems than they solve.
- Optimum security is achieved when your employees perceive themselves as valued members of the team and are permitted and encouraged to participate in the game of loss prevention. Make no mistake, loss prevention is a game. There are official and unofficial rules. There is a playing field, referees, penalties, and ways of scoring. The rules are not always well defined or easily understood. There are good teams and bad. Good guys and bad. There are winners and losers. Without a clear under-standing of the game and its rules, you are destined to end up a loser.
- All the elements of a game are present. The best-coached, hardest working, most dedicated, and most talented teams win. Loss pre-vention encompasses the same elements. Draft the best, coach and inspire them — and trade the losers.

13. What about subsequent follow-up to the orientation?
- Follow-up is critical to the success of the orientation program. All aspects of security awareness and loss prevention must be part of an ongoing process.

14. What methods are used for follow-up?
- Many methods can be utilized to keep the message in the forefront; for instance, here are two: require a semiannual security briefing

and update for all employees. Require security to be on the agenda for discussion at weekly, monthly, bimonthly, and annual meetings.

15. What topics would a typical security agenda include?
    - Ethics-, honesty-, and integrity-related issues
    - Abusive behavior problems and incidents
    - Areas that are vulnerable, weak, and exploitable
    - Types, locations, and frequency of incidents
    - Dollar losses attributable to abusive conduct
    - Actual or suggested countermeasures
    - Cost-effectiveness and efficiency of current countermeasures
    - Relevancy and effectiveness of current security policies and procedures
    - Recommended changes in security policies and procedures
    - Cost-effectiveness of security policies and procedures
    - Recommendations for improving communications within and outside the organization
    - Violations of policies and procedures and action taken
    - Review of off-the-job security topics and exposures
    - Review of emergencies: who, what, when, where, and how were they managed
    - Review of departmental or facility security strategy
    - Review of employee attitudes and practices
    - Effectiveness of disciplinary policy and dispositions
    - Drug and alcohol-abuse awareness
    - Ways of improving responsibility and accountability
    - Maintenance schedule for security hardware, status, repairs, and condition
    - Explanation of how to use the "integrity line," its importance, and anonymity of responder

16. Should meeting minutes be required, and if so distributed to whom?
    - Yes. Distribute to top management and the vice president of security. The names of key persons on the distribution list communicate the importance placed on the subject; employees will pick up these kinds of subtleties. If you fail to include the top management players on the list, then the message is that the minutes and the subject are not important. Corporate politics and turf wars aside, you must do it.

17. Should security be an agenda item for corporate committees?
    - Yes.

18. What committees?
    - Executive
    - Audit

- Personnel
- Safety
- Accounting/audit
- Risk management
- Maintenance

All security-awareness, compliance, and loss-prevention efforts need the involvement of employees to succeed. Take the time and make the effort to insure that every employee knows and understands the organization's position and their personal role in protecting the assets of the respective organization as well as co-workers.

3.10   The Importance of Employee Involvement

The importance of obtaining a high level of employee, customer, and vendor involvement in the loss-prevention process cannot be overemphasized. Employee involvement is an essential element of success. Motivating employee involvement in the asset-protection process requires a systems approach. That's what security awareness is all about.

The underlying thesis of employee security-awareness/compliance and loss-prevention programs is the belief that most people know and understand the difference between right and wrong and are honest. The system assumes that when provided with leadership, direction, and support in a manner in which ethics, honesty, and integrity are reinforced most employees will respond favorably. People want to work and go about their daily lives without fear, coercion, and threats against their welfare. Management, employees, customers, and vendors should share a mutual concern for security because they are all at risk of being victimized by dishonest, irresponsible, and unethical behavior. How to avoid being victimized is the issue.

A few specific considerations are:

- Each organization is unique; therefore, each faces a unique set of vulnerabilities.
- Levels of abusive behavior are different for each organization; therefore, the negative consequences for each organization are different.
- Abusive behavior impacts employees, customers, and vendors on different levels and in different ways as well. Each loss, regardless of which entity suffers, has a negative impact on the organization as a whole and its behavior. That impact will lie somewhere between insignificant and catastrophic.

- Losses are felt relative to the ability of the victim to absorb and recover from them (assuming recovery is possible).

Most employees know, understand, and have experienced the negative personal consequences of an abuse-incurred loss. Those same employees, however, may not understand that when their employer is victimized they are, too, albeit on a relative basis. An important aspect of motivating employee involvement is educating them to the latter fact.

When an employee understands that the dishonest, irresponsible, and unethical behavior of a co-worker is or has the potential to inflict serious consequences on his personal welfare, he takes a much different view of that behavior. The same reaction applies to customers and vendors who interact with employees and depend upon the goodwill of the organization for sales or service. In both situations their rational self-interest tells them to protect themselves. Motivating involvement in the loss-prevention process is not as difficult as might first be thought. The majority of employees act in the best interest of their employers.

The experience of the police in American cities indicates that a relatively small percentage of abusive citizens account for the highest percentage of known crimes and losses. This ratio of people involved in wrongful conduct applies equally as well to the American corporate environment as it does to our communities at large.

The majority of people, whether they are employees, customers, or vendors, reject illegal, irresponsible, and unethical behavior. The motivation for the rejection is simple: people find such behavior threatening to their own interests and disruptive of their sense of personal security. It is this majority (and rejection and fear of victimization by occupational crime and other abusive acts) that is management's most valuable asset in the effort to protect the assets of an organization and its employees from abusive exploitation.

This majority, when motivated and provided with incentives, encouragement, and opportunity to participate in the loss-prevention process, will do so in varying degrees. A well-designed and supervised employee security-awareness/compliance program provides the motivational input, the basis for cooperation, and the opportunity to participate. Employees may then provide the necessary peer pressure to support prevention, deterrence, and early detection of abusive behavior.

Yet no matter what the program offers, there will always be a certain level of apathy among target groups. Not everyone, no matter how well the program is designed, is going to actively participate in the process. From a loss-prevention viewpoint, however, tacit participation is important and has its own value and positive influence on the program.

The employee who buys into the thesis of asset protection, even though he is not vocal about it, is nonetheless important to the success of the mission; apathy is always a concern. While a certain level of apathy will always exist, that level can be reduced, if not eliminated, when a well-planned and concerted effort is made to accomplish that objective. Take action to overcome or reduce apathy and the program will prosper.

Apathy is reduced when the following factors are present:

- Management is committed to ethical standards of performance.
- Management's condemnation of abusive behavior is clear.
- Assurances of concerned support are evident.
- Employee and nonemployee participation is encouraged.
- Guarantees of confidentiality are provided through an anonymous reporting system.
- Management's disciplinary actions are perceived as fair and impartial.
- The messenger never becomes the victim.
- Investigations and audits are conducted professionally.

The most successful loss-prevention endeavors are those that center on motivating the highest level of employee, customer, and vendor involvement in the process: an educational, motivational process that emphasizes the concern of the organization, the importance of individual honesty, integrity, ethics, accountability, and personal responsibility. Customers, vendors, and possibly neighbors are also included for participation in the loss-prevention process; they can be great sources of information.

Customers and vendors deal directly with employees on every level of an organization. They often see employee behaviors in a way the employer does not. They see the good and the bad. They are lied to, exploited, cheated, snubbed, ignored, treated rudely, coerced, threatened, and intimidated. They interact with other customers and vendors. They talk to each other and exchange information and insights. They know who is unethical and who is ethical, who is taking kickbacks and which companies give them, often how it is done and how much is paid; they know or suspect who among them are doing the dirty deeds. When properly motivated, these contacts can be great sources of information, particularly when granted anonymity. Often all they need is demonstrated management interest, concern, cultivation, and encouragement; they already have the incentives to expose a problem if one exists. All they need is an interested and receptive ear. You should provide that ear.

Let customers and vendors know that abusive employee conduct will be properly handled, and if they do choose to identify themselves, assure them that it will not jeopardize their relationship with the organization. Also, make it known that if collusive abuse is discovered and proven, business relationships will be jeopardized. Give them the confidence and trust they need and a box of "secrets" may be opened.

On another scale, neighbors can often be very helpful with information regarding after-hours activity. This source applies primarily, of course, to small organizations. Involve the neighbors and ask for their help where beneficial. If a business offers discounts on products or other incentives, it's surprising what the neighbors already know and will tell, that is, if the trust is there.

3.11 Personal Safety and Security

Whether deserved or not, many employees feel management has little concern for their personal safety and security. Unions may use this theme to drive a wedge between management and subordinates. It is well established that no matter what the company does in this regard, for some employees, it will never be enough. Notwithstanding that fact, the attempt must be made to communicate management's concern because others in the group will see, understand, and appreciate those efforts. Those employees who grasp and understand the organization's concern can become allies, not only in the loss-prevention process, but also in other important business and organizational aspects as well.

Organizational concern and support are not always reciprocated to the degree management deserves. But where it is given, there is greater employee loyalty. In those companies where employees perceive the organization as caring there is correspondingly little tolerance for wrongdoing. Not every employee is ungrateful and unappreciative, even if he does not publicly demonstrate otherwise.

Experience teaches that employees are not too receptive to the idea that what each does individually directly affects the organization. Their universe is on a much smaller scale. Most want to know what you are going to do for them. They do not always ask what they can do for the company.

Therefore, motivating employee participation is more complicated than just trying to educate them about their roles in the bottom line and telling them that abusive behavior ultimately hurts them. That approach must be taken and is an important part of the educational process, but there is more. This is where personal-safety and security considerations can be helpful in many respects, not the least of which is loss prevention, detection, and reporting of occupational crime, and other abusive behavior.

Employees can be fearful off the job and sometimes on the job as well. For the most part, however, employee fears center on home and family. One of those fears is the fear of crime. Crimes that are or may be committed against them personally, their families, or property are of primary concern. In some cities it has become a preoccupation for survival. The threat to the company is not always an employee priority, and one can understand why — given the high level of personal risk in some cities. It is in this area that employees need assistance from the organization, but that is often neglected by a company. Expand the focus of security awareness and loss prevention to include personal safety and the security of employees when they are off the job and make friends on the job.

By raising security awareness and providing solutions and support for off-the-job security problems, the organization demonstrates care and concern in an area vital to the employee. Showing concern for your employee's welfare and then committing resources in this area enhance loyalty. Educational materials designed for off-the-job usage can expand knowledge and security awareness that is brought back to the job. The following is a list of topics that could be used effectively:

- Home security
- Vehicle security
- Automatic teller machine security
- Parking lot security
- Rape prevention
- Burglary prevention
- Neighborhood watch programs
- Home security checklist
- Drug abuse recognition and prevention
- Security for latch-key kids
- Theft prevention when traveling
- Locks, lighting, fences, and alarms
- Prevention of muggings and purse snatchings
- Fire safety in a hotel
- Fire safety at home
- Protection of bicycles
- Vacation security checklist
- Mobile home security
- Hurricane, earthquake, and tornado security
- Emergency item checklist

A great number of security-related communications materials are available. They come in a wide assortment: written materials, coloring books, films, slides, and video and audio tapes. Educational materials can often be obtained free from local law-enforcement and national crime-prevention organizations; those sold are inexpensive. Many organizations have the in-house resources to produce their own. Whatever your situation, take advantage of the resources that are available. Some law-enforcement agencies operate crime-prevention bureaus. They will have resources on a variety of subjects and issues. Often they provide free speakers and seminars related to off-the-job concerns.

One outstanding source of this type of material and crime-prevention programs in general is The National Crime Prevention Council, 1000 NW Connecticut Avenue, 13th Floor, Washington, D.C. 20036. Their "Corporate Action Kit" is loaded with professionally prepared materials that can be put to immediate use. These materials can be distributed in any number of ways: mail, e-mail, CCTV, employee meetings, newsletters, handouts, personnel and security departments, loss-prevention seminars, cafeterias, and employee lounges. This endeavor has a direct positive benefit to the employee and an indirect one for the organization. This supplemental program is a great enhancer of security awareness and asset protection.

3.12   Communicate the Loss-Prevention Message

The materials and media delineated below are used as part of a multidimensional approach in communicating an organization's security-awareness and loss-prevention message to a target group. The target group may be limited to employees, or it may include customers, vendors, and, in limited circumstances, neighbors.

In addition to those methods and media outlined herein, a great variety of creative materials and approaches can be developed within an organization using in-house resources. There are also commercially available, professionally developed media that can be purchased, borrowed, or rented and used to strengthen a program.

What is the purpose of communications? Why does a company need it? What does this kind of approach accomplish? These are good questions and many of the answers follow. Well-prepared communications media promote:

- Personal ethics, honesty, and integrity
- Ethical business and management practices
- The individual employee's responsibility for his own actions
- Compliance with security policies and procedures
- Communication between management and target groups
- Mutual confidence, trust, and respect
- Communication and interaction with security department

- Employee morale and pride in the organization
- Prevention, deterrence, and detection of abusive behavior
- A corporate culture that is conscious of loss prevention
- Security visibility
- Broad-based concern and participation in loss-prevention
- Known or suspected incident reporting

The examples noted below are a representative sample of various media and methods. These media are not original to the author. All of the examples cited have been developed and used by various security professionals in and out of the private sector in serving the needs of their respective organizations. The development of the media examples presented has been an evolutionary process with generously shared input and refinements from a variety of sources over the course of many years. It is because of this shared input and refinements that it has become impossible to credit authorship.

In the design of loss-prevention and employee security-awareness/compliance programs some, if not all, of the methods noted below should be incorporated into those programs. The media are selected and then used to fit the needs and desires of the specific organization. A few examples of communications media are:

- Corporate security theme
- Posters
- Newsletter articles
- Paycheck reminders
- Telephone sticker reminders
- Hard hat sticker reminders
- Letters to customers
- Letters to vendors
- Program kick-off letter
- Specialty videos produced in-house, rented, or purchased from commercial sources
- Voice mail
- E-mail
- Fax transmissions
- Computer bulletin boards
- Telecommunications media
- Personal and organizational security and loss-prevention seminars

The above listing includes only a few examples of the many available communications media and methods that have been used by a number of organizations to effectively communicate their messages; there are others. The only limitation in this area is imagination and creativity. Media should be kept fresh. Do not allow the media or their messages to stagnate. Contests are an excellent method to obtain new material and also involve members of your organization in the process.

One of the associations that has pioneered the professionalizing of the corporate and governmental security practitioner is the American Society for Industrial Security, 1655 North Fort Myer Drive, Suit 1200, Arlington, Virginia 22209–3198. Over the years the members of this organization have conceived, developed, and refined most of the media outlined herein and much more than space limitations permit. Contact with an organization of this nature is very helpful in answering any questions that this book fails to address or in giving professional assistance in any security-related area, including the design and implementation of a program.

3.13 Security Policies and Procedures

In this subsection security policies and procedures are examined. Sample policies are provided for reference. Policies are the law of the organization and should be carefully planned and developed prior to implementation because it is these policies that set the standards for employee performance and place the company on record regarding security-related issues. Once set in place, policies should be enforced.

At this juncture of the planning process, several important components should be in place, for instance:

- Recognition of an abusive employee problem or the potential for one
- The commitment of executive management
- The decision to improve all loss-prevention and detection programs
- The decision to create a new employee security-awareness program or enhance an existing one
- The development of a program philosophy
- The development of the program's goals
- The development of a list of anticipated benefits

Now it is time to develop the security policies and procedures that will form the heart of the employee security-awareness/compliance program and all loss-prevention efforts. Any existing policies should be reviewed and updated as necessary to deal with new problems or meet any fresh goals.

Inadequately planned and utilized security policies and procedures manifest the opposite of the desired effect. With programs that are poorly planned and managed employees lose confidence, trust, and respect for the organization and management. The net result is the increased potential for abuse, lower morale, and higher costs. Oppressive environments are deadly for morale; balance is the key. Policies and procedures must have the same weight as known vulnerabilities and risks.

Policies set forth uniform standards by which the organization is expected to function. Procedures are the means prescribed to carry out policy. Both influence the quality of the work environment, cost effectiveness, efficiency, how the customer is ultimately served, and the profitability of the organization. Well-developed security-related policies are essential to the success of loss-prevention and compliance programs.

Security policies serve to accomplish several purposes, among which are the following:

- Establish the philosophy of the company and security programs
- Establish goals
- Define management and employee responsibilities in specific areas
- Proscribe procedures to be used in policy compliance
- Establish both behavior that is unacceptable and accountability
- Assist with protecting the assets of the organization and its employees
- Assist in the protection of business relationships with customers and vendors
- Ensure fair and impartial disciplinary practices

The chart in Chapter 4: The Support Materials, Exhibit 4.2 outlines a generic policy development and maintenance cycle. The sample development cycle should be modified to reflect the needs and operating circumstances of the organization intending to use it. The planning cycle outlined in the referenced section is a very general representation of what is involved in the planning and review process. Essentially, this planning cycle offers a place to start; the fine points related thereto fall to you.

Security policies that are poorly conceived will be poorly supported and contribute to the problem — not alleviate it. Those policies that are "phony eyewash" send a transparent message of fraud in and of themselves. Employees, stockholders, customers, vendors, regulators, and juries in litigation cases will recognize that transparency as well. Management's attitudes toward ethics are revealed by its practices, not its words.

Periodic policy reevaluation is mandatory. A review cycle should be developed that will ensure the timeliness and effectiveness of all policies and procedures. Do not continue with faulty or out-of-date policies and procedures. If a policy is flawed in some manner, change it.

When and how are the effectiveness of an organization's security policies and procedures optimized? Let's take a closer look and answer those two questions.

The effectiveness of security policies is optimized when:

- The need for the policy correlates with a known or perceived risk.
- The policies are clearly written, easily understood, and fairly and impartially enforced.
- They meet all applicable laws and regulations on the specific issue.
- Security orientation and training sessions are effectively produced and conducted.
- They are fully disseminated and advertised to all employees.
- Each employee has signed an acknowledgment of policy understanding.
- Employees are provided with a copy of security policies.
- All employee questions and concerns are satisfactorily answered.
- Security-related issues are agendas for discussion and review at regularly scheduled meetings throughout the company.
- The policies are reviewed and evaluated for relevancy, effectiveness, and efficiency.
- Compliance with security policies and procedures and overall program support are included in performance evaluations and promotional considerations.
- Security-incident-related discipline is consistent and fair.
- No management double standard exists.
- An effective off-the-job educational program exists for personal safety and security.
- The employee security-awareness compliance program is effectively managed.
- An "Integrity Line" is open, advertised, and supported, and reports received are acted upon.
- A policy on security-related discipline, prosecution, and loss recovery exists.
- Alleged incidents of abusive behavior are competently investigated and resolved.
- A thorough and effective pre-employment screening program exists.
- A thorough and effective exit-interview program exists.
- Thorough, effective, and well-supervised internal controls and audits are in place.
- The security department is professional and supported by management.

Security policies and procedures must be reviewed by a lawyer to ensure compliance with applicable federal and state laws, bargaining unit contract provisions, or other legal considerations related to the subject matter. No policy should be finalized and implemented without thoughtful review and legal concurrence as to compliance with applicable law.

The following 14 sample policies provide examples that can be utilized to assist in the development of security policies for an organization. While they are basic in nature, they nonetheless are a starting point to initiate a policy development program and thus provide a solid foundation that can be built upon over the years. The examples are not intended to imply that only 14 are needed. The number will vary with the subject matter to be addressed; individual organizations determine both.

3.13.1   Code of Conduct

Scope:

This organization is committed to integrity in the conduct of all business relationships. Our reputation for integrity is a highly valued asset. In order to maintain that reputation all members of this organization must make a personal commitment to adhere to high moral and ethical standards in the conduct of their business relationships and in compliance with organizational policies and procedures and applicable law.

Provisions:

- The Code of Conduct and related security policies are a must-read for all employees of the organization including all levels of management and supervision.
- Employees will sign an Acknowledgment of Receipt form, certifying that they have read and understand the Code of Conduct Policy and related security policies.
- Should an employee require clarification of the Code of Conduct Policy or any other policy of this organization, inquiry may be made to the Human Resources, Legal, or Security Department.
- Enforcement of organizational policy is the responsibility of management and supervision.
- Failure of management and supervision to enforce adherence to organization policy can result in disciplinary action up to and including termination. Policy compliance is required of all personnel.

3.13.2   Corporate Security Policy

Scope:

It is the policy of this organization to provide a safe and secure work environment for our employees to conduct the business of this organization and to protect assets from abuse-incurred damage or loss. Illegal, unethical, and irresponsible employee behavior is unacceptable because it is detrimental to the interests of both the individual employee and the organization.

Provisions:

- The company is committed to honest and ethical business practices. Our reputation for integrity has earned us well-deserved employee and public respect.
- We are committed to the maintenance of the highest standards of quality in our products and services, and in our customer, vendor, and neighbor relationships. The character, loyalty, and commitment of our employees are important ingredients that contribute to the success and profitability of the organization.
- The security of our employees and the protection of the assets of this organization are of paramount management concern. Protecting the assets of this company requires a personal commitment to the highest standards of personal conduct while on the job.
- Each of us plays an important role in the prevention, deterrence, and detection and reporting of those actions that could or actually do cause damage to our company, its employees, or customers.
- To further clarify this position the company has developed a group of security-related policies. Those policies will be explained to each employee, and copies will be provided. Compliance with these policies is mandatory.
- If the company is to remain competitive, and if our personal lives are to be rewarded with the accomplishments of our goals, then we must collectively commit to the pursuit of personal and business excellence. Personal and business character is the hallmark of excellence; ethics and integrity are the cornerstones.
- Violations of security policies will subject the violator to appropriate disciplinary action, which may include dismissal and criminal or civil prosecution.

3.13.3   Abusive Behavior Policy

Scope:

It is the policy of the company to prevent, deter, detect, report, and take appropriate remedial action to correct the commission of any illegal, unethical, or irresponsible act committed by an employee or other source. Such behavior is considered abusive and detrimental to the interests of the company and destructive of interpersonal and business relationships.

Provisions:

- Honesty, integrity, and ethics are individual responsibilities. This responsibility cannot be transferred to another person. Each individual employee will be held accountable for his actions. No person, management or otherwise, can compel an individual to commit an illegal, unethical, or irresponsible act.
- Abusive behavior should be reported promptly to supervision or management. If there are mitigating circumstances that reasonably preclude that course of action, reports can be made directly to the security department or through the "Integrity Line." In either instance employees will not be required to identify themselves. The following examples are representative of those behaviors and acts considered abusive and, therefore, unacceptable:
  - Dishonest or unethical business practices
  - Financial, consumer, or vendor fraud
  - Theft of cash, inventory, or equipment
  - Falsification of records
  - Conflicts of interest
  - Accepting or offering unauthorized discounts
  - Sale, use, or possession of illegal drugs on company property or at company-sponsored events
  - Price-fixing
  - Commercial bribery
  - Sale or abuse of proprietary information
  - Possession, use, or display of a firearm or other dangerous weapon on company property or at a company-sponsored event, excluding authorized weapons for security personnel, the training thereof, and certain exempted tools used in work assignments.
  - Sick-leave abuse
  - Sexual harassment
  - Soliciting or accepting gifts
  - Workers' compensation and health insurance fraud
  - Insider stock trading

- Commission of criminal acts
- Any illegal act so defined by law
- The absence of a specific citation from the above list does not relieve an employee of the responsibility to exercise the highest ethical standards and compliance with federal, state, and local criminal laws.
- If in doubt as to the proper course of action to take in any situation that is believed to be covered by this policy, employees should consult their supervisor or the appropriate person in the security, legal, or personnel department for direction.
- Violations of this policy will subject the violator to appropriate disciplinary action, which may include dismissal and criminal or civil prosecution.

3.13.4 Conflict of Interest Policy

Scope:

It shall be the policy of the company that business conducted with vendors and contractors is exclusively awarded on the basis of the best product or service for the most reasonable cost. Independent and objective decisions are required.

Provisions:

- The following activities are prohibited:
  - Any relationship with a vendor, competitor, or other personal interest that conflicts with the interests of the organization.
  - Outside, nonemployment-related activities that are not kept totally separate from your status with the company.
  - Use of employment with the company for outside gain, including discounts based on the purchasing power of the company or its relationship with the vendor.
  - Solicitation or acceptance of any gift, favor, loan, or anything of monetary value from any person, firm, or corporation with whom the company maintains a business relationship or with whom the potential for such a relationship exists. The only exception to this policy is the occasional meal or refreshments of nominal value offered in the normal course and scope of business relationships.
  - Unsolicited promotional items of nominal monetary value are excluded. Gifts, favors, loans, and other items of monetary value should be immediately reported to management and returned, if applicable.
  - The use of information, personnel, equipment, or facilities proprietary to the organization (directly or indirectly) for personal gain

or profit or when used illegally or outside organizational policy to the gain of another.

- Selling goods or services, directly or indirectly, to the organization or its subsidiaries.
- It is specifically recognized that the foregoing prohibitions do not apply to:
  - Stock ownership in publicly traded companies.
  - Investments in which an employee has no direct or indirect ability to control the day-to-day operations of said business, its investments, or business policies in which said business furnishes goods and services to the company.
  - Properties owned prior to the commencement of employment with the company.
  - Acquisition of property from a relative that was owned by said relative prior to commencement of employment.
- Each employee must clearly understand that a conflict of interest can exist without realization of monetary gain. Personal benefit can be derived in many ways.
- Caution must be exercised in the conduct of personal affairs to avoid any conflicts of interest or even the appearance of it.
- Employees are required to immediately disclose any situation that may be in violation of this policy or that even gives the appearance of such a violation.
- Questions regarding the application and provisions of this policy should be referred to management, corporate security, human resources, or the company's legal department for direction.
- Violations of this policy will subject the violator to appropriate disciplinary action, which may include dismissal and criminal or civil prosecution.

3.13.5   Drug Abuse Policy

Scope:

It is the policy of the company to provide a safe and secure work environment for our employees. Drug abuse has produced a national epidemic in crime and a crisis in healthcare. Uncontrolled drug abuse poses a threat to the welfare of our employees, customers, and the interests of the company.

Provisions:

It is in the interests of all concerned that company policy on drug abuse shall be as follows:

- Drug testing will be required as a part of the pre-employment physical examination. Failure of the test will result in the immediate disqualification of the applicant.
- If the organization has a reasonable suspicion to believe that an employee is working with illegal drugs in his system, the employee will be asked to submit to a drug-screening test. That employee will be placed on unpaid suspension, pending the results of the test. The cost of the test will be borne by the organization. All test results are confidential. Refusal to take the test on request will be grounds for discharge.
- Employees tested under reasonable suspicion and found free of illegal drugs will be returned to work with full back pay and benefits, and their personnel files will not reflect the procedure. Employees who test positive will be subject to appropriate disciplinary action that may include dismissal.
- Those employees who test positive will be evaluated as to their suitability for rehabilitation. If upon evaluation the organization deems rehabilitation advisable, then a program appropriate to the situation will be worked out to assist in overcoming the problem.
- Participation in the sale or transfer of illegal drugs voids any consideration for company-sponsored rehabilitation programs.
- Employees who engage in the illegal use, transfer, sale, or possession of drugs or who abuse prescription drugs while on the job, on company property, or at organization-sponsored events, are subject to appropriate disciplinary action, which may include dismissal and criminal or civil prosecution.
- Use of illegal drugs off the job is not exempted from this policy when such use would adversely impact an employee's work performance or could jeopardize the safety of co-workers, customers, the general public, or company equipment.
- Any employee who is arrested and convicted of or who pleads guilty or *nolo contendere* to any on- or off-the-job drug violation will be considered to be in violation of this policy. On-the-job connected activity will be cause for immediate termination. Management will consider the nature of the charges, the employee's performance and tenure with the organization, and any other mitigating factors in the evaluation.
- Notwithstanding the foregoing, any such arrest, conviction, guilt, or plea of *nolo contendere* will automatically constitute cause and trigger a drug-screen test. Failure to test negative for drug use will result in immediate termination. Management consideration and evaluation of the employee's case for off-the-job drug activity will include cause for disciplinary action up to and including termination.

3.13.6   Incident Reporting Policy

Scope:

It is the policy of the company that employees are required to report known or suspected incidents of occupational crime or other abusive behavior. If the organization is to conduct its business in an ethical manner, then every employee must make a commitment to that objective.

Provisions:

- If the organization is to provide a safe and secure work environment, then it must know when, where, why, how, and by whom abusive acts are being committed so that remedial action can be initiated.
- If the organization is to design effective loss-prevention programs, it will need this information. To provide a response appropriate to any given situation, the company must be able to identify and quantify security-related problems. It is for these reasons that the participation of each employee in the prevention and detection of abusive behavior is needed.
- Our employees are the best source of this kind of information. Each person employed by the company suffers a loss, either directly or indirectly, as a consequence of wrongful conduct. Each employee therefore has a vested interest in the prevention or detection of such behavior.
- The organization feels that each employee is a valued member of our loss-prevention team. Each employee, not just management, shares responsibility for the security of our company and the personal property of co-workers.
- Each employee has an individual responsibility to insure the prevention, deterrence, and detection of abusive behavior.
- Instructions are provided for proper and timely reporting of abusive acts. Through the use of the Integrity Line, reports can be made anonymously, if circumstances dictate.
- The organization respects the abilities and dignity of each employee and individual participation in and contribution to the success of the company. Each employee is encouraged to participate in our loss-prevention efforts by assuring that all abusive behaviors are reported.
- Abusive behavior has been defined as those acts or actions that are illegal, unethical, or irresponsible that cause (or have the potential to cause) damage to the company, its employees, customers, or vendors.

Instructions for reporting abusive behavior:

- Any employee:
    - Promptly report to corporate security, management, or the Integrity Line, upon notification or discovery of any actual, suspected, rumored, or attempted act or actions by an employee or nonemployee that meet the definition of occupational crime or other abusive behavior.
- Location management:
    - Report any illegal act known or suspected to have been committed by a nonemployee (such as burglary, vandalism, robbery, etc.) to local police authorities for investigation.
    - Refer illegal or unethical acts known or suspected to have been committed by an employee, customer, or vendor to corporate security for evaluation and investigation or referral back to local management for disposition.
    - Irresponsible acts committed by employees, customers, and vendors are managed and disposed of at the local level.
    - Contact corporate security for instructions if a doubt exists as to what action to take.
    - Corporate security department:
        - Complete form #000, Incident Report; evaluate, review, analyze, and distribute per procedures.
        - Business hours: (Times would be noted in this space.)
        - After hours, weekends, holidays: (Times would be noted in this space.)

Violation of this policy will subject the violator to appropriate disciplinary action, which may include dismissal and criminal or civil prosecution.

3.13.7 Prosecution Policy

Scope:
It shall be the policy of the company to prosecute employees or nonemployees in instances involving the commission of illegal acts against the organization when, in the opinion of the chief executive officer or his designee, such action would be consistent with company responsibility to the community and when determined to be in the best interests of the company.

3.13.8 Price-Fixing Policy

Scope:
It shall be the policy of the company to compete in the marketplace based on the quality of our products and services. Employees are required to comply

with all relevant federal and state laws on antitrust and restraint of fair trade and not to engage in any form of unfair competition.

Provisions:

- Employees are prohibited from:
    - Attempting, or even discussing, the reduction of competition through price-fixing, market allocation, or other illegal or unethical schemes
    - Arbitrarily refusing to transact business with a competitor
    - Requiring other companies to buy from us before we will buy from them or forcing them to take a service they do not want to acquire before one that they do want
    - Engaging in any illegal or unethical act on behalf of the organization
- Each employee shall assume and be held responsible for any legal liability incurred from his violation of this policy including all legal fees, court costs, fines, penalties, and incidentals imposed in a court of law.

Violation of this policy will subject the violator to appropriate disciplinary action, which may include dismissal and criminal or civil prosecution.

3.13.9 Insider Stock Trading Policy

Scope:

As a public company it is policy for all employees to comply with applicable securities laws and regulations.

Provisions:

The company is required to publish certain "material" information in a timely manner. "Material" information is that information that may affect the value of company stock or bonds, or that might influence investment decisions concerning our stock or bonds. Material information would include, but is not limited to, the following:

- Issuance of new stock
- Issuance of new bonds
- New products
- New services
- Marketing plans
- Financial budgets

- Financial forecasts
- Negotiations on new ventures, mergers, or acquisitions
- Labor negotiations and contract status
- Major new contracts
- Changes in dividend rates
- Profit and loss
- Stock splits
- Legal or regulatory issues
- Any unusual developments that would be beneficial to investors

Prohibitions:

- The use by any person, firm, or corporation of material information that has not been publicly released or is not publicly available for investment purposes.
- Disclosure of that information to another person who uses the information for investment purposes.

Any violation of this policy must be immediately reported to corporate security. Violation of these laws not only undermines business relations and public trust, but can result in substantial criminal and civil penalties for the company as well as the individuals involved. It is because of the aforementioned reasons that strict adherence to the policy set forth herein is mandated.

Violation of this policy will subject the violator to appropriate disciplinary action, which may include dismissal and criminal or civil prosecution initiated by the company.

3.13.10 Protection of Information Policy

Scope:

It is the policy of the company to protect and control access to and use of confidential information. Access to confidential information is, therefore, limited only to those employees with a need to know.

Provisions:

Even with the above restriction, large numbers of employees work with confidential information on a daily basis in the course and scope of their employment. It is for this reason that control of such information must be reinforced in an effort to keep unauthorized disclosure from occurring. Each employee shares in this responsibility.

- Protected information:

- Classified proprietary information
- Classified national security information
- Highly valued information that, if divulged, could adversely affect the company
- Restrictions:
  - Disclose to authorized personnel only or as required by law or judicial process

Improper disclosure or use of proprietary information is a violation of this policy and may subject the violator to appropriate disciplinary action, which may include dismissal and criminal or civil prosecution.

3.13.11   Foreign Corrupt Practices Act Policy

Scope:
It is the policy of the company to comply with all the legal requirements of the Foreign Corrupt Practices Act.

Provisions:

- Under the provisions of the Act it is illegal for a U.S. company to make payments to foreign officials or governments with the intent to improperly obtain or retain business.
- The Act requires that the company's books, records, and accounts accurately reflect any and all business transactions conducted with foreign nationals.
- Employees are required to comply with company procedures governing these types of transactions to ensure full compliance with the requirements of law. Absolute compliance is demanded.
- Violations of this Act can result in criminal and civil sanctions, both individually and for the company, which can include substantial fines or imprisonment.

Violation of this policy will subject the violator to appropriate disciplinary action, which may include dismissal and criminal or civil prosecution.

3.13.12   Computer Security Policy

Scope:

- It shall be the policy of the company to provide for and ensure the protection of its computer systems and components from:
  - Intentional or accidental damage

- Intentional or accidental alteration
- Theft
- Fraudulent use or manipulation
- Unauthorized access to and/or disclosure of proprietary information including:

  - Central processing units, software, monitors, keypads, printers, modems, and any other hardware or peripherals used with and comprising a computer system
  - Electronic transmission and collection of data
- Restrictions:
  - Compliance with specific computer security procedures and controls.
  - Personal use of computer hardware or software is prohibited.
  - Software use is restricted to authorized employees and for company business.
  - Copying of software or supplemental materials must comply with licensing agreement requirements and limitations.
  - The sale or transfer of any software, supplemental materials, documentation, or copies thereof to unauthorized persons is strictly forbidden.

Any actual, rumored, or suspected deviations from this policy should be reported promptly to corporate security.

Violation of this policy will subject the violator to appropriate disciplinary action, which may include dismissal and criminal or civil prosecution initiated by the company.

3.13.13   Fidelity Bonding Policy

It shall be the policy of the company to insure itself through the bonding of each employee from losses of money or property resulting from employee dishonesty.

3.13.14   Use of Company Property Policy

Scope:

It shall be the policy of this company to prohibit the use of company property for the personal benefit of an employee unless such use is specifically exempted and authorized by policy. No company property may be used at any time or under any circumstances for any illegal or improper purpose.

Provisions:

- Property of the company cannot be sold, donated, loaned, or otherwise disposed of except when in compliance with policies governing that disposal. No deviations or exceptions from those policies are permitted.
- Each employee who has custody or control of company property is personally responsible and accountable for that property, including its security and safekeeping.
- Actual, rumored, or suspected deviations from this policy should be promptly reported to corporate security.

Violation of this policy will subject the violator to appropriate disciplinary action, which may include dismissal and criminal or civil prosecution initiated by the company.

As you can see, company security policies and procedures set the ethical tone for the organization and the procedures for compliance therewith. From a loss-prevention point of view, security policies and procedures are the foundations upon which all else is built. Plan and develop security policies and procedures very carefully and with careful thought. Once the policies are in place, do not neglect them. Periodically make a careful review and analysis of all policies to ensure not only compliance, but also relevance.

3.14   Pre-Employment Screening

The single most constructive place to begin protecting the assets of any organization, once the previously described elements are in place, is in the employee selection process. Effective pre-employment screening is critical to loss prevention and the stability and well-being of an organization. Background inquiries and verification of certain applicant-supplied information are indispensable resources for evaluating an individual and his suitability for employment.

Hiring the most qualified applicant is not the only objective of the personnel selection process. Ensuring that the prospect is honest, ethical, dependable, and conscientious is also an important element in the evaluation. But employers are discovering that honesty is not the only reason for carefully screening applicants. The legal aspects of "negligent hiring" (i.e., hiring a sexual criminal to work with children) and "negligent retention" (i.e., retaining a sexual criminal in a job that exposes a third party to increased personal risk) can play an important role in the process as well, but that is a topic for another book.

No argument is currently being made, even by the most ardent foes of pre-employment screening methods, that employers do not have a legitimate right and need to ascertain certain kinds of information about a prospective employee. How that information is obtained and how it is ultimately used in the hiring decision are subject to legal and public-policy considerations.

The entire pre-employment screening, investigation, evaluation, and employment decision process must comply with existing federal and state laws in a variety of critical areas, that is, if management is to avoid legal entanglements arising from both government regulators and prospective employees who file complaints or sue.

Discrimination (on the basis of religion, race, sex, or age) continues to occupy employer attention and concerns. But the most important "buzzwords" in the employment area for the next decade will be "workplace privacy." The central thrust of federal and state legislative action and judicial review in the employment law area will center on workplace privacy and the Americans with Disabilities Act issues and concerns.

Each prospective employee, as well as those currently employed, has the right to be free from excessive, unwarranted, non-job-related intrusions into his personal life by an employer. Unfortunately, past employer excesses in these areas have been well documented. The result is that many of the federal and state laws enacted over the last decade are intended to correct perceived employer pre- and post-employment excesses and protect employee privacy. Those laws are supposed to protect the rights of prospective employees from employer abuse. You are encouraged to take this intent seriously.

It is for these reasons and others that pre-employment screening has and will become increasingly more difficult to accomplish. Some personnel and security professionals speculate that obtaining employee work-experience and past-performance reference data will become a thing of the past during this decade.

Evidence of deterioration in this area is already abundant. A survey conducted by the National Association of Corporate and Professional Recruiters found that approximately one half of the companies surveyed had developed policies that prohibit providing references for current or former employees to prospective employers.

The reason? Fear of lawsuits. Many business organizations feel that providing information on former employees is just too great a risk and thus are either refusing to cooperate on inquiries or to participate on only a highly restrictive basis. Many of the companies that do cooperate are restricting the information provided to verification of employment, dates of employment, and job title. No other information is provided — a limitation that is very restrictive — but safe.

Employers are being sued by current and former employees who are turned down for new employment or terminated based upon information uncovered during pre- or post-employment background investigations. The problem often arises when negative information about an employee has been provided that is subjective and is not supportable with documentation. Most of this legal activity focuses on four main areas:

- Libel
- Defamation of character
- Invasion of privacy
- Discrimination

On a relative basis there are not all that many lawsuits, but there can be a lot of publicity when one of those few cases settles for $1 or 2 million. Fear increases each time a settlement is publicized in the trade magazines and papers. With each settlement or suit come additional negative publicity and the increased possibility of more litigation; this points out the importance and necessity of incorporating legally sound pre-employment screening and selection programs into operating policies and procedures.

As regrettable as it is, the employer can no longer presume that a prospective employee has the character traits desired and sought, is free of drug and alcohol abuse, or that the personal, employment, and educational information provided is accurate and truthful. The reality of the situation is just the opposite. The employer must assume the worst until proven wrong, while simultaneously attempting to balance his need to know against the privacy rights of the individual. In far too many instances, prospective employees have been known to lie, distort, and misrepresent personal histories and past employment data. Pre-employment screening identifies and allows the weeding out of those applicants who do not meet selection standards.

Finding the right person is becoming a much more difficult task, both as to qualifications and character concerns. Lowering standards is not the answer, but broadening the recruiting base is. Employers need the largest number of prospective employees they can generate. From that improved applicant base they can then select the most desirable prospects. If current recruiting methods are not gaining the desired results, management must reexamine its methods and look for ways to improve those in use.

Pre-employment screening is the most effective way to eliminate untrustworthy applicants. Applicant screening enhances loss prevention by screening out the problem before it is hired. Dealing with and managing the problem employee post-employment is a major drain on management time and is the least effective and most costly approach; screen out the problem, when and where possible.

Even with the most sophisticated and thorough screening methods in place, hiring mistakes will still be made. But management can guarantee that with proper screening methods fewer mistakes will be made and costly personnel problems in a variety of areas reduced. The latter statement assumes that sound management attitudes and practices exist throughout the organization. The goal should be to eliminate the problem applicant before hiring, not after. Assuming legal guidelines are followed and met, it is certainly much easier (and more cost effective) to deny employment than to try to eliminate a problem person after that individual has been hired.

Do poor employee selection and screening approaches cost a lot of money and executive time? Research from the U.S. Department of Labor estimates the costs of employee turnover in three categories. Those categories are listed below. Estimates of costs are based on employees who failed to complete a 90-day probationary period. The estimates include wasted salary, benefits, employment agency fees, training costs, and severance packages.

- Entry-level employee cost: between $5,000 and $7,000
- Mid-level manager cost: twice salary or approximately $50,000
- Senior executive cost: $100,000 salary; as much as $300,000

These estimates may be low. Careful pre-employment screening is cost-effective. Few companies can afford the costly mistakes illustrated above because of poor or ineffective employment decisions. Search out and hire only those individuals who are the lowest dishonesty risks and who have the highest probability of success.

Those applicants with a history of abusive behavior may be clearly or marginally risky. Reject the clear-cut cases, and where you can legally and ethically do so resolve all ties in favor of the company. Marginal risks may not be worth the time and effort required to ensure success. The marginal risk candidate will present the greatest opportunity for error in the employment decision-making process. That is reason for careful review and pre-employment screening.

Qualities of the least-abusive individual, behavior indicative of the most abusive individual, screening methods used to identify the least and most abusive individuals, and the four federal and state laws governing pre-employment screening and the decision to hire are reviewed in the materials that follow.

When it comes to loss prevention, what qualities does management look for in a prospective employee? Which candidate will offer the lowest risk of abusive behavior? What are the qualities one should look for? Many qualities are desirable and should be sought.

1. Qualities of the least abusive individual
    *   Honesty, integrity, and ethics
    *   Strong work ethic
    *   Strong sense of personal responsibility
    *   Dependability
    *   Strong sense of personal accountability
    *   Respect for rights and property of others
    *   Strong sense of right and wrong
    *   Mental soundness
    *   Physical health, even if handicapped
    *   Strong moral principles
    *   Personal pride
    *   High self-esteem
    *   Emotional maturity
    *   No drug- and alcohol-abuse problems
    *   No criminal convictions (within limits)

2. Behavior indicative of the most abusive individual:
    *   Dishonesty
    *   Ethics and integrity problems
    *   Weak work ethic
    *   Little or no sense of personal responsibility for actions
    *   Dependability problems
    *   Disruptiveness
    *   Severe emotional immaturity
    *   Attitudinal problems
    *   History of high absenteeism
    *   Little or no respect for rights and property of others
    *   Situational concept of right and wrong
    *   Questionable or known mental instability
    *   Physical unsoundness for the specific job
    *   History of disciplinary problems
    *   Questionable morals
    *   Marginal productivity
    *   Frequent job changes
    *   Criminal conviction
    *   Poor driving record
    *   Lack of personal pride
    *   Debilitating low self-esteem

    • Drug or alcohol abuse

3. Screening methods used to identify the least and most abusive individuals:

The only way to insure hiring decisions that will minimize the risk of employing an abusive person is through an in-depth background investigation. Pre-employment screening is a process, one intended to discover the assets and liabilities of a prospective employee and to determine suitability for employment.

Proper screening attempts to remove the veils of deceit and to expose any lies and misrepresentations that may have been made by a candidate in his application or employment interviews. Screening verifies who the applicant really is, his qualifications, and the lack or misrepresentation thereof.

To assist management is the pre-employment screening process. The National Employment Screening Services, Source Publications, Inc., of Tulsa, Oklahoma publishes a comprehensive source directory entitled *The Guide to Background Investigations*. The *Guide* provides a complete listing of names, addresses, and phone numbers for gaining access to federal, state, and county repositories for criminal, educational, workers' compensation, and driving records of candidates for employment. This comprehensive guide to pre-employment screening also provides information on important legislative developments that will affect the pre-employment screening process. The Internet is another asset. Government Web sites will often have a wealth of information from public records and provide legal inputs.

If you are not inclined to do your own searches in the pre-employment screening process, commercial database services will do it for you. Subscribers to these services can access national information including criminal conviction histories, credit reports, driver license histories, workers' compensation claims, past employment histories, professional license standings, educational verification, and much more. They offer on-line computer service right from your office or direct toll-free access.

Recruiting, interviewing, screening, selecting, and hiring a competent, productive, honest, and ethical workforce are becoming increasingly difficult to accomplish. Social changes and legal constraints contribute to this complexity. These are very challenging times for employers. The screening process is critical to the life of a business, even though fraught with myriad legal trapdoors.

Many methods are used in the pre-employment screening process. Outlined below are some of those employers use in their evaluation and assessment of an applicant. Many of the same methods are used for high-level promotional considerations as well. Detailed assessments are usually only undertaken for certain levels or classifications of employment.

Generally, employees being seriously considered for a position undergo a preliminary screening procedure. Prior to the actual hiring decision, a more detailed screen is completed. This detailed screening may include additional interviews, medical examination, drug screening, and background data collection. This information is then used in finalizing employment decisions.

The scope and depth of screening inquires are generally determined by how important or sensitive a specific position is. Specific levels of the screening and methods to be used can be designed for each position, occupational grouping, or some other criteria that are appropriate to the situation and need.

In defining screening levels be sure to take into consideration negligent hiring exposures. Negligent hiring lawsuits are on the increase. Just what is negligent hiring? Well, simply defined, it means failing to conduct a thorough background check on an employee that would have detected problems, and that employee subsequently causes harm to a third party while on the job.

The emphasis in negligent hiring is to discover the individual who has a criminal history indicating a record of violence or a propensity to the same. You must also protect against any other background information that would raise legitimate concerns about the attitudes or emotional stability of the individual, particularly if those indicators signal a potential negative impact on the safety and security of those persons who would interact with him.

If this type of individual is not found during pre- or post-employment processing and he later causes harm to a customer, vendor, or co-worker, a major lawsuit for damages can be expected. Monetary damages from those actions can be significant. The caveat here is that there is no guaranteed way to be protected from this exposure. Not only that, but the background search must conform to federal and state guidelines.

The best thing to do is to conduct a bona fide background investigation. Even if the search does not reveal a criminal conviction in a state that applicant said he had lived, in the case of *Ponticas v. K.M.S. Investments, 331 N. W. two-dimensional 907 (Minn. 1993)*, the court has ruled that a legitimate attempt to discover facts "would have been a significant factor in determining whether the employer exercised the degree of care necessary to avoid liability." Do your homework.

Upon completion of this screening-methods review, discussion of four of the most important laws that dictate legal compliance in the employment decision process will be included.

Pre-employment screening methods and resources:

- Employment application

- Paper-and-pencil honesty and psychological testing
- Pre-employment physical examination and drug testing
- Inquiries to former employers
- In-depth personal interview
- Personal reference inquiry
- Criminal history review
- Review of workers' compensation claims
- Motor vehicle record review
- Credit history review
- Civil records review

The methods listed above are the foundations of basic pre-employment screening. Some business and governmental organizations use techniques that go far beyond those listed. Screening is a function of need, and the methods devised will reflect that need. For most business organizations, however, the generic pre-employment screening approach will serve them well. If the generic approach is insufficient in some area, then the program should be expanded to satisfy any deficiencies.

Summary of each of the above referenced screening methods:

1. Employment Application
   - Nondiscriminatory
   - Meet EEOC guidelines
   - Verify employment listed
   - Verify education listed
   - Verify dates of employment listed
   - Verify licenses listed
   - Verify professional certification listed
   - Verify references listed
   - Verify home addresses listed
   - Verify job title and description of work listed
   - Verify work experience listed
   - Verify military history listed
   - Obtain written permission to inquire and for release of all information to be collected in the pre-employment screening process.

2. Paper-and-pencil honesty and psychological testing (still legal in most states, but its usage is coming under increasing attack; check legality in your state prior to use). It should:
   - Be easy to use
   - Be completed within 1 hour
   - Reveal attitudes toward theft

- Reveal attitudes toward other abusive behavior
- Reveal other patterns of negative behavior
- Indicate work ethic
- Show drug and alcohol abuse
- Be selected carefully
- Be nondiscriminatory
- Be job relevant
- Be applied equally
- Meet EEOC guidelines
- Review validation tests (verify from independent source)
- Provide measurable and verifiable results
- Originate from a reputable company
- Be impartial and nonthreatening
- Allow for computer and phone scoring
- Provide specific programs for specific needs and be cost effective on the scale used
- Supported by management

3. Pre-employment physical examination and drug testing should determine:
   - Medical history
   - Any illegal drug use
   - Current physical condition
   - High blood pressure
   - Heart disease
   - Known disease
   - Drug screen
   - Concealed disease
   - Mental stability
   - Fitness for specific job
   - Vision limitations
   - Physical limitations
   - Concealed injury
   - Relevancy of problems to job

4. Inquiries to former employers
   - Failure to check and document inquiries risks negligent hiring liability.
   - Search for information on the candidate must be job related.
   - Attempt to verify applicant-provided information.
   - Many companies are reluctant to provide negative data.
   - Some companies will cover up or hide past dishonesty.

- Check all discrepancies that occur in interviews or on the application thoroughly.
- View subjective evaluations with caution.
- Refusal to provide reference may or may not indicate problem employee. Inquire further.
- Bypass previous company's personnel department and go directly to last supervisor.
- Attempt to develop names of co-workers to contact.
- Performance evaluations, test scores, salary histories, and medical records are privacy issues. Access to them affects screening process. If wrongfully disclosed, the employer is liable for an "invasion of privacy suit."
- Ask about the person's eligibility for rehire.
- Ask if there was evidence of drug or alcohol abuse.
- Personal information must be job related.
- Ask if the person had ethics or character problems.
- Explain intention to check with past employers and references. Obtain written authorization to do so, along with a release and waiver of liability for prospective employer and information provider.
- Explain procedure. Tell the applicant what checks will be made and obtain appropriate releases.
- Data collected must be job related.
- Treat provider input confidentially.
- In-depth personal interview should:
- Explain reasons for leaving previous job(s)
- Explain distortions and misrepresentations
- Verify identity of applicant
- Verify Social Security number
- Verify driver's license
    - Explain conflicting dates on application
    - Explain any unanswered questions or blanks
    - Explain unsigned application
    - Explore applicant's level of motivation
    - Explore applicant's initiative
    - Explore applicant's ambitions and goals
    - Explore applicant's background

- If past employer refuses a request for a personal reference on an applicant, ask the applicant to explain the reason for that refusal.
- Request copy of applicant's last performance appraisal
- Plan questions carefully

- Design questions to elicit specific information
- Do not give even the appearance of discrimination
- Do not violate the applicant's right to privacy
- Keep inquiries to job-related requirements
- Use generalized and specific questions to obtain full disclosure
- Supplement personal feelings or impressions with verifiable objective information. Interviewer cannot rely solely on gut feelings; integrate such feelings or impressions with a complete evaluation of background data.
- Get a detailed explanation of duties and responsibilities

5. Personal Reference Inquiry
   - Can be a waste of time. Check anyway.
   - Named references and letters are sometimes fraudulent. Check them carefully.
   - References are sometimes negative but can be open, fair, and objective
   - Ask for names of other persons who know applicant
   - Ask for a list of past employers and the reasons association terminated
   - Check with past employers. Look for those not listed on application.
   - Verifications can be accomplished in person, on the phone, or in writing.

6. Criminal History Review
   - A criminal history should not automatically preclude employment.
   - Evaluate the whole person. Don't limit review to one issue.
   - Records of arrest and conviction are two totally different things.
   - An arrest is made on probable cause and is not a determination of guilt. A person is presumed innocent until proven guilty in a court of law.
   - Rejection based on conviction record is not permitted without sufficient evidence indicating the record and decision are based on job-related issues. Reference EEOC TITLE VII guidelines.
   - Convictions are determinations of guilt.
   - Conviction is grounds for rejection when offense is job related.
   - Record and acts must be inconsistent with safe and efficient business operations for rejection.

Evaluate:
- Nature of job and responsibilities

- Nature and frequency of crimes
- Age at time of conviction
- Whether crime is misdemeanor or felony
- Elapsed time from last occurrence
- Employment history prior to and after incident
- Rehabilitation efforts and evidence of same

7. Review of Workers' Compensation Claims
   - Frequency and nature of injuries
   - Lost-time accidents and duration
   - Settlements and washouts
   - Cross-reference with data furnished by candidate
   - Follow-up as required to insure accuracy and truthfulness

8. Motor Vehicle Record Review
   - Number, type, and frequency of traffic citations
   - Vehicle accidents
   - DUI arrests and convictions
   - Type of license
   - Status of license
   - Restrictions
   - Any suspensions or revocations
   - Current standing

9. Credit History Review
   - Federal and state laws restrict use of credit data for employment purposes
   - Must be demonstrably job-related
   - Notify applicant of inquiry, how and what will be checked
   - Retain only a reputable credit agency to make inquiries
   - Explain procedure applicant can use to review data produced
   - Explain procedure applicant can use to correct, amend, or dispute any file data
   - Obtain written consent from applicant
   - Limit inquiry to job-related data
   - Maintain confidentiality. Do not share data with others.
   - Comply with provisions of Fair Credit Reporting Act

10. Civil Records Review: Public records
    - Tax Assessor
    - Real property holdings
    - Filings

- Lawsuits
- Judgments
- Divorces
- Bankruptcy filings and dispositions
- Mental Health
- Business ownership
- Professional Licenses
- Name changes

11. Four Laws that Impact Pre-Employment Screening:
   - The Employee Polygraph Protection Act
   - Civil Rights Act of 1964
   - Fair Credit Reporting Act
   - Arrest or Criminal Conviction Records

Now, a synopsis of each of the areas noted above will be provided, but before that, a few qualifying comments are in order. Contrary to what many of those involved in the applicant-screening process may believe, the legal restraints set forth in the laws reviewed herein are not designed or intended to eliminate pre-employment screening. The purpose of these laws is to ensure that the decision-making process is fair and any decision to hire or reject a prospective employee is based on pertinent job-related information and is nondiscriminatory. These laws also protect the individual's right to privacy.

The following laws impact the methods used to collect data and how that data is used to make a hiring decision about a prospective employee. Employers must become very knowledgeable about these laws or risk noncompliance and paying sanctions that can become very expensive.

1. The Employee Polygraph Protection Act
   Prohibits private employers from requiring, requesting, or suggesting that a prospective employee take a polygraph examination as a prerequisite to employment qualification.
   Exempts federal, state, and local governments and national defense and federal security contractors from the same pre-employment constraints and use in criminal investigations.
   Polygraph examinations can be legally requested and used with severe limitations by private-sector employers during investigations of drug or criminal abuses. See the law first. Penalties provided for noncompliance.

Any adverse employment action must be based on independent evidence and not solely on an individual's refusal to take the examination or his failure to pass same.

2. Civil Rights Act of 1964

   Title VII prohibits all discrimination in employment based on race, color, religion, sex, or national origin.

   Applies to all employers with 15 or more employees.

   Covers all terms and conditions of employment.

   Employer is held liable for any discriminatory acts or practices irrespective of who actually makes hiring or rejection decisions.

3. Fair Credit Reporting Act

   Restricts use of applicant's credit record when used for employment purposes.

   Sets guidelines and regulates consumer reporting agencies that compile credit and other background reports on individuals that are prepared for and submitted to a client.

   Requirement of good credit for employment consideration must be job related. May violate privacy provisions if it invades free speech, beliefs, or private associations.

   Always obtain written consent.

   Information must be treated as confidential.

   Do not conduct any pre-employment screening or background inquiry or internal investigation without knowledge and compliance with the provisions of this Act. A copy with opinion letters and pending legislation can be found and downloaded from the Internet. Keyword: Fair Credit Reporting Act.

   The purpose of this Act is to insure that all information on file is accurate, timely, and given only to persons making credit or employment decisions.

4. Arrest and Criminal Conviction Records

   U.S. Department of Justice has authorized states to enact laws or issue executive orders permitting employers access to the criminal history data of employees or prospective employees. Most are available directly from state files and data-collection centers.

   Many laws are now on the books. Most regulate classes of employers who have access and information that will be provided.

   Some states permit access to both arrest and conviction data. Others restrict to convictions only.

   With few exceptions, arrest and conviction records are still obtainable as public records from the local courthouse. The problem is having to check every courthouse in a state or employ a search service that provides relevant information on a statewide or national basis.

These services can be contracted with providers who specialize in this area. Many also provide data related to workers' compensation histories and other worthwhile background information.

Several national database services are available that tie in with state services permitting nationwide checks.

Be sure to understand the laws and regulatory requirements for an individual state, and comply with any restrictions on collection, use, and processing.

3.15   Security Committees

The employment of committees in business is a well-established practice. These committees are identified by many different names, and their uses are as varied, for example, executive, finance, audit, risk management, human resources, and safety committees. How they function as well as their purposes, scope, and authority are also as varied as the organizations they are intended to serve.

Basically, the committee concept is used to bring together an assortment of employees to collectively pool their backgrounds, education, knowledge, and experiences. Theoretically, this collection of people forms an asset that improves the decision- and policy-making process. The quality of the committee system, its input, effectiveness, and impact on the organization will vary within the organization and from organization to organization.

The purpose of this section is not to debate the merits or liabilities of the committee system; instead, it is to point out how a security committee is organized, its purpose, and some outcomes that can be reasonably expected if it is put to use. In some instances, safety and security concerns have been combined and a committee formed to address safety and security; in other situations, the security committee stands alone.

As with safety and other business committees, the security committee may exist on corporate and facility levels or on one or the other. In the following material, both the corporate- and facility-level committees and their organizations and purposes are addressed.

1.   The Corporate-Level Security Committee
     Membership:
     - Management
     - Committee chaired by security manager
     - Prepares monthly report for CEO

     Meets:
     - Monthly

Purpose:

- Identifies corporate-wide security requirements
- Interfaces with security department
- Reviews, revises, and approves security-orientation program
- Reviews, revises, and approves employee security-awareness program and media materials
- Reviews, revises, and approves security policies and procedures
- Reviews and evaluates all security programs to determine effectiveness
- Performs oversight function to assure that security policies and procedures are enforced and enforcement is consistent and fair
- Performs oversight function to ensure that management and subordinates are meeting their security responsibilities
- Monitors, reviews, and evaluates compliance with policy and the effectiveness of disciplinary actions arising from abusive behavior
- Reviews security-related activity and incidents. Reviews recommended remedial action.

2. The Facility-Level Security Committee
   Membership:
   - Management
   - Chaired by facility security manager or appropriate management
   - Represented by each department
   - Prepares monthly report for management (copy to corporate security manager)

Meets:
- Monthly

Purpose:
- Identifies facility security requirements
- Works to improve understanding and compliance with security policies and procedures
- Reviews, evaluates, and contributes to the off-the-job security program

- Reviews, evaluates, and contributes to the effectiveness of any employee, visitor, or vendor security-orientation programs
- Reviews and evaluates effectiveness of security communication methods and media
- Reviews and evaluates effectiveness and relevancy of security policies and procedures
- Performs general management oversight function to ensure that security policies and procedures are enforced and enforcement is consistent and fair throughout the organization
- Performs general oversight function to ensure that management at all levels is meeting its security responsibilities
- Monitors, reviews, and evaluates compliance with policy and the effectiveness of disciplinary actions arising from abusive behavior
- Reviews security-related activities and incidents
- Recommends countermeasures

The security committee, although new to the business committee concept, is nonetheless emerging as an important committee function. When developed and used effectively, this committee can serve a useful purpose for any government, private, or commercial organization.

The committee should be designed to fit the culture and needs of the organization. Use creativity and imagination to produce a productive, stimulating, and effective structure. Membership on the committee is important. Staff the committees with those employees who will take the task seriously and perform duties conscientiously.

Interest and concern are more important than security expertise in the beginning. For those members lacking specific knowledge and background, the necessary security knowledge will develop later as the process matures.

3.16 Investigations

Investigating allegations of known or suspected abusive acts is a fundamental element in the prevention and detection of losses. Determining what will be investigated and when, how, and by whom are all questions that need to be answered. Management must make that determination and, in doing so, many factors must be considered. These answers will influence the quality and, thus, the success of this important function. An investigative strategy that is too broad in scope may be viewed as intrusive and oppressive. Conversely, too narrow an approach will be largely ineffective.

Making the final determination of the scope, authority, and responsibilities of those who will perform the investigative function in the organization is important; achieving balance is the key, though it is not an easy task. The following questions aid in the analysis, evaluation, and decision process.

What is an investigation?

- An investigation is a thorough and systematic, official, management-sanctioned inquiry into an actual or suspected wrongful activity. Its purpose is to determine the truth of the matter and to gather related evidence that either confirms or invalidates any concerns arising therefrom.

What matters will be investigated?

- Management will make that determination. Many factors will go into the decision-making process. A good place to start is the development of an incident-classification system that identifies those behaviors and acts considered abusive. Once an incident-classification system is in place, guidelines can be developed that will determine which incidents will be investigated.
- Those incidents and behaviors with the greatest potential to negatively impact the company, its employees, customers, or vendors are selected for investigation. Some allegations of abusive conduct or specific incidents of such behavior may automatically be investigated, while others may have to reach a specific dollar threshold before an investigation is made.
- All reported incidents are recorded, analyzed, and evaluated, but not all incidents are investigated. Preliminary inquiries are used to test allegations or suspicions. Upon completion of the preliminary inquiry the decision is made to either terminate further inquiry or to conduct a full investigation. Investigations can be time-consuming and expensive, but they are an essential element in the loss-prevention process.

When should the investigation be conducted?

- Investigations should be initiated in a timely manner. In some instances, a timely manner may require an immediate response; in others, delays will vary from hours to days. In the worst case, weeks may pass. If an investigation is to be made, the sooner it begins the better. The longer a decision to investigate is delayed the greater the probability that valuable evidence will be lost; that evidence can be either physical or provided by a witness. Inappropriate delays can severely damage the prospect of a successful conclusion. Once an incident meets investigative criteria, the process should begin without delay.

Who investigates?

• Larger business and governmental organizations have in-house security professionals and staff investigators. Most smaller companies do not have in-house security personnel. In the smaller organizations, management will often conduct the investigation. Depending on management's background, education, knowledge, motivation, and experience, this approach can have disastrous consequences for the manager and the company.

Conducting an investigation into an actual or alleged incident of misconduct is not an assignment for an amateur. Except for minor policy violations, investigations require highly skilled and trained personnel. For this reason, small companies are often advised to seek the services of a competent contract security organization or consultant to handle investigations. Even if police authorities are involved, in-house or contract services often make the difference between success and failure. Specialists working with the authorities can prove very beneficial.

The conduct of any investigation entails a certain element of risk of a lawsuit. Use professionals to avoid or minimize legal expense. An improperly conducted investigation can generate civil actions for defamation of character, discrimination, false arrest, false imprisonment, and other actions.

The proper and legal conduct of an investigation requires specialized legal knowledge and investigative techniques. The proper and legal conduct of an investigation, therefore, demands the highest levels of professional competency. This is not an area to economize on too stringently. Professionalism, as you have probably already noted, is not obtained cheaply.

No investigation should ever be conducted by internal staff personnel or investigators without their full and complete knowledge of the provisions of the Fair Credit Reporting Act and compliance with its provisions. Every inquiry, from pre-employment screening to investigations into actual or suspected wrongful conduct, whether conducted by internal staff or third parties under contract, is subject in varying degrees to the provisions of the

Fair Credit Reporting Act or a combination of other federal or state laws governing same. For instance:

The Federal Trade Commission has interpreted the 1996 amendments to the Fair Credit Reporting Act to mean that employer use of independent third parties such as private investigators, attorneys, and human resource specialists to conduct investigations into known or suspected illegal acts was subject to the provisions of the Act. Those provisions provide that the employer must:

- Notify the suspect employee before beginning an investigation.
- Obtain the suspect's written authorization to conduct an investigation and authorization from all other employees subject to an investigation resulting therefrom.
- Make full and complete disclosure to the suspect employee of the nature and scope of the investigation.
- Provide suspects with a complete and unedited copy of the investigative report upon request and prior to initiating any adverse action against them.

These provisions have been highly contested, are subject to continuing debate, and may be modified. Until and unless modified, do not fail to comply. Become knowledgeable and compliant with all provisions of all federal and state laws applicable to pre-employment screening components and the legal conduct of criminal or other investigations, whether by internal staff or third-party suppliers.

The Association of Certified Fraud Examiners, 716 West Avenue, Austin, TX 78701 can be a valuable source of information on the investigation of fraud. Certified fraud examiners (CFE) have met testing, background, ethical, education, and experience standards to receive certification. When outsourcing fraud investigations, seek out an investigator who is a certified fraud examiner. Check with the Association for the name of a CFE in the area.

What do investigators do?

- Establish predication
- Prepare investigative plans
- Investigate
- Interview witnesses
- Take statements
- Gather and preserve evidence
- Analyze data and draw conclusions
- Develop suspects

- Question suspects
- Identify perpetrators
- Recover stolen property
- Determine if policy was violated or a crime was committed
- Prepare written reports
- Testify in administrative or criminal proceedings
- Prepare for civil recovery of damages

The importance and role a competent post-incident investigation brings to the quality of any inquiry and its outcome cannot be overemphasized. Without a professional and legally competent investigation the organization subjects itself to inferior work product and, thus, inferior decisions.

3.17   Discipline, Prosecution, and Recovery of Losses

Despite the best efforts of management some level of occupational crime and other abusive behavior will always exist in any organizational environment. If an employee security-awareness/compliance program is in place and working properly, the probability of early detection of abuse is increased. Thus, management must anticipate demand and then plan and devise methods for dealing with abusive behavior and those employees responsible for its commission.

Policies should be uniform in their application, consistent in their dispositions, and fair to all. Every effort must be made to remove any ambiguity as to how an abusive incident will be handled by management. This program sets the standard for consistency and fairness. Both elements are critical components in achieving a successful disciplinary program. It is particularly true if disciplinary actions are to serve as a deterrent to abusive behavior.

Employee discipline is but one area that may require substantial review and revision. Questions regarding what has been done in the past and what is going to be done in the future about the abusive employee raise many legal and practical issues for management. Resolving those issues can be a very difficult and time-consuming task.

Now a look at a few of the specific issues that need to be resolved to assure that a disciplinary system is reasonable, consistent, and fair, and one that will gain the respect and confidence of all employees. A few questions of concern that address these issues and raise many legal and personnel issues follow:

- How does management currently discipline the abusive employee?

- What methods of discipline will be used?
- What about the degree of punishment?
- What behavior will require termination or prosecution, if any?
- Will abusers be allowed to resign? Under what circumstances?
- Will all violators be prosecuted for losses above a certain dollar limit?
- Will all violators be discharged for losses above a certain dollar limit?
- Will a combination of progressive measures be used?
- Will anyone be prosecuted? Some, none, or all? If so, how will cases be selected?
- Who will make the determination to prosecute, and what criteria will be used? Will they apply in all instances of abuse or just some? Should the determination be based on the nature of the abuse, a dollar amount, or the employee's level, tenure, or job classification?
- Who will evaluate cases from a lawsuit risk standpoint?
- What criteria will be used in the evaluation process?
- Are applicable provisions of the Fair Credit Act incorporated and complied with?

This is but a representative cross section of those questions that need to be asked and for which answers must be found. Many more arise in the course and scope of the analysis, and many more answers must be sought. All these questions address complex issues, some with significant legal implications; therefore, they require careful consideration and well thought out answers prior to incorporating them into policy or prior to making any changes in existing policy.

There is nothing elementary about answering the questions posed above because of the complicated organizational, social, and legal issues (and the ramifications thereof) that must be considered in the evaluation and decision-making process. For these reasons it is important that management solicit competent input from its security, personnel, and legal staffs prior to finalizing any new policies or making any changes in existing policies or procedures.

Let us examine this matter more closely. We begin with a broad conceptual framework to put the situation into a logical, if only a summarized, perspective.

There are two broad categories into which employee misconduct falls: policy violations and crimes.

Policy violations are violations of corporate policy. Generally, they are administratively disposed of internally by the company. They can also technically be crimes. Whether they are treated as such depends on the seriousness of the offense and other business and legal considerations. Crimes, when reported and suspects identified and prosecuted, are processed in the criminal justice system. Policy violations are generally disposed of administratively using internal procedures.

Policy violations may or may not involve the commission of a crime. There are also differences in definitions, intent, and degrees of damages or loss. For instance, executive embezzlement is not the same as taking home a package of notepads. Both are policy infractions; both are wrong; both are thefts; and technically, both are crimes. But the intent and degrees of the loss are different, thereby creating a distinction in the two instances unless restricted or prohibited by federal or state laws.

Reasonably, management would not be expected to discharge or prosecute the person taking the notepads, but such action would be expected in the case of embezzlement. Unless the employee who took the notepads is a repeat offender, discharge would be excessive and unfair. The executive might or might not be prosecuted for his crime. His employment might not even be terminated or otherwise affected. Both incidents might be treated as policy violations and not as crimes.

As noted, policy violations and crimes range from minor to very significant, from those acts deserving of a mere verbal warning to those resulting in loss of job or imprisonment. Both can be fraught with legal complexities, particularly when contested. How these two areas are managed and how decisions are made regarding what course of action a company will initiate in either situation become very important to the business.

Inadequate or sloppy disciplinary practices not only open the company to legal retaliation from the aggrieved employee, but from government sources as well. Ill conceived and poorly thought out prosecution decisions can also be disastrous. Employees lose confidence and trust in management when disciplinary actions are perceived as unfair, unreasonable, or selectively enforced. How does management avoid this circumstance? Some answers are provided in the following paragraphs. If a labor union exists and an employee suspect is a member, then the guidelines may have to be amended to reflect procedures proscribed by collective-bargaining agreements.

The hallmarks of an effective disciplinary program are:

- Reasonable
- Fair
- Impartial
- Applied equally to all employees
- Lacking in double standards
- Unambiguous
- Unequivocally enforced
- Commensurate with misconduct
- Prescribed levels of punishment

- Meets or exceeds applicable laws
- Meets due-process criteria
- Nondiscriminatory
- Complies with the requirements, restrictions, and limitations of the provisions of applicable federal and state laws and regulations related to the subject matter.

The negative aspect is that the process can be time-consuming and, therefore, expensive. Expediency in the employee discipline area can be very expensive, much more so than the time and effort it takes to insure consistency and fairness. Management may think that cutting disciplinary corners is cost-effective and efficient. That may be true in some situations where time may be saved on an individual case or on several cases. The questions, however, are how much was lost in employee confidence, trust, and respect and what will that ultimately cost? Another question is, do you know what case is going to blow up in your face and cost significant amounts of money to defend? Haphazard disciplinary procedures are not cost-effective or efficient. To the contrary, such actions can be very expensive and damaging to employee relations. Inferior disciplinary procedures actually contribute to the abusive-employee problem.

Unfortunately, the disciplinary approaches of many companies fail to even marginally meet the guideline's criteria. When well developed and managed, the disciplinary process can be a highly effective loss-prevention tool and management asset. Consistency and fairness are not management's adversaries — they are management's allies.

Management attention and efforts directed at creating an atmosphere of concern, fairness, and certainty of punishment are very important to the control of abuse-incurred losses. Punishment should, of course, fit the abusive behavior. Discharge for proven thefts of a specified dollar amount and other categories of gross misconduct involving ethics, honesty, or integrity issues set high standards.

A combination of progressive measures for less serious violations is usually effective. Disciplinary actions may vary from verbal to written warnings, suspension, probation, and termination for certain classifications and for repeat offenders. Record all actions and review files for purging of incidents on some reasonable periodic basis, such as annually with pay reviews. Standardize the approach and the punishment prescribed.

Crimes are defined by law, committed by internal and external sources, generally managed and disposed of in the criminal justice system, and may also be litigated in civil court.

There are those who would argue that every property crime above a certain dollar amount should result in both termination and prosecution of the employee offender. Every crime committed by a nonemployee, the argument goes, should be prosecuted. Many sound reasons for that advice and the advocacy thereof exist.

Other arguments, however, are just as persuasive against the prosecution of offenders, be they employees or not. The decision to prosecute or not may become a business decision, one that not only has organizational and legal implications, but societal ones as well. The decision to prosecute should be made with great caution.

Many company executives are extremely reluctant to report crimes to the police or file criminal complaints against employees, particularly those in management. Criminal action is seldom taken against executives and infrequently against the rank-and-file worker. If the source of the criminal activity is a nonemployee, managers are more inclined to report and file criminal complaints. One of the criteria set forth in *Chapter Eight,* when defining an "effective" compliance program, places significant constraints on managerial discretion in reporting internal criminal behavior. If applied, management is required to report known or suspected criminal incidents to appropriate authorities and to cooperate with investigators. If the incident is not reported and later becomes known to authorities, and someone is prosecuted and convicted in a federal criminal court, and the organization is charged and convicted in connection therewith, failure to have reported and possibly not cooperated can result in unmitigated sanctions.

Most employees identified with a criminal loss are simply terminated. Many times the underlying problems that contributed to the occurrence are never addressed or solved by management. Management's attitudes and practices are infrequently reviewed or changed.

Who you are, who you know, and what you know are frequently the most important determinants of the class of disciplinary action, that is, if disciplinary action is taken. Seldom is anyone from an executive suite ever prosecuted, civilly sued, or subjected to efforts by the bonding company to recover the loss. If a choice is provided, an implicated senior manager is generally required to resign.

In some of these predicaments the accused or suspected executive may even negotiate the terms and conditions of his departure. Some implicated executives have sauntered away with severance packages that included pay, extended health benefits, stock options, a bonus or other perks, and a letter of recommendation.

Why do business executives devise these kinds of decisions and enter into arrangements with wrongful colleagues? Many sound (and some not so sound) business reasons influence those decisions. Some examples of the reasoning used by managers are provided below. You must make your own judgment as to their validity and wisdom, the ethics involved, and then decide if you agree with the thought process. Some influencing factors are:

- Lack of confidence in and respect for law-enforcement authorities
- Costly and disruptive nature of extensive and extended investigations
  Fear that any investigation will escalate and expand into other areas
- Fear that local authorities will bring in federal or state investigators
- Fear of adverse and damaging publicity
- Lack of confidence in the quality of prosecution
- Lack of confidence in and respect for courts and judges
- High probability of lightly imposed judicial sanctions
- Little to no expectation that the loss will be recovered
- Potential for loss of productive time for key employees tied up in investigations, depositions, and trial
- Fear of retaliatory employee lawsuits
- Time consuming, disruptive, and expensive legal actions
- Cost-effectiveness
- Adverse effect on employee relationships
- Friendship, favoritism, compassion
- Adversely reflection on management
- Forced reinstatement of an acquitted miscreant employee with back pay and benefits
- Damaged civil recovery efforts following acquittal

The above examples make it obvious why management is often reluctant to become involved with the police or the criminal justice system. From a business perspective, many negatives can influence the decision to prosecute or not. Sometimes prosecution of offenders is just not justified as a rational course of action. In some instances, it is just more cost-effective and prudent to walk away from a given situation and not risk other exposures to loss. As hard as it may be to do, sometimes the latter course of action is the best. Given other circumstances, however, there are many sound reasons why prosecution must be undertaken. A review of a few of those circumstances appears later in this section. Prior to that, however, this discussion continues with an outline of responsibilities that management must assume once the decision to prosecute has been made. Management must be willing to:

- Ensure that the investigation meets the highest standards of competency, whether conducted by the police, in-house, or contract personnel, prior to agreeing to proceed with prosecutorial action.
- Finance the costs once the decision is made to prosecute.
- Withstand any criticism and/or bad publicity that may accrue.
- Face the possibility and accept responsibility for any lawsuit arising from that decision.
- Commit the time and personnel necessary to a successful prosecution.

- Be committed to a successful prosecution.

Given these responsibilities, it is easy to understand that the decision to prosecute an individual can initiate an expensive, time-consuming, and overall unpleasant experience for management. It is for these reasons and others that management is often reluctant to prosecute anyone, employee or nonemployee. Management sometimes feels it is best to discharge the employee or let him resign without fanfare, just prevent further losses, take the loss and forget it, or correct the problem and move on.

Making sound decisions can involve a complex decision-making matrix. One criterion used in the process is to analyze the negatives that might be encountered if a certain action or set of actions is initiated, for example:

- Make a list of the potential negative consequences to be expected if a specific decision or combination of decisions is made.
- If a certain course of action is taken, then what? What are the worst possible consequences to be expected from the course of action, and can you live with that outcome?
- What will the contemplated action cost?
- What return can be expected on the investment of time and money? Is it worth it?
- What is the most cost-effective and efficient way to dispose of the problem?

Even in the face of what is oftentimes compelling negatives, prosecution frequently remains the correct course of action. Why? Any number of reasons would justify that decision. For example:

- The loss sustained by the company may be grievous; thus, to take any other action would be unreasonable.
- To do otherwise would violate stockholder trust and responsibility.
- Prosecution would clearly serve as a deterrent to others.
- The point must be made that the organization will not tolerate criminal behavior.
- It is necessary for the public record to absolve management of any complicity in the crime.
- There must be a public record of conviction for the individual involved, the by-product of which is that any prospective employers who investigate the individual will be put on notice of his criminal past.

- There must be a legal determination of guilt that will aid in the civil recovery of damages.
- Fiduciary responsibilities must be fulfilled.

Now a look at some other issues related to the same subject that will need to be resolved. For example:

- Will the police be notified in all instances of criminal activity, or just certain types of crimes and dollar amounts?
- Will only crimes known or suspected to have been committed by external sources be reported to the police? Will that decision be based on a dollar amount?
- Will the police be notified of internal criminal activity on just a case-by-case basis? What will that basis be?
- Will employee losses be reported to the police? How, when, and by whom? If not, why not?
- If a police investigation develops a suspect, who will make the decision to prosecute or sign an affidavit?
- Will all external crimes be prosecuted?
- Will all internal crimes of a certain dollar amount be prosecuted, or just selected cases?
- Will no internal crimes be prosecuted?
- Who will work and coordinate with the police?
- If criminal conduct is not reported to police, who will investigate? In-house security department? Contract service?
- What role, if any, will the security, personnel, and legal departments play in the decision to prosecute?
- Who will assess and evaluate potential or actual negative publicity and attempt to control it?
- Who will determine costs? Damage to reputation? Initiate remedial action? Manage oversight of corrective actions?

One hundred percent recovery of a loss is infrequently made. In most instances the "fruits of the crime" have been consumed or otherwise disposed of by the miscreant prior to discovery. Beyond any initial recovery, most companies rarely seek legal alternatives to recover losses directly from the individual or business involved.

Generally, most individual offenders do not have the amounts or class of assets that encourage seeking legal remedies in making a recovery. There are, of course, exceptions. In a few instances, some offenders do have sufficient assets to justify recovery efforts, but even the "haves" are seldom pursued.

While it is true that recovery may be possible in some cases, the process can be time-consuming and expensive. Therefore, most victim companies just choose to absorb the loss and return to business as usual as quickly as possible. As is observed from the following discussion, however, there are incentives for seeking legal remedies other than realistic expectations of recovering a loss.

You should not get too discouraged at the poor prospects of recovering a loss. Perseverance still has its rewards. Restitution is not always the primary motive for pursuing a miscreant anyway. Pocketbook penalties may be the only real punishment imposed on most violators, and in the final analysis, imposing those penalties may be the foremost deterrent of all to abusive behavior.

When practical, striking an offender in his pocketbook can have a great spillover deterrent effect in the workplace. Out-of-pocket defense costs can be severe for an individual. No only that, but the public record of an action can have its own negative consequences on a person in a variety of ways. Of course, cases would have to be chosen carefully. A win is mandatory, or the organization might have to pay the defendant's costs.

You would not sue an indigent laborer and expect any positive result, but this would not be the circumstance with a person who owned a home, had to seek gainful employment after discharge, had a family, an education, managerial or professional skills or accreditation, and some expectation of further career growth and development. In the latter instance, legal action can put all of the above in jeopardy, and judgments last a lifetime, unless satisfied.

Pursuing legal alternatives for recovery may be an effective recourse for management in ways not previously recognized. Fear of facing legal action will not impact all employees to the same degree or in the same manner, but it can have a very sobering effect on a few if carefully managed. Somewhere, sometime, somehow, some negative consequences must be imposed on the abusive individual if the problem is ever to be controlled.

In most instances of misconduct that occurs in a business environment offenders walk away with only minor inconvenience, maybe some embarrassment, and, at worst, in a few instances the loss of a job. Without a successful criminal prosecution, including a conviction and finding of guilt, the employer cannot reveal the reason for a discharge or forced resignation to a future prospective employer for fear of a retaliatory lawsuit from the discharged employee.

The offender is often quite able to seek out and acquire another position, and his new employer is now at risk. The fruits of the offender's last exploitative act are his to enjoy, and the entire process can begin again — hardly a fair and equitable situation for the employer–victim.

Yet another negative with which the employer has to deal is that co-workers know or often accurately speculate on the reason for a specific employee's departure. These same co-workers also understand the position that management is often in with respect to these matters as well as the advantages to the abuser. They observe the lack of negative consequences to the individual or the relative minor nature. Management is oftentimes perceived as doing nothing in these instances, and in far too many cases that perception is accurate.

The appearance to subordinates of a do-nothing attitude on the part of management by subordinates encourages and contributes to the existence and growth of an abusive-behavior problem within the respective organization. Management, through its attitudes and practices, may create a "catch-22" situation. All the wrong messages can be sent, with the net result a totally inequitable situation that requires alternative solutions and approaches in order for the problem to be resolved.

If criminal prosecution is not a viable alternative, then seeking other remedies may be an appropriate and effective course of action. Pursuing some form of administrative or civil recovery may be the most effective recourse available in many situations. For example:

- The burden of proof is less than in criminal cases.
- Chances of recovery are improved.
- A public record of the abuse is established.
- Pocketbook penalties are imposed.
- Deterrence is enhanced.

When civil remedies are sought, those individuals who have sufficient assets may be forced to make whole or partial restitution. Those without sufficient assets cannot savor the fruits of their excesses because of the cost and aggravation of defending themselves. Concerning the costs of recovery, the company may break even or lose money.

Prior to pursuing one or more of the alternatives illustrated below, evaluate the merits of each case. Such an evaluation would include the amount of the loss and the estimated cost of recovery. Evaluate and determine any legal liability that might be incurred if the matter is pursued. Determine the payoff management wants and expects from its investment in the recovery efforts. Determine who will provide that payoff and how. Some examples of payoffs include:

- Imposition of pocketbook penalties
- Making an example of the individual
- Cost-effective recovery of the loss
- Deterrent value

- Maintenance of discipline
- Integrity of security policies

Outlined below are several methods that can and have been used to meet various business objectives arising from abusive employee behavior. Each method is evaluated for effectiveness and frequency of use for each category.

Prosecutorial Disposition

- *Guilty — Court-Ordered Restitution:* Seldom effective on an individual basis because the court is limited in enforcing its own order. Frequently used but little more than eyewash for the victim in most instances. Looks good on paper and can be effective if a business organization or an individual with assets is involved.
- *Plea Bargain:* Effectiveness is improved if restitution is included as part of the plea bargain. Even in this instance there is no guarantee that partial or full restitution will be made. Used in conjunction with sentencing, such as a condition of probation. Can be effective if properly supervised or if individual is an executive with another company that has resources. In those instances when the individual does not have the legitimate means or wherewithal to repay the loss, collection often becomes an exercise in frustration and futility.
- *Parole:* If the subject was incarcerated, he may be considered for parole. If management of the victim company asks to participate in the process, it can lobby for restitution as a condition of parole. Not always effective.

Civil or Administrative Disposition

- *Recovery of Stolen Goods:* Full recovery is seldom made; partial recovery is sometimes achieved. Most items recovered are in poor condition and may not be resalable or usable.
- *Recovery of Stolen Cash:* Offenders rarely volunteer to return any money still in their possession upon discovery and admission. If any money is left, offenders are likely to lie and deny.
- *Restitution:* Seldom made because the sums involved are usually too large, but is sometimes effective for relatively small sums.
- *Recovery from Bonding Company:* Can be an excellent source of restitution, assuming the individual is bonded and coverage is sufficient; however, it is often insufficient to cover the loss. Preparation of "Proof of Loss" can get complicated and may require an expert to effect recovery. Claims are seldom made, even when coverage exists.

- *Recovery from Theft Insurance:* Can be a source of restitution. Loss and other coverage limits, including high deductibles, may severely limit recovery.
- *Recovery Using Termination Agreements:* Can be source of restitution with certain levels of employees, assuming they are not drug and alcohol abusers. This can include provisions for the subject to obtain a loan for repayment from a third-party source, or installment reimbursement can be used. In the latter case, the company sets up an account in the name of the offender and bills him each month. This method can be interest free or require interest payments. Another approach is to have the offender sign a "quit claim" to real property he owns. Creative agreements can be reached with offenders who are attempting to avoid defense costs associated with civil litigation, criminal defense, or public exposure of their criminal behavior. Companies must use contracts and meet all legal requirements to protect future interests. If the offender defaults on the agreement, sue. This is seldom used.
- *Recovery through "Work Off" Agreement:* Can be effective in those few situations involving smaller amounts of money. It is an excellent method if the employee is critical to the business and termination will cost more than the loss. It has also been used for larger amounts under very special circumstances. Contracts are a must. Payroll deduction should be used. Full payment is due upon termination. This approach is seldom used.
- *Recovery through Civil Lawsuit:* Can be effective if the offender has assets or has the potential to build assets in the future. Evaluate use in all cases and determine viability. Can be very expensive to defend, if defended at all. This tactic has the potential to impose pocketbook penalties on the violator. Judgments or liens that will be paid off at a later date can be obtained. Can create adverse publicity for the offender that can benefit the company. The threat of a suit often generates some form of settlement; an actual suit can be costly for an organization to pursue. This method is used mostly against business organizations where a high expectation of recovery exists. It is seldom used against individuals. The threat of a suit can generate a countersuit and more costs. It is not without risks and should be evaluated carefully prior to initiating.

As this analysis demonstrates, management has alternatives other than to write it off and forget it when an employee is caught in an illegal act resulting in a loss to the company. Each loss situation is different and must be evaluated on its own merits. Each case should be carefully considered prior to a final decision on the dispositional method to be implemented.

3.18   The Integrity Line

As was noted in Chapter 1: The Problem, Section 1.5, "Management Attitudes and Practices," item no. 3, "No one to tell it to," alternative methods of reporting abusive behavior (other than to location management) should be available to both employees and nonemployees. There is no need to restate the argument for this now, but you are urged to refresh your memory by re-reading Section 1.5. The purpose here is to outline the key ingredients to understanding this alternative approach and its success.

For the purpose of discussion, the alternative reporting program is called "The Integrity Line." This name was selected because it is descriptive of security-awareness and loss-prevention objectives. By definition, integrity means a commitment to high moral values or a state of incorruptibility. The Integrity Line is a communications program set up to serve management and others concerned about the welfare of the organization or themselves.

This type of program provides the means and encourages employees, customers, and vendors to report known or suspected abusive behavior to someone other than site management. This action is necessary when the direct reporting of the problem to site or higher management is not feasible, or when anonymity is desired.

Alternative methods for reporting abusive behavior may, therefore, be needed because management is suspected or actually involved, management is not trusted or respected, the miscreant is close to the complainant, or the complainant wishes to remain anonymous for any reason.

Integrity lines are not new. Their use has proliferated with the increase of abusive behavior in our society. Programs of this type are known by many different identifiers such as "Hot-Line," "Tips-Line" and are used in government and business. They encourage the reporting of drug sales, child abuse, missing children, crimes, etc. Most operate on a 24-hour basis and are toll-free. When properly advertised and managed they can be an effective tool. The Association of Certified Fraud Examiners at EthicsLine, The Wilson Building, 800 West Avenue, Austin, TX 78701 provides one such fee-for-service program. The service provides a toll-free telephone number and intake 24/7 by trained professionals including contact police officers and certified fraud examiners.

These programs are not, however, infallible and have their own imperfections and shortcomings. Most of the inefficiencies are management and operator centered. Generating input is possible, but the proper collection of data and follow-up are often weaknesses that ultimately undermine user confidence and trust, which then cuts off the exchange of information.

Programs that are well managed (with operators trained to handle sensitive in-calls) are effective, productive and can be an important facet of loss-prevention and detection of wrongdoing for businesses. Use and trust will vary depending upon several key ingredients. For example, they must

- Be well publicized and their use encouraged
- Establish credibility
- Be managed effectively
- Have trained personnel to handle in-calls
- Carefully assess input
- Follow up the investigation competently
- Assure anonymity and confidentiality
- Link to number identification if a reward program exists
- Contract to outside service if necessary
- Use in-house security personnel
- Use a 24-hour toll-free number
- Involve employees, customers, and vendors

The initial credibility of any information received must be suspect because in-call lines are subject to abuse by disgruntled persons; proceed with caution. All input must be carefully reviewed and analyzed for credibility prior to acting on it, and any follow-up investigation requires the highest levels of competence.

Usually, a preliminary inquiry is made to test the credibility of any information prior to the initiation of a formal investigation. If not managed properly, this is the type of program that can cause more problems than it cures. Execute the program with the greatest degree of sensitivity, planning, and careful thought.

3.19   Security-Related Exit Interviews

Conducting exit interviews with departing employees has been a long-accepted management practice. Human Resources departments seek these interviews in an effort to identify problems so that remedial action can be initiated. The interviews focus on the reason for voluntarily resignation, the person's reaction to a termination, or upon retirement.

It is believed that a person leaving an organization may be more open, forthright, and inclined to discuss and identify problem areas than those still employed by the organization. This intuitive attitudinal assessment may or may not be accurate. In some instances, however, some disgruntled departing employees disclose important areas for management concern and interest.

Interviewers who conduct exit interviews pursue information on employee morale, working conditions, personal experiences, management attitudes and practices, etc. By identifying problem areas management can move to correct any legitimate deficiencies or inefficiencies in itself or in operations and thereby reduce turnover and other costs. As with any program, this one has met with varying degrees of success. Again, the individuals who conduct the interviews determine the quality of the end product. Properly conducted exit interviews have proven to be an effective management resource.

Security professionals saw the value of the exit interview and have adopted it for their purposes. In some companies, the security aspect is included in the company's regular exit-interview format and protocol, while in others it is conducted separately by security professionals. Whether used by the company's personnel department, management, or security personnel, the professionally conducted exit interview is a potentially valuable resource.

Security-related topics and issues offer a valued enhancement of a company's security-awareness and loss-prevention efforts. The following information provides a basic outline of the approach used in the conduct of security-related exit interviews.

- Voluntary terminations: Resigned or retired
- Involuntary terminations: Discharged because not suited to task or inability to perform

The following questions and answers clarify some aspects of the security-related exit interview:

1. Who conducts the security-related exit interview?
   The security department
   The personnel department
   A contract service
   Management other than the employee's immediate supervisor
   Direct report to supervisor or management group
2. How is the interview conducted?
   Face-to-face interview is most effective.
   Put person at ease and explain purpose of interview
   Explain that any information provided is kept confidential
   Request openness and honesty. Concern over job reference can impact
      openness and honesty.
   Use structured format
   Keep detailed notes
3. Ineffective interview methods:
   Telephone interviews
   Mailed questionnaires
   Harsh, demanding, or threatening tactics
   Use of trickery
   Lies, distortions, misrepresentations

Threats or other coercive tactics

Veiled offers of reward

Record with permission only

4. When and where is the interview conducted?

Voluntary termination:

> During phase-out process
>
> In private

Involuntary termination:

> As soon as practical. Conduct at work or at home. Must be conducted in private and confidentially.
>
> Those discharged or forced to resign because of illegal, unethical, or irresponsible behavior should only be interviewed by investigators.
>
> Exit interviews are included in the investigation process.

5. What is the purpose of the interview?

> To gather information to assist management in the evaluation of the company's security-awareness, loss-prevention, and security department functions.
>
> To gather information on any known or suspected illegal, unethical, or irresponsible employee behavior.

6. A generic question format:

> How do you view the company's employee security-awareness/compliance program?
>
> How do you view the company's loss-prevention efforts?
>
> How do you view the business practices of the company?
>
> Do you view management as ethical or unethical? Why?
>
> How do you view the company's audit program? Effective or ineffective? Why?
>
> How do you view the Integrity Line?
>
> How do your co-workers view the Integrity Line?
>
> How do you view the "off-the-job" security program?
>
> What would you do to improve security?
>
> Do you know of or suspect any current or former employee of:
>
> Theft of employee or company property?
>
> Misappropriation of company assets?
>
> Violations of company policy?
>
> On- or off-the-job drug sale or abuse?
>
> Conflicts of interest?
>
> Kickbacks?
>
> Misuse of company property?
>
> Irregularities in employee purchases?
>
> Drinking on the job?

Sexual harassment?
Falsification of paper work?
Fictitious invoicing?
Forgery?
Workers' compensation or health insurance fraud?

The above list provides a sample question format. Each organization's format should be designed to test company policy compliance and seek out abusive acts. In the design, abuses that are specific to the industry or organization should be highlighted. Check the questions with lawyers for compliance with applicable law prior to using.

A word of caution about exit interviews:

- Any information or allegations received in an exit interview should be suspect.
- The interviewer should question the accuracy, motives, and credibility of the person's input. Attitude, feelings, personality, mental state, and prejudices influence the accuracy and credibility of his input.
- You are cautioned not to take information obtained in an exit interview at face value and then to act upon that information.
- All information must be carefully analyzed and evaluated prior to taking any initiative related thereto.
- Look for patterns of behavior indicative of deception, and examine every possible motive.

Not withstanding some inherent shortcomings, the security-related exit interview can be an effective adjunct to any employee security-awareness/compliance and loss-prevention program. In addition to the collection of important data, an additional deterrent effect is achieved.

Individuals leaving a business organization do not always terminate the personal relationships they have established with former co-workers and, specifically, with those still employed. Relationships are maintained, to varying degrees, over extended post-employment time frames. The fact that security-related inquiries are being made will be noticed from within the organization.

Any security questions and many of the concerns expressed in the interview have the potential for being communicated to those friends and associates who are left behind. The mere fact that security inquiries are being made has a deterrent effect on abusive behavior. The violator never knows when a current or former co-worker with knowledge of abuse will choose to report it. With this approach several messages are communicated:

- The company's security concerns
- The importance placed on security
- The welfare of the employee
- The importance of ethics, integrity, and honesty
- The willingness of the company to act on security-related issues

3.20 Conclusion

Employee security-awareness/compliance programs, integrated with other internal controls, assist in filling the people void usually found in most loss-prevention efforts and can be effective in achieving loss-prevention objectives.

Employee security awareness is:

- Knowing what the organization's expectations of employee conduct are.
- The policies and procedures governing employee conduct.
- Being aware and conscious of those actions occurring around the person that will or could result in a loss to an individual or the organization.
- Knowing the negative personal effect abusive behavior has on each individual employee.
- Knowing what action to take regarding any recognized security exposures or risks.

Protecting the assets of a company is too important a process to be left solely to management and other specialists, such as auditors and security practitioners. Why limit the protection of assets to so few people when the entire employee, customer, and vendor base can be educated, trained, and encouraged to participate? Why assume that only the specialists know what they are doing and are, therefore, the most effective? Why assume that only the specialists care? By not overtly utilizing the entire people base a company severely limits its loss-prevention potential and in fact may contribute to the problem.

The barriers to communication and the exchange of information up and down an organization are legendary. Territorial imperatives, turf wars, and egos isolate, fragment, and impair efficiency and negatively impact the bottom line. Insofar as loss prevention is concerned, this maze of competing interests can be bridged with the assistance of motivated employees, customers, and vendors who are encouraged to prevent, detect, and report abusive behavior. All of these people can be educated, trained, motivated, and encouraged to participate in the loss-prevention process because they view loss prevention and the detection of abusive behavior as part of their jobs and responsibilities.

Make employees feel as if they are part of the team. Let them know they are appreciated and that the company cares. When employees, customers, and vendors know of the company's concern, abuse-incurred losses are reduced. Successful businesses are not run on fear. Employees treated with respect are not as likely to develop resentment and hostilities toward management and the company. Resentment and hostilities are ultimately vented on the company, co-workers, customers, and vendors.

Effective employee security-awareness/compliance and loss-prevention programs:

- Contribute to and build feelings of mutual trust, confidence, and respect.
- Build peer pressure against abusive behavior and increased fear of detection
- Shield against fiduciary liability for executives and directors.
- Contribute to building cooperative relationships between management and target groups.
- Contribute to the development of team spirit and link that spirit with company interests and personal safety.
- Educate employees to link satisfaction of personal goals to those of the company.
- Benefit every aspect of a business.
- Eliminate double standards that create an "us vs. them" mentality.
- Supplement and enhance an existing security department.
- Diminish employee hesitation to get involved in the loss-prevention process.
- Aid in mitigating federal criminal sanctions levied against convicted organizations under *Chapter Eight, Sentencing of Organizations.*

Well-developed employee security-awareness/compliance and loss-prevention programs contribute to organizational excellence and pride. Why does this benefit result from these types of programs? Well, there are many sound reasons:

- People like to work in an organization they respect and that reciprocates that respect.
- The people most companies want to employ take pride in themselves and want to work for an organization that they can take pride in.
- People like working for the best. They want to know that the organization they work for hires only the best. Excellence attracts excellence.

- People feel good about belonging to a company that seeks excellence, hires excellence, and produces excellence.
- People want to be associated with an organization that has a public reputation for ethics and integrity.
- People want to be part of a company that cares about employee safety and security, both on and off the job.

Abusive behavior is present in every business or organization. Only the levels and damages vary. No matter the effort or the effectiveness of management's loss-prevention efforts, no organization will ever be totally abuse proof. Management, therefore, must maintain an ever vigilant and watchful eye to ensure that losses from abusive acts are kept to a minimum, detected when they do occur, disclosed as early as possible, and resolved effectively. This effort requires careful balancing of corporate and employee interests. The danger here is to become so effective in the prevention and detection of abusive behavior that the organization's creativity and purpose for existing are disrupted. That consequence must be avoided.

Overly restrictive policies and procedures will destroy the organization's effectiveness and alienate the groups whose support is sought. Balance is the key. Do not overdo a program, but do not let the fear of overdoing it keep efforts ineffective or marginally effective.

Most organizations do not do enough and suffer because of it. The idea is to get people involved in the loss-prevention process by recognizing and accepting individual responsibilities. They thereby contribute to their own security and commercial success, and that of the organization.

The level of wrongdoing in any organization is a direct reflection of the management's character and that of the rank-and-file employee. Therefore, an abusive-employee problem identifies its own cause. Finding the solution is more complex. The effectiveness of all loss-prevention efforts will also reflect the organization's character level and management commitment.

All you have to do now is use the information contained in this book in a manner consistent with your own objectives, to reach your own goals based on your own belief system, knowledge, and experience. In this way you will produce an employee security-awareness/compliance program that will enhance your organization in the most meaningful way. As you make your way through this task, remember that management indifference breeds employee indifference and that management corruption breeds subordinate corruption. Do not let yourself or your organization get caught in either of these two traps.

As has been shown in these pages, the corrupting of America is a high-stakes game in which we have everything to lose and nothing to gain, a game in which even those who perceive themselves as winners are actually losers. And as in any game, the loser's mentality will affect the outcome of the game in the most negative and substantive way. To tolerate the corrupt among us is to guarantee our own corruption.

Support Materials

4

Objective: To provide examples of support materials used in the planning, development, and implementation of an employee-security-awareness compliance program and in communicating the organization's loss-prevention message to a targeted group.

4.1 Overview

The materials presented in this section relate to the planning, development, and implementation of an employee security-awareness/compliance program and the methods and media often used to effectively communicate an organization's loss-prevention message. The message and media can be used to target employees and other groups such as customers, vendors, and, where appropriate, neighbors bordering your facilities.

The materials presented can be used individually or in some combination to deliver the message and improve the organization's overall security awareness. Previewing these materials and their various applications may stimulate your imagination in the creation of materials unique to your organization and intended uses. Bear in mind that their purpose is to assist in not only communicating your loss-prevention message but keeping it fresh and prominently displayed. This is necessary if the program and the message are to avoid stagnation and lose credibility with the target group.

The methods and materials represented in the following pages have been field tested by some security-sensitive organizations and may prove to be cost-effective and efficient for your intended purpose. They should supplement management oversight, hiring practices, internal controls, audit practices, training, security policies and procedures, the disciplinary process, management practices, and leadership. These methods and concepts are not original to the author, and individual credit cannot be attributed. Most if not all have evolved from shared knowledge and experience exchanges between security and security-related practitioners in the private and public sectors.

193

A media program is not a stand-alone project. It is part of an approach that either contributes to and makes the program effective or undermines its purpose. The employee security-awareness/compliance program is used to integrate all loss-prevention efforts into a cohesive, cost-effective approach. The message is simple: security — the prevention, detection, and reporting of occupational crime and other abusive employee behavior and protecting the assets of the organization and its membership — are the responsibility of each person who benefits from his association with the organization.

The key element that motivates responsiveness to this thesis is the realization that abusive employee conduct translates into a threat to the personal welfare and security of the individual employee, customer, or vendor. Unethical, illegal, and irresponsible employee conduct can and does undermine the organization's purpose. This message must be conveyed to employees, customers, and vendors in a graphic and repetitive way to gain their support and participation in the prevention and detection of abusive behavior.

In the subsections that follow a variety of materials are introduced that can be used to communicate a loss-prevention message in a proven, efficient, and cost-effective way to any target group that is selected for participation. Each provides a brief description of the purpose of the example and some suggestions on how to make use of it.

4.2 Policy Development, Evaluation, and Maintenance Cycle

Exhibit 4.1 is a format that can be used in the development of an organization's security policies and procedures, their evaluation, and maintenance. On examination you will observe that the chart cycles through a process that begins with the perception of need and concludes with a

STEPS		
1.	Perceived need	14.	Gather input
2.	Gather input	15.	Draft revisions
3.	Draft policy	16.	Draft changes reviewed
4.	Draft policy reviewed	17.	Policy revised
5.	Policy revised	18.	Policy spell checked, edited
6.	Policy spell checked, edited	19.	Policy approved
7.	Policy approved	20.	Policy printed
8.	Policy printed	21.	Transmittal memo prepared
9.	Transmittal memo prepared	22.	Policy distribution list prepared
10.	Policy distribution list prepared	23.	Policy distributed
11.	Policy distributed	24.	Policy enforcement
12.	Policy implementation/enforcement	25.	Periodic review
13.	Periodic policy review	26.	Repeat prior process

Exhibit 4.1 Policy development and evaluation, and maintenance cycle.

review and evaluation. Naturally, the cycle should be developed to fit individual needs.

Overall the policy development, evaluation, and maintenance cycle as presented here consists of 26 steps, 13 of which make up the basic development process, with the remaining dedicated to proper review and maintenance of the policy.

If policies are to be effective, they must be reviewed and evaluated for need, relevancy, current accuracy, and usage. The cycle presented in this subsection will aid that process. For optimum effectiveness the development, review, evaluation, and maintenance cycle should be adapted to conform to the needs and idiosyncrasies of your organization.

4.3   CEO Program Kick-Off Letter

Exhibit 4.2 is an example of a typical letter to be used to inaugurate an organization-wide employee security-awareness/compliance program. A letter similar to the one in this subsection should be prepared and signed by the chief executive officer and sent to each employee. Company letterhead may be used, but if the CEO has a personalized version, then its use should be considered. Optimum effectiveness is sought. Use of the CEO's personal letterhead places an importance on the subject not otherwise achieved. Use it for maximum effect.

Of course, once the program is announced, the initial security orientation program should also begin. Until the entire agenda is complete with a full implementation schedule prepared, new employees of the program should not be noticed. Once all current employees are introduced to the program, then new hires, temps, etc. should be similarly oriented. This new employee orientation would be conducted in a manner proscribed by policy.

4.4   Customer Security Letter

Exhibit 4.3 is an example of a generic form letter that is used to communicate the organization's loss-prevention concerns to its customer base. The letter is designed and intended as a statement of the organization's commitment to quality products, service, honesty, and ethical conduct in the discharge of its business relationships.

The letter solicits the customer's input should the customer feel that the standard to which the organization is committed is not being met. Specific mention is made of both staff and management's business performance and conduct. A high level of importance is generally placed on this type of communication because the chief executive officer has signed it.

XYZ Corporation
2000 Old Town Street
Every City, USA

Dear Fellow Employee:

Soon you will be hearing about and asked to participate in the most comprehensive Employee Security-Awareness and Loss-Prevention program that our company has ever undertaken. The program is called "Security! Whose Job Is It Anyway?"

Why do we need such a program? If we are to stay competitive in the marketplace, we must, among other things, reduce the cost of doing business. Preventing, deterring, and detecting abusive business behavior will help make us more efficient and cost-effective.

What is abusive business behavior? This behavior is defined as "….any illegal, unethical, or irresponsible act that creates a loss or harm to the company, its employees, or customers."

Do we have a problem of abusive behavior? No; and we sure don't want one. That's what prevention is all about. Are we incurring costs from abuse-related conduct? Yes. Do we have an increased exposure to these kinds of losses in today's environment? Yes. Every company in our country is exposed to and experiencing some level of internal security-related losses.

This program offers a new way of addressing the risk and preventing, detecting, and reporting detrimental conduct within our company. With your full cooperation and participation we can continue a company spirit based upon the personal commitment of each of us to the highest ethical and service values, a spirit that will set in place a defensive system that will protect both personal and company interests from the negatives of abusive conduct today and into the future.

Let's all rise to the challenge. Security is your job. Thank you for your continued best efforts.

Very truly yours,

John Q. Executive
Chief Executive Officer

Exhibit 4.2 Chief executive officer program kick-off letter.

The CEO's signature signals his intent and personal commitment to the stated objectives and follow-up. Implicit in the letter is the CEO's solicitation of any information related to illegal, unethical, or other improper conduct on the part of his subordinates. While somewhat veiled, the message is still discernible to the sophisticated recipient. The CEO's assurances

---

XYZ Corporation
2000 Old Town Street
Every City, USA

Dear Valued Customer:

The business relationship we currently enjoy with you is a highly valued one. We anticipate the future with the expectation that we will continue to deserve your confidence and will grow and prosper in a mutually beneficial business relationship.

It is our intent to serve you with the highest quality products and service. We will enhance our relationship by always meeting high standards of ethical business practices. We shall employ, train, and support a staff who will meet our demanding performance, ethical, and service requirements. We seek unquestioned integrity in our business relationships.

Should a situation ever arise that causes you to question the intent of our company or that of any individual staff member or management, I request that you contact me personally (or name of person to be contacted) so that the issue may be resolved to our mutual satisfaction. You have my personal assurances that the resolution of your concerns will be managed on a confidential basis.

Very truly yours,

John Q. Executive
Chief Executive Officer

Exhibit 4.3 Customer security letter.

of confidentiality in the management of any expressed concerns further reinforces the implicit message contained in the letter. This message also places the customer on notice that he is expected to conduct his business relations on the same level.

Any information received from a source solicited in this manner, assuming that the source identifies himself, should receive a confirming letter from the CEO. This confirmation should contain not only an expression of appreciation for the concern or information received, but also the name of the person who has been assigned responsibility to follow up and resolve the matter.

Unless the person providing the information has requested anonymity, then his cooperation in meeting with the CEO's designated representative should also be solicited in the letter. Once the matter has been resolved, the responder should be notified of the outcome, if only in the most general and nonspecific terms, with a solicitation of cooperation in the future should the need arise. This approach will serve to build continuing support and mutual respect.

This type of correspondence, and the message it contains, should not be used unless there is total commitment on the part of management to achieving the objectives set forth therein. Any attempt at eyewash will be immediately recognized as such by the customer's management and will only serve to undermine the organization's purpose for the program.

Generally, a message of the nature described is mailed quarterly. A schedule designed to fit individual needs and objectives can be adopted. As a guide, once a month is too much, and annually is too little. This timing places the necessary importance on the issue, keeps it in the forefront, and assists in maintaining an up-to-date, accurate mailing list.

4.5   Vendor Security Letter

The vendor security letter (Exhibit 4.4) is also in a generic format. As with the customer security letter, this dispatch is used to communicate the organization's loss-prevention message to the target group. The letter is also designed and intended to convey the organization's position on important security-related issues, two of which are specifically addressed in the letter. Those two important security concerns are conflict of interest and the gift or kickback exposure.

Now take a moment to examine the content of the letter and what is intended to be accomplished. In its opening paragraph the letter establishes the value placed on the existing business relationship and the desire for its equitable continuance, "equitable" being the operative word. The message of the letter links the concept of what is equitable to the elimination of any misunderstandings that could affect the relationship. Equitable not only implies quality, favorable pricing, and service, but also adds the two other issues that, if violated, will have a far-reaching negative impact on the business relationship.

Once respect for the vendor and the business relationship is established, the two issues of primary concern are outlined. Other than the ambiguities implicit in the qualifying exceptions related to ownership or employee status as defined by organizational policy, the positions on these two issues are clearly stated. If the ambiguity needs clarification, questions and concerns are solicited and can be directed to the author of the letter. This correspondence diplomatically sets the importance that its author places on the stated policies and the vendor's compliance with them.

In the concluding paragraph the letter's author makes it clear that the vendor's failure to comply with the policies outlined or its failure to notify him of any violations of same will jeopardize the continuation of any existing

---

XYZ CORPORATION
2000 OLD TOWN STREET
EVERY CITY, USA

Dear Mr. Vendor:

We have long valued the business relationships we have established with our various suppliers. We look forward to the equitable continuation of those relationships. In an effort to ensure that there are no misunderstandings arising out of certain issues of importance to our company and yours I'm asking that you please review the following information carefully.

First, our employees are prohibited from being an owner, consultant, or employee of any business organization seeking or doing business with our company, except as exempted in our conflict of interest policy. Secondly, our policy prohibits the offering or acceptance of gifts or gratuities to or from any person, firm, or corporation doing or soliciting business with our company.

We take these policies and the compliance therewith very seriously. Should a situation arise that calls into question your compliance with our intent or to your knowledge that of any of our staff or management, I request that you contact me personally (or designee) so that the issue can be resolved. You have my personal assurances that your concerns will be managed on a confidential basis, if requested. I'm sure we both share a mutual concern that neither of us will, by our actions or lack thereof, jeopardize our current relationship.

Thank you. If you have any questions please direct them to

Very truly yours,

John Q. Executive
Chief Executive Officer

Exhibit 4.4 Vendor security letter.

business relationship. This letter sets a high ethical tone that will influence all future relationships with the vendor.

Correspondence of this nature and importance is generally distributed on a quarterly basis. If quarterly does not seem appropriate, develop your own timetable. The letter is distributed to existing vendors and immediately upon entering into any new vendor relationships. It is addressed to the vendor's executive management from the CEO, as well as to divisional, regional, and local levels. If a right-to-audit clause is included as a part of all contracts or purchase orders, then a reminder of that right might be asserted.

4.6 Employee Security-Awareness Pamphlet

The pamphlet (Exhibit 4.5) referenced here is a generic model of the type to be handed out to all existing employees in a start-up program, to new employees post-start-up, and temporaries, and to part-timers upon reporting for work. Its purpose is to inform each person working in an official capacity with the organization how management feels about the commission of wrongful conduct. The information in the pamphlet places responsibility for the ethical, legal, and responsible conduct of the organization's business. Instructions are also provided for reporting wrongful conduct.

Our example is relatively concise. You are not limited to our example. Ours served its purpose and is inexpensive to produce. Some organizations have extensive handout materials and cover a number of core issues important to the employee and the organization. Some are very impressive in both content and art work. You are limited only by your objective, imagination, and budget constraints.

A pamphlet of this nature can be used on a stand-alone basis or as handout material in conjunction with a more formal security orientation program. If distributed on a stand-alone basis the pamphlet and its message are a mini-security orientation. As mentioned, the pamphlet defines organizational attitudes on the subject, places responsibility, and provides instructions for reporting wrongful behavior.

If either of the frameworks described above is used, the expected results are enhanced if someone in personnel or security takes a few minutes to explain the contents of the pamphlet, as opposed to just handing the material out along with other printed information. Some organizations have designed their pamphlets with key ethics and security policies in them and a tear-out acknowledgment for the employee to sign. The signed acknowledgment is then placed into the individual's personnel file as a part of the permanent record.

If your pamphlet is used in conjunction with a formal security orientation program, then it becomes one part of the composite security profile presented in that session. For security orientations other than for management, many organizations find it difficult to allocate the time to conduct formal sessions for new hires, existing employees, or temporaries. It is for the latter reason that the pamphlet can become an important part of the organization's loss-prevention program as a handout at the beginning of employment. When used appropriately, this handout material can play an important part in the success of the program.

If this medium is to be effective, then the pamphlet must be professionally prepared and printed. The presentation of this important message must be done in a manner that will not only emphasize the program, but also

COMPANY LOGO

SECURITY!
WHOSE JOB IS IT ANYWAY?

(THEME)

(Title page, 8.5" × 11" folded in half)

An Employee
Security-Awareness and Loss-Prevention Program

TOGETHER
WE CAN PREVENT
ILLEGAL, UNETHICAL, AND IRRESPONSIBLE BEHAVIOR

To discuss a security problem, report abusive behavior, or any vulnerability to loss, contact one of the following:

1. Your supervisor
2. Management at any level
3. The Security Department

COMPANY LOGO

(Pamphlet-Backside)

If you wish to remain anonymous, or for any other reason,
contact our *Security Department* directly
at: 1-800-123-1234

or

Call *The Integrity Line* anytime: 1-800-123-1234.

Security!
Whose Job Is It Anyway?

Figure 4.6 Exhibit 4.5A Employee security-awareness pamphlet.

SECURITY IS YOUR JOB

This pamphlet reaffirms the importance of maintaining a high standard in our business conduct.

As an employee, you have an obligation to practice good business ethics. Integrity is a personal responsibility. You alone are responsible for your actions. No one can justify an illegal or unethical act by claiming it was ordered by someone in higher management. No one can compel an employee to commit an illegal or unethical act.

YOU MAKE THE DIFFERENCE

Protecting our assets and promoting security awareness is everyone's job at XYZ. Your Security Department is charged with the responsibility of coordinating those efforts to assure maximum results.

The Security Department's primary purpose is to assist everyone in the prevention of losses and in protecting those personal and corporate assets we have worked so hard to acquire.

If you know of a situation that needs special attention in preventing or resolving a threat to the integrity of our company, call the Security Department at 1-800-123-1234. You will not have to give your name, just identify the problem.

TOGETHER, WE CAN MAKE A DIFFERENCE

Mr. John Q. Executive
Chief Executive Officer
XYZ Corporation

(COMPANY LOGO)

SECURITY? IT'S YOUR JOB

SECURITY!

WHOSE JOB IS IT ANYWAY?

"Security! Whose Job is it Anyway?" was selected as the theme of our security-awareness and loss-prevention program because each of us at XYZ is a member of the security team. Each of us is in a position to set an example that ensures sound security and ethical practices.

PREVENTION

Your personal commitment to honesty and integrity is a necessary and inseparable part of our loss-prevention efforts in identifying problem areas and in finding solutions for them. Who you are and what you stand for will determine whether you will be part of the problem or a part of the solution. It's your decision: A commitment to excellence, or less than you can be.

DANGERS

It has been estimated that America's business community loses as much as $400 billion a year to dishonest, abusive, and irresponsible behavior. Company employees account for the majority of that loss.

Theft of equipment, inventory, and cash, and drug and alcohol abuse, workers' compensation and health insurance fraud, kickbacks, vandalism, and burglary are examples of the problem. The actions of dishonest, abusive, and irresponsible employees can severely damage a company.

Not only companies are victimized. Many families are devastated by drug and alcohol abuse. Homes are burglarized, individuals robbed, and possessions accumulated over a lifetime are lost to thieves. Security is a concern both on and off the job.

RESULTS

At a minimum, a company victimized by employee abuses and irresponsibility would have to raise prices (which would have a negative effect on their competitive position), scuttle plans for expansion, reduce benefits, lay off personnel, and stop pay increases in an effort to curtail their loss.

Exhibit 4.5B Employee security-awareness pamphlet.

contribute to its credibility. Poorly written and printed materials will diminish rather than enhance organizational credibility on the subject of security.

4.7   Cover Jacket for Loss-Prevention Kit

Whether your organization is using an employee security orientation presentation to communicate its message or just handing out loss-prevention materials on a one-on-one basis, it is helpful to package those materials in a manner that will enhance their importance and credibility. One way of doing that is to present your communications media, policies, policy summaries, etc. in a manner designed and intended to ensure that their purpose is accomplished.

As seen in Exhibit 4.6, the method suggested to package security-awareness materials for presentation to a target group or individually to members of that group is in a specially prepared and printed envelope. The example presented here is a 6 × 9″ white envelope. The envelope, of course, can be any color and any quality paper. The size should fit the intended use. Print and logo colors should be tailored to the organization. If materials are printed on standard 8.5 × 11″ paper, then the envelope must be sized to accommodate those materials.

Typically, the envelope contains a letter from the CEO, security-related pamphlets, certain security policies and procedures or summaries of same, and any forms for written acknowledgment of the receipt and explanation. As you can see, the envelope approach is a handy, cost-effective, and efficient way to package security and loss-prevention materials. Of course, many other methods can accomplish the same purpose. Regardless of the method selected, keep a keen eye on the quality of all materials; do not skimp. They are a direct reflection of the importance placed on the project.

The envelope in this example is clearly identified with the company logo, the information contained within and at the bottom, and the security theme of the organization. Anyone reading the cover notations is aware of the originating organization, the purpose of the envelope, and its contents. The fact that the company has gone to the extent it has in the preparation and presentation of the information the package contains places a degree of importance not found otherwise.

4.8   Employee Security Responsibilities

Exhibit 4.7 is a summary of a company policy prohibiting abusive behavior. This summary not only recapitulates a listing of prohibited conduct, it also explains the negative effects of such behavior on both the individual employee and the company. In the explanation of why wrongful conduct is detrimental

```
┌─────────────────────────────────────────────┐
│          ╱                           ╲        │
│         ╱                             ╲       │
│  ┌──────────────────────────────────────┐    │
│  │                                        │   │
│  │      ⟨ COMPANY LOGO ⟩                  │   │
│  │                                        │   │
│  │                                        │   │
│  │            EMPLOYEE                     │   │
│  │       SECURITY-AWARENESS                │   │
│  │             AND                         │   │
│  │        LOSS-PREVENTION                  │   │
│  │              KIT                        │   │
│  │                                        │   │
│  │                                        │   │
│  │      (6" × 9" white envelope)           │   │
│  │                                        │   │
│  ├────────────────────────────────────────┤   │
│  │           SECURITY!                     │   │
│  │    WHOSE JOB IS IT ANYWAY?              │   │
│  └────────────────────────────────────────┘   │
└─────────────────────────────────────────────┘
```

Exhibit 4.6 Cover jacket for loss-prevention kit.

to personal and corporate interests, it clearly removes any pretext of a double standard in the application of security policies and procedures. The message is that security policies and procedures apply to every employee regardless of rank or title. Compliance is required and disciplinary action mandated when violations occur.

This statement of employee security responsibilities places a shared responsibility for the protection of company and co-worker assets on the individual employee. The distinction is often made that the protection of assets is the responsibility of security personnel or management and not that

Illegal, unethical, and irresponsible employee behavior is damaging to the interests of the individual employee and the company. Abusive acts undermine not only business relationships, but those of a personal nature. Lost employee, stockholder, customer, and vendor confidence, trust, and respect — thus extracting a costly toll. Abusive employee behavior, therefore, is unacceptable in this organization. This applies to all employees regardless of position or rank. As a matter of policy we choose to conduct the business of this organization on an ethical basis. Many of the security policies and procedures of our company will be explained and your questions answered in the security orientation session. We will make every reasonable effort to ensure that each employee knows and clearly understands his or her responsibilities as it regards this subject. That is the purpose for the security orientation and all handout materials. You are expected to do your part to ensure that you understand and comply with the standards set forth. You will be held to that standard.

Protecting the assets of our company is the collective and individual responsibility of each employee. Each employee has the responsibility to ensure that our assets are protected and ethical business practices are adhered to. Failure to comply with the security policies of the company will subject the violator to disciplinary action up to and including dismissal.

The conduct outlined below provides examples of those behaviors that are unacceptable in this organization. These examples are provided so that each employee understands the company position. It is your individual responsibility to personally comply with all security policies and procedures and the ethical intent of the company. To avoid any possible confusion on security-related issues, policies, and actions complicated by you that may conflict with policy, direct your questions to your immediate supervisor for clarification.

BEHAVIOR PROHIBITED BY POLICY

Use, sale, or possession of illegal drugs on company property or at sponsored activities

Abuse of prescription drugs on company property or at sponsored activities

Use, sale, or possession of alcoholic beverages while working

Use or unauthorized possession of firearms on company property or at sponsored activities

Theft of company property or that of a co-worker, customer, or vendor

The willful destruction or damage of company property or that of a co-worker, customer, or vendor

Workers' compensation fraud

Group insurance fraud

Unauthorized use of company personnel, materials, equipment, or other resources

Conflicts of interest

Falsification of records or reports

Taking or giving unauthorized discounts

Offering or accepting unauthorized compensation from a customer or vendor

Sexual harassment

Engaging in restraint of trade

Unethical business practices

Financial, consumer, or vendor fraud

Industrial espionage

Physical assaults

Abuse of sick leave

Cheating or other abuse of co-workers, customers, or vendors

ABUSIVE BEHAVIOR DEFINED

Any illegal, unethical, or irresponsible act that causes loss or harm to the company,

its employees, customers, or vendors.

Exhibit 4.7 Employee security responsibilities.

of the rank-and-file employee. This delineation of wrongful conduct and the individual employee's responsibility in the prevention and detection of such behavior assigns clear accountability for compliance with the organization's ethical standards as well as its security policies and procedures.

The statement should be included as a part of the employee's security orientation, whether that orientation occurs on a one-to-one basis with local management or in a group setting. Customarily, each employee is required to read the statement and provide assurances that he or she clearly understands and subscribes to its mandate as a condition of employment. A copy of the statement is provided along with any other position statements, policy and procedure summaries, or actual policies where used as part of the orientation.

Statements of this nature should be included in an employee security-awareness/compliance and loss-prevention kit. They are part of the loss-prevention foundation and should be treated as an important part of the program. It is imperative that time be taken to ensure that each employee understands the purpose of the statement and its importance in the prevention of abuse-incurred losses and that compliance is required to avoid disciplinary action. Any reasonable employee questions or concerns should be addressed and resolved to avoid confusion on any of the points or issues raised.

4.9 Acknowledgment of Individual Security Responsibilities

Exhibit 4.8 is a generic form used to certify the receipt of the employee security-awareness/compliance and loss-prevention orientation materials. When referring to a copy of the statement note that the certificate clearly states that the individual understands his responsibilities in the prevention and detection of abusive conduct. It confirms that certain security policies and procedures were explained to the employee and that he understands them. Further clarified is the fact that any questions raised were answered to the employee's satisfaction.

In the statement space is provided in the heading to identify the date and time the presentation was made, the person making the presentation, and the name and signature of the employee receiving the orientation. A copy of this and all materials used in the presentation are given to each recipient for personal use and records. The original signed acknowledgment is then permanently placed in the employees personnel file. Annually, each employee should acknowledge and sign a restatement of their individual responsibilities as proscribed by policy.

CERTIFICATION

This will certify that the person whose name and signature appear below has participated in the XYZ Corporation's security and loss-prevention orientation. By my signature affixed below I further certify that I know and fully understand my personal responsibilities in the prevention and detection of abusive employee behavior. The following company security policies and procedures were clearly explained to me, and any questions I had concerning those policies and procedures were answered to my satisfaction. I know that should I have any further questions in the future I should refer them to my immediate supervisor for clarification. Furthermore, I was provided an *Employee Security-Awareness and Loss-Prevention Kit* that contained the materials noted below for my personal use and files. I have also been provided a signed copy of this certification.

EMPLOYEE
SECURITY-AWARENESS AND LOSS-PREVENTION KIT

Pamphlet *Security! Whose Job Is It Anyway?*

POLICIES:

Employee Security Responsibilities

Acknowledgment of Individual Security Responsibilities

Instructions for Reporting Abusive Behavior

Security Reminder – Wallet Card

(List all security-related policies and procedures reviewed and distributed. Annually, every full-time or part-time employee and temporary worker should sign a new certification of their individual responsibilities confirming that they understand the policies related thereto. This procedure also ensures that any revisions to policies are provided and acknowledged by the individual.)

Date: _____

Time: _____

Print Employee Name: _____

Employee Signature: _____

Print Presenter Name: _____

Presenter Title and Signature: _____

Exhibit 4.8 Acknowledgment of individual security responsibilities.

4.10   Instructions for Reporting Abusive Behavior

Exhibit 4.9 is a companion piece to the other materials that make up the employee security-awareness and loss-prevention kit. Its purpose is to provide the individual employee with written instructions for the reporting of abusive behavior.

ABUSIVE BEHAVIOR DEFINED

Any illegal, unethical, or irresponsible acts that create a loss or harm to the company, its employees, customers, or vendors.

OUR OBJECTIVE IS TO PREVENT OR DETECT AND REPORT ABUSIVE BEHAVIOR

It is impossible to meet this objective without the direct involvement of our co-workers and their personal commitment to making it a reality. No one individual or department can do the job alone. It will take each of us working together to achieve this objective. If we are to design a loss-prevention program that is cost effective and that provides an appropriate protective response, then we must have your input. We must know about and be able to accurately identify and quantify a problem if one exists, and then move to fix the problem. We must know if abuses are occurring, and where, how, and by whom they are committed. You are the best source of that information. Abusive conduct has a very negative impact upon all of us and impairs the ability of the company to stay profitable and in business. Please follow the instructions below to report any abusive conduct known to you.

INSTRUCTIONS FOR REPORTING

To report any act of abusive employee behavior or to discuss a security problem or vulnerability to loss, contact any one of the following:

1. Your supervisor

2. Management at any level

3. The Security Department

If, for any reason, you wish to remain anonymous or have your identity protected, contact our Security Department directly or use the Integrity Line.

SECURITY DEPARTMENT

1–800–123–1234

INTEGRITY LINE

1–800–123–1234

Exhibit 4.9 Instructions for reporting abusive behavior.

As this item makes clear, abusive behavior is once again defined for the employee. This repetition is intentional and designed to reinforce the importance placed on the issue by management. Also found in the text of this handout is a statement of the organization's objectives regarding loss prevention and the detection of wrongful conduct. This item also contains a commonsense explanation of the need for the policy as well as the importance of the individual employee's cooperation and participation in the organization's loss-prevention efforts.

The specific instructions for reporting wrongful conduct are clearly stated, reasonable, and offer maximum flexibility to the individual with something to say. The various alternatives provided for reporting incidents or concerns are clearly explained. The toll-free telephone number for the organization's security department or other entity is given as is the toll-free number for the special line that is set up to receive communication from those persons who wish to remain anonymous when making their report. This form is distributed at the time employees receive their security orientation.

4.11 Ideas for Corporate Security Themes

Exhibit 4.10 contains suggestions or ideas for use as a corporate security theme. The theme is the name or slogan used to identify the organization's security-awareness program. Whatever it is should be used on most if not all communications media and materials.

An example of a theme is found in the employee security-awareness pamphlet, Exhibit 4.5. The one used in the pamphlet is "Security! Whose Job Is It Anyway?" This slogan appears throughout the pamphlet and on posters and other media used in a campaign. It becomes the centerpiece of the organization's employee security-awareness orientation program.

The central thesis of a theme is used to communicate and build a team concept in loss prevention. In very succinct terms the poster should promote the importance of individual character and ethics in building a successful organization, loss prevention as a shared responsibility, and encourage participation in your program. Posters can influence a broad audience, depending on how and where they are placed. Customers, vendors, and visitors are all examples of target groups that can be influenced with posters. Select poster placement with that objective in mind. Lobbies, sales counters, hallways, and offices are great areas for poster placement. You will think of other appropriate locations.

A theme should be catchy and easy to remember while simultaneously capturing the essence of the program. While they should be kept simple and short, they can be enhanced with artwork. A nice logo says a lot. Do not be afraid to use your imagination in the presentation of the security theme.

Security!

Whose Job Is It Anyway?

Security!

You Make the Difference.

Security!

It's Your Job.

Security!

It's a Team Effort.

Security!

The Good Guys Win.

Security!

It Requires Excellence.

Security!

Honest and Proud of It.

Security!

Get Involved.

Security!

Get Committed.

Security!

Ethics, Honesty, and Integrity.

Security!

It's Us.

Exhibit 4.10 Ideas for corporate security themes.

The slogans provided with this example capture the point in both form and substance. They may be used as is or as a stimulus for more fertile imaginations to create their own. Soliciting ideas for security themes through contests is a great way to improve employee participation in the entire process and to build a sense of ownership in the program. You may be surprised not only at the interest in loss prevention these contests will generate, but at the quality of the poster ideas and suggestions received from your employees or their family members.

If the contest method is used, be sure to provide the winner with proper recognition. A nice gift, such as cash, a weekend for two at some nearby resort, time off, or some security-related item like an alarm system for the winner's home or car is always helpful. It is an excellent means of generating employee interest and support. A photo of the winner in the organization's newspaper or letter is also a great way to kick off a program.

4.12   Do-It-Yourself Security Poster Ideas

The security poster (Exhibit 4.11) is an important part of any security-awareness program. Posters keep the message in front of the target groups. They should be placed not only for employee viewing but for customer and vendor consumption as well. Be careful not to select themes and slogans that can be easily altered to change the intended meaning. For example, if your poster reads, "Crime does not pay here! Have you joined the team?" and the word "not" obliterated, you can see the result is not the message you intended to convey.

The following ideas are examples of text that could be used in a company-generated poster program. The ideas presented are simple. They are limited only by imagination and creativity.

Abusive Behavior?

Any illegal, unethical, or irresponsible act that creates a loss
or harm to the company, its employees, customers, or vendors.

Security!

Speak up, the loss is yours.

Security!

It's in your interest.

Security!

It's an attitude at XYZ

Security!

Honesty improves performance.

Security!

Don't keep abusive conduct a secret.

Security!

Don't stand for it. Stand against it.

Security

At XYZ ethics is more than just a word.

Security!

Ethics. Honesty. Integrity

Security!

It's personal pride and self-respect.

Security!

You manage it.

Exhibit 4.11 Do-it-yourself security poster ideas.

In some organizations security posters have become an art form. Poster-design contests have produced creative success. The examples of poster text and presentation presented here are about as simple as you can get. You want your poster message to be clear and succinct, but that does not mean you cannot use imagination and creativity in their design. Colors, creative use of fonts, or artwork can really improve both the delivery of the message and the credibility of your program. Some commercially produced posters are available. Check them out for applicability to your use.

Posters and their message must remain fresh. They should be changed frequently enough to attract attention. This medium should be changed no less than once a quarter for effectiveness. Some organizations change them monthly. Quality gets and retains attention. Use materials that communicate the importance placed on the message.

4.13   Sample Security Poster

Exhibit 4.12 is self-explanatory. As can be seen, it is a simple 8.5 × 11″ presentation on poster board stock. This particular example picks up the organization's security theme and delivers the message that security is the job of each employee. Employees are reminded to prevent abusive behavior and are provided with the toll-free telephone number of the corporate security department. If there is a hot-line, then that number should be advertised as well.

Posters can be designed to convey any security message you desire. The example shown here is simple and to the point. Posters should be displayed at key locations, high-traffic points, and restricted access areas throughout the organization. The number of posters should be sufficient to keep the message in front of your target group, and its size should fit the intended use and space constraints. One size may fit all, or multiple sizes may be produced. Some may be billboard size. You decide based on your situation and the needs and objectives of your program.

4.14   Security Telephone Sticker Reminders

In Exhibit 4.13 are samples of communications media designed and intended for use as an attachment to all company telephones. Once again the intent is to keep the security-awareness, loss-prevention message in front of your employees. Telephone stickers are attached to the front, side, or handset in plain view. Keep the message fresh. Change it. Purchase stickers that are removable. A quarterly change is recommended.

SECURITY!

WHOSE JOB IS IT ANYWAY?

SECURITY IS YOUR JOB!

SECURITY DEPARTMENT

1–800–123–1234

INTEGRITY LINE

1–800–123–1234

(Logo)

PREVENT ABUSIVE BEHAVIOR

Exhibit 4.12 Sample security poster (8.5 × 11″ poster board stock).

4.15   Security Hard Hat Sticker Reminders

The security hard hat sticker (Exhibit 4.14) is designed to be placed and prominently displayed on the outside surface of a hat. As with all communication media the placement and message imprinted on the sticker are important. This medium can also be used by attaching the stickers to clipboards, vehicle dashboards, or to any other applicable surfaces. The program can be mandatory if hard hats or other equipment is owned by the organization or voluntary if the targeted equipment is the personal property of the employee.

Design the scheduled timeframe for sticker rotation to fit the organization's needs. During the first year of a new program you may want to rotate stickers once a month for the first 3 months, quarterly thereafter. This approach can be used to supplement a poster or other attention-getting program or as a stand-alone project.

Telephone stickers are designed to attach to sides, front, or handset of each company telephone. Easy peel-offs are best. Examples of text messages are

SECURITY IS YOUR JOB!

Illegal, unethical, and irresponsible behavior robs you.

Don't justify, excuse, cover up, or tolerate it.

Security: 1-800–123–1234

SECURITY IS YOUR JOB!

Speak out — the loss is yours.

Don't justify, excuse, or tolerate abusive behavior.

The Integrity Line: 1–800–123–1234

YOU MAKE THE DIFFERENCE!

Don't tolerate, excuse, or cover up illegal on-the-job drug abuse, sale, or possession.

Security: 1–800–123–1234

YOU MAKE THE DIFFERENCE!

Insist on honest and ethical business practices.

The Integrity Line: 1–800–123–1234

SECURITY!

Integrity is more than just a word.

Security: 1–800–123–1234

SECURITY!!

There is no valid reason to cover up for a thief.

The Integrity Line: 1–800–123–1234

SECURITY!

Fraud or thievery takes money out of your pocket.

Security: 1–800–123–1234

SECURITY!

Think! You could be the next victim.

The Integrity Line: 1–800–123–1234

Exhibit 4.13 Security telephone sticker reminders.

Stickers are designed to be attached to the sides, front, or rear of a company-owned hard hat. The same sticker can be placed on clipboards, car and truck dashes, etc.

Proud to be union and proud to be honest.

No drugs or alcohol on this job.

Crime *does not pay* here.

Security is my job.

If you can't do the time, don't do the crime.

Bringing back ethics.

Don't ask me to steal or cover it up.

Integrity! It's more than a word at XYZ.

Integrity is the measure of EXCELLENCE!

All employees at XYZ are part of the loss-prevention team.

Fraud and dishonesty are destructive to our company.

Integrity!

It's a matter of integrity.

Security!

Have you joined the team?

Exhibit 4.14 Security hard hat sticker reminders.

This is another medium that fits well with an employee-based contest for ideas, suggestions, and artwork. Employees often get their children involved in these types of programs by submitting entries. Encourage family involvement in any contest that you run. Prizes and recognition incentives are nice motivators that promote employee participation, involvement, program validation, support, and buy-in when thoughtfully initiated and managed.

4.16   Security Paycheck Reminders

Exhibit 4.15 is a sample set of security-related paycheck reminders. These reminders are periodically included with or attached to employee paychecks or verification slips for direct deposits. As can be seen from the examples, they contain a motivational message and instructions for contacting the organization's security department. If no security department exists, then the contact person or contract service should be identified. This medium is ideally suited to business card size presentations. The message is placed on the front of the card and contact information on the back.

Paycheck reminders are attached to or included with employee paychecks, or imprinted on electronic deposit validations. They contain a motivational message and security contact information. These reminders are ideally suited to business card-size presentations.

The front of the card contains the message and the back has contact data.

THINK SECURITY!

Abusive behavior has a direct negative impact on you and your family.
It reduces the cost-effectiveness and profitability of our company.
Lost profits and efficiency impact wages and benefits.

THINK SECURITY!

If we earn 5 cents on each dollar of sales, then we must produce
$20 in new sales for each $1 lost to abusive behavior.
Fact: abusive behavior hurts each of us individually.

THINK SECURITY!

Abusive behavior: any illegal, unethical, or irresponsible act
that creates a loss or harm to our company, employees, or customers.

THINK SECURITY!

At a minimum, a company victimized by employee abuses
might have to raise prices, scuttle plans for expansion,
reduce benefits, lay off personnel, and withhold pay increases
in an effort to stay in business.

THINK SECURITY!

Each of us has an obligation to practice sound business ethics.
Honesty and integrity are an individual's responsibility.
You alone are responsible for your actions.
No one can justify an illegal or unethical act based on the claim
that someone in higher management ordered it.

THINK SECURITY!

Our ethics and security policies and procedures
assist in protecting each employee from exploitation
and assist in keeping our company competitive
in the marketplace, profitable, and efficient.

Exhibit 4.15 Security paycheck reminders.

The reminder's message is centered on money and emphasizes the direct negative effect that abusive conduct has on the individual employee. When this message is linked with the employee's paycheck you will often get improved recognition of and a new perspective on abusive behavior. Personalize the message. Emphasize the fact that wrongful conduct takes money directly out of the pocket of the individual employee and thus should not be tolerated.

The messages should also emphasize the importance of individual honesty and integrity and that each employee is responsible for his personal conduct and shares the responsibility with his co-workers for the protection of the organization's assets and each employee's personal property. These types of reminders are a necessary part of any security-awareness program. As with all media, identify the organization and use appropriate artwork to improve the attractiveness and attention-getting potential of the piece. This is also an excellent contest item.

The frequency of these reminders is based on the same criteria as other media. Need and effectiveness are paramount considerations. With the initiation of a new program message, changes should be made based on the pay period. If weekly, change every 2 weeks for the first 3 months; thereafter once a month might provide the desired results. If paydays are every 2 weeks or monthly, adjust accordingly. Stay flexible and modify your program as needed. Sloppy materials send a like message. Importance is assigned by the importance assigned.

4.17 Security Wallet Card Reminder

The security wallet card reminder (Exhibit 4.16) defines itself and its use by the title. The card is designed and intended for placement in an employee's wallet or purse. Its purpose is to be a simple, handy reminder of key security information that is easily stored and readily available. The size of the card is that of a standard business card. Larger sizes are not easily accommodated in a wallet or purse.

The distribution of this medium is generally made at the security orientation, as a periodic attachment to a paycheck, or as a handout in another forum. Because of space limitations, the desired message is printed on both sides of the card. In the example provided here, one side of the card identifies the sponsoring organization, the security theme, and a request to prevent abusive conduct. On the flip side is encouragement for the employee to speak up on security problems, and three different levels of reporting instructions are printed. To enhance retention value calendars or a compact directory of key internal telephone numbers can be added to the card. Of course, well-planned, one-sided cards can also be effective.

(Front)

SECURITY! WHOSE JOB IS IT ANYWAY?

PREVENT ABUSIVE BEHAVIOR

(Insert company logo)

(Rear)

SPEAK UP!

To discuss a security problem contact:

Your supervisor, management at any level, or

security department.

To remain anonymous contact:

The Integrity Line 1–800–123–1234

Security wallet cards are printed on standard business card-size stock.

Exhibit 4.16 Security wallet card reminders.

In addition to the suggestions already made, key facts can also be used to reinforce the importance of everyone's participation in the loss-prevention process; for example: "in the year 200X abusive conduct cost our company $2.3 million!" or "in 200X your participation in and support of our security programs resulted in a savings of $500,000."

As with a business card, the manner of data presentation and the quality of the material that the data are printed on convey a message themselves. Quality shows and sends a like message. Inferior messages, printing, and card stock send a message of their own. Your employees will translate the importance you place on the message by the quality of the method used to transmit it. The better the presentation the more likelihood that your message will be favorably received and the card kept for future reference. This method of communicating the loss-prevention message and solicitation of support has proven to be very effective when properly used.

4.18   Security Newsletter Article

This subsection presents an example of a specifically written and designed security-related article that is intended for use in a security-awareness and

Just because an unknown phone caller asks for information, don't feel obligated to tell

☐ Always avoid giving the following:
☐ Information about your money investments
☐ Plans for vacationing
☐ Plans for moving out of your home
☐ Charities to which you contribute
☐ Businesses you deal with and societies or clubs you belong to
...TO PEOPLE YOU DON'T KNOW.

Exhibit 4.17 Reprinted with the permission of The National Crime Prevention Council, 1000 NW Connecticut Avenue, 13th Floor, Washington, D.C., 20036, (202) 466–6272.

loss-prevention program (Exhibit 4.17). Articles are written for inclusion in the organization's newsletter or paper. Articles of this nature might even be used in connection with security bulletins or alerts prepared by a security department for distribution to employees, customers, or vendors.

The article used in this example came from the Corporate Action Kit produced by ADT, Inc. and the National Crime Prevention Council. The kit contains 15 sections. Each section is devoted to an individual security topic that relates to on- and off-the-job security concerns.

Topics range from suggestions for improving home protection to on- and off-the-job drug and alcohol abuse. To further supplement efforts in loss-prevention the kit also includes a *McGruff* (the crime-prevention dog) product catalog and a directory of loss-prevention audio-visual materials.

Each of the 15 sections in the kit contains camera-ready masters that can be used for brochures, newsletters, posters, and other applications in your program. The central thesis of this material is that loss prevention is a shared responsibility, a partnership between employees and management.

Security and crime-prevention education will not only assist in deterring the victimization of your employees off the job, but will complement on-the-job efforts as well. Through the use of programs like "Working Together," which is presented in the Corporate Action Kit, you let your employees know that you care about them and their families.

XYZ Corporation
and subsidiaries

Assignment	Classification:	Case Number:
Division:	Location:	Phone:	LYTD:
Region:	Reported By:	Status:	Time:	Date:	Day:
Area:	Police Notified:	How Notified:	When Notified:	Police Case #:
Other:	Assigned:

Synopsis

Materials and Equipment Stolen, Destroyed, or Damaged

Asset Number	Brand Name/Model Description:	Serial Number	Model Number	Check One			Purchase Price	Cost to Repair	Cost to Replace
				Stolen	Destroyed	Damaged			
							Sub-Total		
									Total

Other Loss or Damage

	Cost
Cash, damage to building, etc.	
Other (lost time, production, cleanup, etc.)	
	Grand Total

Prepared By: Approved By: Date:

Exhibit 4.19 Incident Report

4.19 Incident Report

An example of an incident report included here is a very basic one-page form (Exhibit 4.18). Incident reports can become very sophisticated multipage documents. The entire document or a section thereof can be designed for computer or manual completion. The ultimate data-collection format and the manner in which data are collected are up to you. The decision will be determined by the intended purpose and the necessary analysis to be made.

Basically, the information you will want to start collecting will answer the questions of who, what, where, when, how, by whom, and at what cost. Your report should be designed to collect this basic data, if known. Incident reports are generally used to collect preliminary or first-report-type information, which sets in motion official recognition that some category of incident has occurred and the collection of basic information is assured with the report's completion. More detailed accounts are included in follow-up investigative reports (should the decision be made to make further inquiry). Follow-up reports are supplemental to and become part of the original incident report.

In Chapter 2, Sections 2.4 and 2.5, Essentials of Data Collection and Problematic Issues, respectively, information to aid in understanding the incident report and its purpose is reviewed.

Index